ALSO BY PEREGRINE HODSON

*Under a Sickle Moon*

# A CIRCLE
# ROUND
# THE SUN

# A CIRCLE
# ROUND
# THE SUN

## A FOREIGNER IN JAPAN, INC.

## PEREGRINE HODSON

ALFRED A. KNOPF
NEW YORK   1993

THIS IS A BORZOI BOOK
PUBLISHED BY ALFRED A. KNOPF, INC.

Copyright © 1992 by Peregrine Hodson

All rights reserved under International and
Pan-American Copyright Conventions.
Published in the United States by Alfred A.
Knopf, Inc., New York. Distributed by
Random House, Inc., New York.

Originally published in Great Britain
by William Heinemann Ltd., London,
in 1992. Portions of this book were
published in *Granta*.

Library of Congress Cataloging-in-Publication Data
Hodson, Peregrine.
A circle round the sun: a foreigner in Japan /
Hodson, Peregrine. — 1st American ed.
p.   cm.
ISBN 0-679-42102-5
1. Japan—Civilization—1945–
DS822.5.H59   1993
952'.04—dc20          92-31858
CIP

Manufactured in the United States of America

First American Edition

*For Tara*

You have caught the disease of the profession, suspicion.

Graham Greene, *The Human Factor*

He that has two pairs of trousers, let him sell one pair and buy this book.

Lichtenberg

## ACKNOWLEDGEMENTS

I am grateful to my friends and those who showed me kindness during my time in Japan; Their Imperial Highnesses Prince and Princess Takamado; Andrew Fayle; Yoshiko Wakayama; Christopher Case; Futaba Shiotani; Derek Masarella; Kiyoko Osone; Joseph Tuma; John Nakada; William Miller; Junzo Sawa; Simon and Takako Prentis; Murray and Jenny Sayle; Tiziano and Angela Terzani; also Alan; Sachiko; Shigeru; Mariko; Hideo; Phillip and Kinuyo; Ron and Roy.

In the world outside Japan, I have been helped and encouraged during the writing of this book by Felix Pearson; Peter and Cynthia Rockwell; Gillon Aitken; Tom Weldon; Melissa Merryweather; Napier Miles; Bill Buford; Bob Tashman; Carolyn Watts; Nicholas Wolfers; Lesley Walker; Eric Elstob; Tina Richards; Marc Galberg; Pippa Shaw; Richard Berkley-Dennis; Suzy Olsen; Chris Shamwana; and Lesley Walker.

London
February 29th 1992

While I was in Japan I kept a diary, and made recordings. I have used passages from the diary and excerpts from the recordings for some of this book: the rest is from memory.

A thousand years ago, Sei Shonagon, a Japanese woman at the Heian imperial court, collected together her writings about her daily life. She called her collection *The Pillow Book* and it became the prototype for a genre of Japanese writing known as *zuihitsu* or random notes. *The Pillow Book* seemed an appropriate model for a book about Japan and I have written with the example of Sei Shonagon before me. The form of this book is also imitated from Japan, where it might be described as a *shi-shosetsu* or I-novel. But it is not fiction: it is a personal account in a style the Japanese call *shasei* or drawing-from-life.

# A CIRCLE
# ROUND
# THE SUN

For a while I'd been wanting to go back to Japan.

I wanted to drink *sake* and see the snow on Mount Fuji, and there was someone I used to know, who I hoped to meet again.

The last time I saw Sachiko was in London. She was alone, I was with a friend. We talked for a minute or so as if we hardly knew each other and then Sachiko said goodbye, and as she stepped into the sunlight of the open doorway I realised I loved her.

I became a barrister, went to Afghanistan, wrote a book and arrived in the Japanese department of a European bank. As a Japanese speaker, I was supposed to develop business in Japan, but my status was unclear since I was the only person in the Japanese section. My immediate superior was called Bob, and he reported to the old men on the fifth floor who were invisible.

Bob was from the United States but he liked living in England. During the Vietnam war he captained patrol boats along the Mekong River. Then he went into investment banking. In his spare time he was a sculptor; he made human figures which were life-like except they had no faces. His initials R. F. L. were embroidered on the sleeve of his shirt and his cufflinks were gold dollars.

One afternoon Bob asked to see me.

We sat in a room drinking machine-made coffee from plastic cups and he told me what the old men on the fifth floor were thinking.

Attitudes towards Japan were changing. A while back, the CIA said Japanese investment overseas was a Trojan horse. Now people wanted Japan's money. Everyone who was anyone wanted someone in Japan selling to the Japanese. The old men wanted me in Tokyo: the initial posting was for one year, renewable by mutual consent. They hoped I would stay a long time in Japan; the longer the better.

"That's your mission," said Bob. After ten years in London his sense of humour was almost English.

I said I would give my decision in a couple of weeks.

○

Yesterday evening I saw Julian again. We had dinner at a Thai restaurant. He's going back to Pakistan and asked if I wanted to go on another trip inside Afghanistan. I mentioned Japan.

"What do you want to do for the rest of your life," he asked, "play golf and grow roses?"

Sometimes, in the dealing room, flicking through the electronic pages of a company on the Reuters terminal, I remember speaking another language, with different people under a foreign sky. It's like another lifetime, or the Emperor of China who dreamed he was a butterfly.

The past isn't just another country, it's another universe. The mystery is how we get from there to here.

○

Today I had lunch with Terry. We hadn't seen each other since Tokyo. Now he's in charge of Yamaichi's bond trading operation in Europe. He thought a trip to Afghanistan was a bad idea. "Sit on a mountain in the Hindu Kush, freezing your bollocks off, looking at sheep's droppings," he said. "Someone's got to do it but not me thank God."

We talked about the market. Terry said there were signs of a large-scale movement out of equities into bonds. He thinks the bull market is almost over: too many stupid people making too much money too easily.

He's been in the business a long time. After Oxford he went to the Middle East, just as the first wave of petrodollars poured into the world's financial system and he recycled them into loans to South America. Later he sold US Treasury Bonds to Japanese investors. He knows the market: if he says the bull market is over, it's over.

○

This evening I was sitting on the floor of Miles' place smoking an Indonesian cigarette when someone put on Malcolm McLaren's *Madam Butterfly*. The music and the smoke of the cigarette reminded me of evenings in Tokyo with Joseph, sitting in the garden of his house in Setagaya, smoking Kretek cigarettes and listening to the sound of the cicadas. The man's voice was American and he sounded a bit like Joseph. When he started talking about a girl called Cho-cho-san, I thought of Sachiko, and the colour of her eyes, like sunlight in the water of a lake in the forest.

Miles reprogrammed the music, back to the beginning of the aria from *Madam Butterfly*.

"Imagine a story of love," he said, "the cold common sense of the Anglo-Saxon, the curious passion of the Japanese, the romantic spirit of the Italian." Someone told him to change the music. He smiled and pressed the button.

I lit another Kretek and listened to the music and thought of someone singing the aria before I was born. The girl beside me said it was Italian sentimentalism, and a banker just back from a business trip to Tokyo began talking about a culture gap between Westerners and Japanese. He said he wouldn't live in Tokyo for love or money. Someone called Raffery disagreed with everyone. He said Japan was boring: it was like anywhere else—nothing special.

I imagined Sachiko beside me listening to the conversation and saying nothing. I remembered her face. I wanted to hear her voice. I wanted to see her smile. I thought of the Japanese word for little squirrel and decided to go back to Japan, for love if possible, for money if necessary.

○

Johnny Tallis is dead. I heard this afternoon. He fell out of a third-floor window in Tokyo and died eight hours later from internal bleeding. The rumour is that he'd taken drugs; knowing Johnny, it's possible. He was with an American and two Japanese girls. The American had brought some LSD or Ecstasy from Thailand and they all took some. Johnny took too much, got too close to the window, or the edge of the balcony to the flat, lost control and fell over. He survived the fall and was staggering around on the pavement covered in blood, when two policemen appeared and asked him what he was doing. Someone called an ambulance but it took a while to arrive: by the time they got him to hospital he was unconscious and for some time after his arrival, no one knows how long, he received no treatment. The hospital authorities refused to treat him until they knew what drugs he'd taken. All this time he was bleeding inside. His spleen was ruptured. Around ten o'clock in the morning, Tokyo time, he died.

The last time I saw Johnny was in a bar in Roppongi: he was working with a British firm selling whisky to the Japanese. He had a problem with his employers and was looking for a change. He wanted to work in a bank. I told him some people he should see and the sort of questions they might ask. After that we went to some bars he knew from selling whisky. We went to the Cavern Club and listened to a Japanese group of Beatles look-alikes singing sixties songs, and somewhere else we watched a striptease by girls who were transvestites and towards dawn we ended up eating noodles, while Johnny talked about a sky burial he'd seen in Tibet. Now he's dead.

○

This morning I called Roddy in Tokyo to find out if he knew when Johnny's funeral might be. He said I was too late: Johnny was cremated yesterday.

I asked how it was so quick. He said a drug scandal in the banking community was bad publicity with a new round of banking licences being offered to foreign institutions. "Imagine the headlines," he said.

Money talks, money keeps silent and silence is golden.

The speed with which the body has been cremated is somehow more shocking than the way he died. Writing about it I notice my hand trembling. Perhaps it's the coffee. Johnny's death has affected me badly. I don't want to think about it. At the office I hear phrases like "termination fee," "opportunity loss" and "the negative cost to the individual" and I feel as if I'm about to be sick although my stomach is empty.

○

This afternoon I went to the Japanese Embassy to apply for a work visa. The room was full of Japanese filling in forms, smoking cigarettes. There were a few foreigners. The Japanese looked clean and smart and the foreigners looked dirty and untidy. I took a form from the counter and sat down at a table. It was difficult to concentrate. I was walking along a London street, I'd opened a door and suddenly I was in Japan.

The room was like a busy ward office in Tokyo. The people behind the counter looked bored and irritable. It wasn't funny:

they'd come halfway round the world to help their fellow coun-trymen fill in forms claiming tax relief. The room was full of cigarette smoke and there was a baby crying.

I filled in a visa application form and took it with my passport to the counter. The man at the position was in his mid-thirties. He was wearing a Hermès tie. He pointed to the space between the grill and the surface of the counter and fluttered his hand like someone in a street market gesturing for money. I asked him in English who dealt with visa applications but he just pointed and fluttered his hand again. I handed over my pass-port and visa application. He took the papers without a word and went into the office behind him.

I sat down and thought how good it was to be away from the office: all those people talking about money. There was a tap on the glass. The man at the counter was gesturing at me. He pushed my visa application towards me and pointed at the top of the page where I'd written my name and forenames, then opened my passport and pointed at the page containing my family names. It took a few seconds to see the problem: there was one more name on my visa form than on my pass-port. He was observant; the people at the passport office had made a mistake and forgotten one of my names. I smiled and told him not to worry; the visa was correct.

"Cross it out or do it again," he said. His voice was flat with a slight American accent. I asked why I had to cross out my name; I'd given the correct number of names on my application form, technically my passport was incorrect. He just repeated what he said before. "Cross it out or do it again." I said it was my name and I didn't see why he should tell me to cross it out.

"What is the matter?" he said. There was a disagreeable flicker in his eyes but the muscles of his face didn't move.

"In this country we think it's more polite to use the word 'please,' " I said.

A sly expression flitted across his features. "This is Japan," he said.

"In Japan," I said in Japanese, "my teacher taught me the importance of *reigi*."

"People are waiting," he said in English, "cross it out or do it again. That is the law."

"It's my name," I said.

"Cross it out or do it again. That is the law. Do you understand what I am saying in your language?" He was working himself into a bureaucratic tantrum. "That is the law! If you refuse to do what I say, take these papers and go." He pushed my passport and application form towards me.

I opened my passport, inserted the missing name and handed it back to him.

"That is very wrong," he said.

"It's my name," I said.

He looked at my papers again and pursed his lips together in a slit of disgust as if there was a bad smell, then nodded and told me to come back in ten days. I thanked him and walked out into the street. It was good to be back in London.

○

I woke up a few minutes ago to a phone call from Yamaguchi. He wanted to check that everything was all right. Was the flight OK? Did I have any problems finding the hotel? Had I eaten breakfast? Welcome to Japan.

It's nine o'clock, Tokyo time, and a taxi will be coming to collect me in half an hour. The sun is shining. The trees are bare. The wind disturbs the water surrounding the Imperial Palace, and the branches of the willow trees wave in the sunlight.

I remember this kind of weather from the first time I was in Japan: I recognise the light, I know how cold the wind can be on mornings like this. It's strange, as if the memories I have belong to someone else. I feel like someone visiting a place for the first time who says, "I've been here before."

o

The journey to the office took less than a quarter of an hour. The driver stopped by an off-white building that could have been designed by a committee. There were men in suits walking in and out of the sliding doors at the base of the building. I paid the taxi driver and became one of them.

The office was on the seventeenth floor. The glass doors of the office opened into a grey carpeted reception area. There was no one about, only an empty desk, a large weeping fig tree beside two armchairs, a low table and a waste-paper basket. On the wall was a framed print of blue, orange and lilac flowers.

A sign said, "PLEASE RING FOR ATTENTION." I pressed a white plastic button, the door in front of me opened and a middle-aged woman appeared. The look of polite surprise on her face vanished when she saw I was a foreigner. Instead of bowing as she might have done to another Japanese, she lowered her eyes and apologised for keeping me waiting.

She spoke in English, with a precision that made me wonder if she'd learned from a human being or a tape-recorder. I gave her my name and said Yamaguchi was expecting me. She bowed slightly, opened a door on my left and closed it behind her.

She reappeared and smilingly informed me that Yamaguchi would be with me in a few minutes. She asked if I'd like some coffee or green tea while I was waiting. I asked for coffee and she smiled, as if I'd passed a test, proving some unwritten rule that foreigners drink coffee and Japanese drink green tea.

It was exactly as I remembered it. The indeterminate colours of the walls and ceilings, the woman's appearance, the way she greeted me, the controlled gestures, the smiles, the silences at the end of sentences, the emptiness of the room and the stillness of the weeping fig tree, even the picture hanging on the wall in front of me; it was all exactly as I remembered it. Japan.

She brought a cup of coffee on a tray and asked if I'd like some milk in it. I said I was jet-lagged and preferred the coffee black. She smiled again, as if I'd passed another test, proving that foreigners drink black coffee because they're tired from working Japanese hours or jet-lagged or hungover. I smiled and thanked her. I was beginning to think Japanese.

I picked up a copy of the company magazine that was lying on the table and read an article by the chairman of the bank about the organisation. Halfway down the page there was a photograph of a man with a large face and bags under his eyes. He looked as if he should take more exercise. He believed financial markets offered exciting opportunities for people of talent and creative intelligence.

A foreigner went past. He was wearing a yellow shirt and a tie with diagonal stripes. I guessed the type; more bonds than equities.

I was reading about the company's international operations when the receptionist reappeared. It was almost ten o'clock. I asked if Yamaguchi was busy. She apologised with a smile of embarrassment and hurried away. The delay didn't bother me but I was puzzled. I wondered why Yamaguchi hadn't sent a message. Perhaps I'd offended him. I thought back over the half dozen telephone conversations we'd had together about exchange rates, and plane time-tables and hotel reservations. Perhaps he wanted to emphasise his status by keeping me waiting.

The door in front of me opened and Yamaguchi appeared. He was smiling. I smiled back. He apologised for keeping me waiting: first there was a call from the London office and then a call from a valuable customer for a large and complicated order. He smiled again and I nodded and smiled back at him. It seemed a bit early for a call from London.

"I very much hope for your understanding in this matter," he said. "As you may know, we Japanese are a polite people and we work hard."

I said I understood perfectly and looked forward to learning from him how to achieve large orders in a bear market. He laughed. "You must go to the same university as your customers," he said. "The same school is even better. Please do not think I am always serious," he added, "it was a joke."

I smiled as I looked at his face. I was out of practice. After being away from Japan for a while, I couldn't interpret the look in his eyes.

We walked along a white-walled corridor with dark wood doors set at regular intervals on either side of a grey carpeted walkway. Neither of us said anything and our footsteps were silent as we passed the doors which were all closed. At the end of the corridor Yamaguchi stopped. On our left a door was half open; there were men in shirtsleeves sitting or standing between rows of computer terminals. I had a heavy sensation in my stomach. I wished I were back in the hotel, reading *The Bonfire of the Vanities* or back in England asleep. It was two o'clock in the morning London time and the thought of being introduced to a room full of Japanese didn't make me feel any better.

Yamaguchi asked if I was tired after my journey. I nodded; I was grateful for his sympathy. I remembered how easily some Japanese can read the faces of Westerners. He gestured to a room on our right and suggested coffee.

The room was big and light; two sides were windows and there was a long empty table in the middle of the room with bright tubular-steel chairs neatly arranged on either side of it. Yamaguchi walked towards the window.

"On clear days it is possible to see Mount Fuji," he said and pointed to a gap between a grey office block and a big square sign advertising Mitsubishi. I looked for the familiar outline of the mountain but I could only see a colourless haze of sunlight in the morning mist. Yamaguchi moved to the other window.

"We also have a good view of the Imperial Palace." He placed his hands together and assumed an expression of exaggerated respect, then smiled as if he'd just told a slightly risqué story and was waiting for me to laugh. I looked across the shimmering water of the Palace moat and the massive sloping stone walls towards the pale green copper rooves of the Palace, half hidden in the darker green of the surrounding pine trees.

"It's beautiful," I said.

He turned and gestured at the room behind us and said it was used for meetings. He asked me to sit down while he picked up a telephone receiver and asked for someone called Tamura, in Japanese. His face altered as he switched to English to ask if I preferred milk, tea or coffee. He smiled when he spoke Japanese.

Yamaguchi sat on the opposite side of the table and talked about the market. He said confidence was low, people were uncertain, and trading volumes were down. I'd heard the same story in Hong Kong and my attention wandered.

His face has changed since the summer: there's a puffiness which wasn't there before. I guess the pressure of trying to get orders in a weak market is getting to him. He looks as if he's drinking too much.

There was a light knock at the door and a young woman came in carrying a tray. Yamaguchi didn't react as she placed the cups on the table beside us. She withdrew silently and bowed and was already at the door when he called out to her.

"Tamura, wait a moment." He continued to look at me as he spoke to her. He introduced me as someone from London. She made a polite bow of greeting and began to open the door but Yamaguchi hadn't finished. He turned in his chair to look at her.

"You speak English, don't you?" he said. "Say something in English."

She shook her head and raised her hand to her mouth to cover an embarrassed smile. He was persistent.

"Say something in English, Tamura, show how international we are here in the Tokyo office." A faint pink coloured her cheeks but she didn't say anything. "You understand what I'm saying, don't you?" he said.

She nodded and whispered that she was shy. Her hand remained in front of her mouth. I wanted to say I was sure she could speak excellent English but Yamaguchi went on.

"Say something in English, Tamura. Can't you remember what they taught you in school?" Hesitantly she took her hand away from her mouth and greeted me in English.

"Very good, Tamura," said Yamaguchi. "Are you learning a lot of new words from Mr Casey?" She raised her hand to her mouth again and blushed a deeper pink. Yamaguchi turned and said in a voice loud enough for her to overhear. "Tamura likes foreigners. She wants to marry one." He gestured towards the coffee and suggested we drink it before it was cold.

The door closed silently behind him.

Yamaguchi took a cigarette from a box of cigarettes on the table and smiled.

"Tamura is a good girl, she likes to kid around." I wondered where he learned the phrase "to kid around."

He clicked a Dunhill lighter and lit a cigarette. Someone had told him that I went to Afghanistan to write about a war. Now I was in Tokyo banking. He said it was unusual for Japanese people to change their jobs and he wanted to know why I went to Afghanistan. It wasn't a place to go for a holiday: no whisky, no girls, no *sushi*. I said I went as a freelance reporter. At first I thought he was pointing at me.

"Zero, zero, seven," he said. He shaped the fingers of his hand around an invisible pistol, the middle finger twitched and his face widened in a grin. He'd made a joke but I'd missed the punchline. He raised an eyebrow.

"Like James Bond?"

"No," I said.

He asked who I was working for. I said I was working for myself. He frowned. Then I told him the trip was tax-deductible and he smiled.

"*Naruhodo!*" he exclaimed. "Now I see—a tax holiday!" He laughed and I grinned and we both finished our coffees. It was time for work, but first he had to introduce me to the head of the office, a man called Laroche. He got up and I followed him into the room I'd seen earlier.

It was big, brightly lit and full of people. One side of the room was glass, floor to ceiling. Long white lines of fluorescent lighting converged over a giant display of luminous orange numbers which flashed and changed at random intervals. The room was divided into parallel rows of desks, each with its own telephones, Reuters screen and computer terminal. Most of the people looked Japanese but there were several foreign faces.

In a corner of the room, behind a wall of filing cabinets and a large castor oil plant, a middle-aged Japanese woman was sitting at a grey metal desk. She didn't look up as we approached. Yamaguchi greeted her but it was several seconds before she raised her head. Her face was round and white and her lipstick was purple. Her black hair was cut short, with a fringe over her eyebrows like the Beatles, early 1960s' style and she was wearing a thick brown tweed suit.

She greeted Yamaguchi without smiling. They spoke in English. He asked if Laroche was free and she raised the gold *diamanté* spectacles hanging round her neck and leaned forward to examine the pages of an engagement book. Yamaguchi pursed his lips and glanced at his watch.

Laroche had no appointments but he was talking to someone on the telephone. The woman cast a wintry smile in Yamaguchi's direction and asked who I was. Her name was Noguchi. She apologised for Yamaguchi's failure to introduce us.

"I am afraid he is a traditional Japanese gentleman," she said. Yamaguchi turned towards me.

"Noguchi is in charge of the secretaries. She likes to know everyone's secrets," he said.

"The less we hear about your secrets, the better, Yamaguchi," she said. It might have been amusing if there had been the slightest trace of humour in her face, but there wasn't.

"Yamaguchi is trying to say I am a dragon," she said. Perhaps there was a twinkle in her eyes, I wasn't sure. I knew

Yamaguchi was watching me. I tried not to show any reaction. I bowed and made a mental note to treat her with caution.

A little red light on her desk vanished and she gestured us towards a door. Yamaguchi knocked and someone shouted "Hi!" or it could have been "*Hai!*" in a loud, drawling voice. Yamaguchi opened the door and we stepped into a light, white-carpeted room. A man was sitting at a desk. His head and shoulders were silhouetted by a window: the dirty grey-and-white mosaic of Tokyo, and a blue sky. He got up as if he was doing me a favour and stretched out his hand. He was heavily built and he had a powerful handshake. His spectacles were light-sensitive and I couldn't see his eyes. He showed a lot of teeth when he smiled.

Yamaguchi apologised and said he had to get back to the trading desk. Laroche gestured towards a chair. The door closed and he leaned forward. He said he would come straight to the point.

He wasn't consulted about my appointment here in Tokyo. Until now every foreigner in the office had been interviewed by him. The rule was very clear: only people who had his approval worked in the office. My case was exceptional. He had only seen my curriculum vitae last week. He had already told London he was very annoyed by the way things had been handled.

I said I was sorry and looked at his eyes which were still half hidden by the sepia glass of his spectacles. He showed his teeth in another smile.

"It's nothing personal," he shrugged his shoulders, "it's procedure. I am sure you understand my position." I asked if he understood mine. "Sure," he said, "I just wanted you to know how things are done here." His teeth reappeared in a big grin. "Money. That's the name of the game, isn't it?" I sensed his eyes looking at me through the sepia lenses. I said it didn't grow on trees. He smiled.

"Good," he said, "we understand each other." He pressed

a button at the corner of his desk and as he leaned back in his chair I heard the door opening behind me. I glimpsed his eyes through the darkened glass, looking at me. They were dark. He saw I was looking at him. I smiled. He lifted his gaze over my shoulder towards the door and asked Noguchi to show me to my desk.

I stood up and thanked him. I said "Thank-you," so that Noguchi would hear. Laroche remained seated. "Any time," he said and picked up the telephone a bit too quickly, like an actor in a television drama. On the back of the door was a framed sign, in black letters on a Day-Glo yellow background: "DOING NOTHING IS SPECULATING."

I followed Noguchi into the noise of the dealing room. Yamaguchi's desk was at the far end, under the wall of luminous orange numbers. He was on the telephone and gestured to me to sit down on the other side of the desk. I looked at the numbers: beside them were the characters of Japanese companies arranged by industry section. The market was quiet: some financials were moving and a few pharmaceuticals.

On my right, the window looked out over a sprawl of office blocks and department stores, with the gantries and cranes of Tokyo Bay in the distance and two ships like model boats floating on a glittering stretch of water open to the sea. A little grey aeroplane emerged from the haze over the horizon, taking off from Haneda. It was the sort of view to make a person feel good, even in a bear market.

The screens in front of me were dead and I couldn't find a way to switch them on so I looked at Yamaguchi. He was nodding his head a lot. He frowned once or twice but he didn't say anything. The person at the other end of the line was too important to be interrupted. He glanced in my direction, and as he looked away I had the feeling that the person on the other end of the line was talking about me. Yamaguchi nodded again and without a word put down the receiver and wrote something on a piece of paper. Maybe it was Laroche.

I asked if he needed anything and he said I might as well go for lunch. So here I am.

It's twelve-thirty in the afternoon Tokyo time and I'm sitting in an underground coffee shop called The Café Human on the third basement level, with the remains of a mixed sandwich of ham, egg and cucumber in front of me, talking into a micro-recorder.

It was difficult to get the waitress to come over to the table. Eventually I managed to catch her eye and she found the courage to approach me. I spoke in Japanese. It was a simple order, "*Kohi hitotsu*—one coffee," but she repeated it twice before she felt confident enough to write anything down.

She's young and pretty in a bland sort of way: neat eyes and mouth in a round, slightly chubby face that reminds me of the country girls in Ibaraki prefecture. She looks as if she's just out of school; she isn't wearing any lipstick and her hair is cut short, the way her parents and her teachers would prefer.

At the table next to me two men in suits are drinking iced coffees through straws and smoking cigarettes. They're in their mid-forties: typical *salarimen*, with enamel badges of their company logo on their lapels: the three diamond-shaped leaves of Mitsubishi. They're talking about new arrivals to the firm. The one with tortoiseshell spectacles does most of the talking. His companion, who's a few years younger, keeps nodding his head and agreeing with everything he says. The one with the tortoiseshell spectacles is talking about discipline.

Different languages, different worlds.

Yesterday I was a foreigner. Now I'm a *gaijin*.

The younger of the two men at the next table is looking at me. Maybe he heard me using a Japanese word. He's altered the focus of his gaze so he's no longer looking at me, but through me or at the wall just over my shoulder, and now he's shifted his gaze again, back to the face of his companion.

Here's the waitress. I smile at her and she blushes. First she puts an empty cup and saucer on the table in front of me, carefully adjusting the cup so that the handle is pointing towards my right hand, and arranges the teaspoon in the saucer so that it's parallel to the handle of the cup. Next she puts the small, one-person-size glass percolator of coffee beside it and finally a little aluminium jug of milk a little to one side. The rhythm and precision with which she does these things reminds me of the tea ceremony: every action has its formula.

She makes a tiny, almost imperceptible bow and hurries away. I look at her legs; they're the sort schoolboys call *daikon-ashi*—radish legs, thick and white. She's wearing little lacy ankle stockings which make her calf muscles look even bigger. Looking at her stockings makes me feel sad.

○

When I got back to the office everyone was at lunch and the dealing room was almost empty. There was a message from Yamaguchi telling me to report to Maria Santini in Administration on the fifteenth floor. I'd heard about her in London. Bob called her the "Ice Maiden" and said she had as much sex appeal as a plate of raw fish.

Her office is a small, glass-walled box with Venetian blinds in a corner of Administration. I knocked on the door and a woman's voice answered in Japanese. She was sitting at a grey metal desk, half hidden by a computer terminal and a dark green potted plant with waxy-looking leaves.

She got up to greet me and stretched out a hand that rustled and tinkled with pieces of gold jewellery. There was something about the smile that reminded me of a silent-movie actress.

"Welcome to Tokyo," she said and gestured towards a tubular-steel armchair. She had big, sapphire-blue eyes, white teeth and cherry-red lipstick. She explained who she was and why she'd sent for me. She talked and smiled at the same time. As chief of Administration she supervises the payment of salary and accommodation. She gave me an envelope containing an advance against my salary and told me my housing allowance. I took the envelope and thanked her.

"Don't thank me," she said, "it's from the company." She typed a sequence of keys on a grey plastic terminal, peered into the screen in front of her and frowned. For the first time I saw her face in profile. Her nose was more Roman than Etruscan. She didn't have any information about the currency in which my salary was to be paid. She looked round the side of the screen and asked if I wanted to be paid in yen, dollars or sterling. All the foreign-exchange dealers had chosen yen, so I said yen would be fine.

She tapped some more keys on the terminal, got up from her chair and held out her hand again and smiled like a timid schoolgirl. The change in her manner puzzled me and I shook hands clumsily.

"Welcome back to Japan," she said.

"*Domo*," I said, "thank-you," and bowed slightly.

Back at my desk in the dealing room I thought about the moment of little-girl shyness—like a Japanese girl. She must have been here a long time.

Yamaguchi wasn't back from lunch so I looked through the pile of research reports on the desk beside me. The papers were like archaeological strata, with gaps and overlaps, but it was possible to reconstruct what happened.

In the beginning the London office was the only source of information. A lot of the reports had notes in the margin. There were several unbroken sequences. Then one or two reports from European offices appeared: at first these were annotated as well but as the flow of information increased, the comments in the margins disappeared and the sequence began to disintegrate. Some of the more recent reports were still sealed in the envelopes in which they'd been sent from London. From the weeks before the crash there were no reports from London, just a couple of reports in Japanese, one from the Nomura Research Institute and one from Morgan Stanley.

I imagined Yamaguchi reading the jargon-filled reports from the London office, trying to follow unfamiliar companies through a stockmarket collapse. It looked like he was suffering from information overload.

Yamaguchi appeared a few minutes after four o'clock. He smiled and asked if everything was all right. He seemed in a good mood. He asked if I had jet-lag and I said, "Yes, culture-lag too," which confused him. I tried to explain and he smiled and said, "Now I understand." I think he suspected I'd made a joke about Japan.

The telephone on his desk started bleeping. He answered in the company's name and his face was expressionless but he smiled when he heard the caller's voice. Whoever it was, Yamaguchi gave them the full performance: polite language, honorifics and formal verb endings. Every few sentences he grinned and bowed to the invisible person at the other end of the line. He apologised for not having contacted the person before and began talking about the German economy. What he said was like an editorial in a business magazine. I couldn't see anyone valuing the information, but when he put down the handset he was smiling. It was a call from one of the company's most important clients. "He will buy some stock soon," he said. I asked why he was so optimistic.

He had been talking to Saito-san who works in one of the big life-insurance companies. Saito-san is the head of the department which invests in foreign shares.

"He will buy a lot of German shares," said Yamaguchi, "he has no choice."

I asked why.

It was simple. Saito had already decided to buy the shares. He was just checking to see if there was any reason not to buy. "I know Saito's mind," said Yamaguchi.

"Really," I said, then repeated in Japanese, "*Ah so, desu-ka*." Perhaps the intonation was wrong; Yamaguchi raised his eyebrows.

"*Honto da yo!*" he said. "It's true! We Japanese can know each other's minds. We are a homogeneous society: same schools, same universities, same culture, same language, same minds. *Mondai nai.* No problem." He smiled like he'd proved something. I was going to ask what he meant by "homogeneous" but the telephone on his desk interrupted. It was London. Yamaguchi switched the line through to my telephone and a woman with a Liverpool accent told us to stand by for the morning conference call.

It was dark outside. There was a click and we were in the middle of Beethoven's "Pastoral" Symphony. Yamaguchi shrugged and looked resigned.

The music made me feel sleepy. I could almost see the little pastel-coloured creatures in *Fantasia.* I opened my eyes and looked at the evening sky and the lights of the ships on Tokyo Bay. The music was from another country. Europe was a long way away. I guessed Tanya was asleep.

I could imagine the people in the London office at their desks in the dealing room: Matthew eating a fried-egg sandwich, checking the overnight share prices in New York and Tokyo; Ferdinand Chow drinking a cappuccino and calculating the prices of gold and the major currencies before opening the conference call; Bob sitting beside him looking stern and authoritative, like they taught him to look in the course of assertiveness training.

The music stopped in mid-flow and the woman with a Liverpool accent said, "London, you have been joined by Paris, Brussels, Frankfurt, Geneva and Tokyo." Her voice was impatient. She didn't sound as if she liked her job.

After the operator, it was good to hear Ferdinand Chow. I looked at Yamaguchi. He was leaning on the desk supporting his head in his left hand, holding the telephone receiver in his right. His eyes were closed.

Ferdinand Chow ended the economic summary by telling everyone to have a nice day. Then Bob commented on the numbers and Arif talked about the budget deficit in the US. Yamaguchi's head dropped a little lower over the desk. His eyes were still closed. The telephone was slipping and the mouthpiece was against his ear.

Arif said the US had to reduce its trade deficit or suffer economic catastrophe: Americans were spending money they did not have to buy a lifestyle they could not afford.

"There are no free lunches," Arif said. Even through the intercontinental telephone system I could hear the anger in his voice. "You pay for what you consume. Sooner or later American consumers, which means everyone, will have to pay for what they've consumed. All the people who've been partying on credit. It's time to pay the bill."

Yamaguchi grunted and tried to reposition the handset against his ear. He looked more asleep than awake. I wanted to go back to the Imperial Hotel and adjust to the local culture by watching television. Arif was still talking and I was thinking how it's more fun being a prophet of doom than listening to one. Then the line went dead.

Yamaguchi put his telephone on the desk in front of him.

"There's something wrong with the system," he said, "it often stops in the middle." I asked how to reconnect with London. He said it was difficult. I thought there was a shadow of a smile at the edges of his mouth, but perhaps I imagined it.

○

The office isn't far from the hotel. It's good to be outside. The darkness is alive with headlights and neon signs, like a slow-motion waterfall of golden characters on a red background, advertising insurance policies, glittering on the wall of the building opposite. On the other side of the road the station loudspeaker is telling people to stand back behind the line as a train's arriving in the next few seconds. There are *salarimen* and office girls and a foreigner looking awkward and out of step with the people hurrying along the pavement. The electricity of crowds is in the air, quickening the pulse like adrenaline, making the lights seem brighter and everything more foreign than I remember.

○

It's ten o'clock in the evening.

I've had a hot bath and I'm lying on the bed in a cotton *kimono* with an ice-cold Kirin beer beside me, comparing an Englishman in a *kimono* with a Japanese in a kilt.

It's been a long day. I've recorded most of what I can remember: time to celebrate arriving back in Japan by calling room service for some *sushi*.

○

It's eight o'clock in the morning Tokyo time, it's midnight in London and I'm watching a Japanese woman dressed as a rabbit singing nursery rhymes to a group of children on the television. In half an hour I'll be sitting in front of a Reuters screen in a room full of Japanese people speaking English with American accents.

○

I was only just in time for the morning conference call with New York. Everyone was already sitting round the big table in the middle of the room. A woman in a pinstripe suit dialled the New York office and switched on the speaker system. There was a soft electronic hissing, then a dialling tone from the speakers and everyone stopped talking: thirty or forty people in a room in Tokyo saying nothing, waiting for someone in New York to pick up a telephone.

Yamaguchi looked like he'd had a late night. There was a newspaper on the table in front of him and he was leaning forward with his hands shading his eyes, as if he was reading it, but from where I was sitting I could see his eyes weren't moving. Next to him a woman with a wide face and a small mouth was checking through a newspaper and pencilling figures on to a note pad.

A young woman's voice said, "Hi! Tokyo? New York!" from the loudspeakers and began a litany of numbers, went through a list of buy and sell orders in New York, and ended with a prayer for help with a bond issue. "Jesus," she said, "there's got to be a bunch of Japanese investors who want this sort of paper." The way she spoke, Japan sounded like a big wastepaper basket.

Rex Matsumoto, the head bond trader, a tiny man with a smooth, professional manner and a deep West Coast drawl, said investors in Tokyo weren't interested.

"For fuck's sake Rex," snapped the voice, "don't be so negative." For a couple of seconds nobody said anything. Rex Matsumoto, one of the most senior men in the Tokyo office, had just been insulted in front of everyone by a junior bond dealer in New York, a woman.

Next to Rex Matsumoto a plump man in shirtsleeves leaned towards the central microphone.

"What Rex means," he said, "is that Japanese investors are adopting a wait-and-see attitude at present."

The plump man in shirtsleeves had done the right thing. Like a loyal *samurai* throwing himself in front of an attack on his leader he had *giri*, the sort of thing that gets a man a bigger bonus.

"OK Tokyo, I hear you," said the voice. "But get this. If everyone plays wait and see, nothing happens, there's no market, there's no business and we have no job." There was a hint of hysteria in her voice. Rex leaned towards the microphone.

"Listen, Carla. We understand your position." He sounded like John Wayne, telling his troops not to surrender. "But, as you know, we Japanese have a different perspective. We appreciate your efforts, we really do. Thank-you." He flicked a switch and the conference call was over.

An Englishman with a long nose and a face like an undertaker's told everyone they should talk to their clients as much as possible. After a couple of sentences I sensed people's attention slipping into a stupor of indifference. Looking out the window, I could just see Hakone; a pale view of distant hills like frozen waves on the horizon.

The Englishman with the long nose and the boring voice finished. Rex thanked him and a girl started talking in Japanese. People shifted their positions and looked more alert. She spoke very quickly about a survey of clients' requirements. Then she thanked everyone for their attention, Rex thanked her and the meeting was over.

The Englishman introduced himself as we were going out of the conference room. "Nicholas Clather, spelt C-L-A-T-H-E-R. Rhymes with 'gather.' " He had a weak chin and a nervous mannerism of licking his lower lip: the type of person Keith would call "middle-management cannon fodder."

He was wearing gold cufflinks that might have come from Aspreys and the sort of military-looking tie which bogus majors wear. His face said one thing, his clothes said another: weak and ambitious, a dangerous combination. I asked how long he'd been in Japan. He'd come out to Tokyo at the same time as Laroche, eight years ago.

"Jean, Maria Santini and myself," he said. "We had one room. Three desks, three chairs, three telephones and two waste-paper baskets. Only two waste-paper baskets. You can imagine what it was like." He smiled and gazed into the middle distance like an old soldier remembering former campaigns. He gave me a *meishi* name card and said he had an appointment. He had the manner of someone who's always busy, like Rabbit in *Winnie-the-Pooh*.

Yamaguchi had taken off his jacket, loosened his tie and was smoking like a gangster, taking the smoke in through his bared teeth. I said "good morning" and he said "*Ohaiyo-gozaimasu*" and took another pull on his cigarette. I guessed the cloud of smoke meant he didn't want to be disturbed. I took off my jacket and went to get some coffee.

People were making the first calls of the day: looking at screens, talking numbers, smiling, frowning, pressing buttons, lighting cigarettes, drinking green tea, switching screens, calling out each other's names and waving across parallel rows of desks, like survivors of an invisible catastrophe in a geometrical sea of lights and noises.

While I waited for the coffee to percolate I looked out of the window towards the Imperial Palace. The sky was overcast and the waters of the moat were like a misted-over mirror in which the only reflection was the silver-grey colour of the sky.

It was difficult to connect the dealing room behind me and the view in front of me. The darkness of the trees was like the shadow of a valley in the mountains, as if a remote part of the country had somehow materialized in the centre of the city. On the other side of the water the traffic stretched as far as the Diet building.

○

It's one-fifteen in the afternoon and I'm walking towards the Ginza.

It's good to be outside. Sitting for hours under high-intensity, fluorescent lighting, in front of screens of numbers, breathing recycled air-conditioned farts at a steady seventeen degrees centigrade, it's easy to lose touch with what's happening. People get information overload, knowing everything, seeing nothing: screen-blind, brain-dead people-machines. God help us.

Outside a noodle shop a man is dismantling a cardboard box. He folds it flat and adds it to the top of a neatly stacked pile like a miniature cardboard pagoda. He could have jumped on it and kicked it into a corner but he's Japanese and this is Tokyo and even though I'm a foreigner it feels good to be here. *Kimochi-ga-ii!*

Black hair, pale skin, dark lips, bright yellow silk under a grey sky, brown eyes, a half-familiar sweetness in the air, the smell of noodles and cigarette smoke, flashing lights and the electronic thunder of wargame machines. A man clapping his hands beside a fruit stall decorated with pyramids of oranges and tangerines shouting "*Irashai! Irashai!*"

○

It's one-forty-five and I'm drinking a coffee in The Café Human. I have to be back at the office by two o'clock.

Yamaguchi has explained my duties to me. I check the Reuters terminal for the final levels of the major European stock-markets and calculate the percentage increase or decrease on the previous day's levels. Then I check the movements of the major currencies against the dollar, convert them into yen and calculate the percentage change against the dollar. That's all. If I take it slowly it might take half an hour. When I asked about a client list he said it would be better to wait until the situation was clearer.

This morning I met another foreigner who works in the company. His name is Kit Casey and he comes from California. He works in the accounts department. We were by the photocopying machine and we could see along the row of secretaries. Kit told me their names and ages, whether they were married or had boyfriends and who they'd slept with in the company. He said there's a rumour that Yamaguchi has slept with every woman in the dealing room except for Laroche's personal assistant Noguchi and the switchboard operator called Tamura.

I asked about someone with long black hair and a short skirt. He laughed and said I was too late. She has a boyfriend in

Yokohama and the person operating the company switchboard has put several calls through from Laroche's office. I guess the switchboard operator is Kit's girlfriend. If he's as thorough with accounts as he is at finding out about people's private lives, the company's in good hands.

○

It's just after five o'clock and I'm walking back to the hotel.

The wind's cold and I wish I had an overcoat. It's the same wind as it was three hundred years ago, when the poet Basho made his journey on the narrow road to the deep north, and I think of him walking into the cold shadow of a late autumn evening with only the wind for company.

Someone's getting into the rear seat of a large black car. He looks very old. Half a dozen men in suits are standing with their arms rigidly by their sides watching him. The old man finally manoeuvres himself into the car, someone closes the door, nods to the chauffeur and the men in suits bow deeply as the car draws away. As I walk past, one of the men complains of the cold.

At the pedestrian crossing the lights are red. Everyone is waiting obediently for the lights to change. But the road is clear. There are no cars—I'm going to walk across the road even though the lights are red. I check again, there are still no cars coming. All clear. Here goes.

Thirty yards away, on the other side of the six-lane highway, there's a group of twenty or thirty people waiting. I'm walking at my natural speed, or trying to. I'm conscious of the people on the other side waiting and watching and waiting. I have the feeling some of them want a car to come from nowhere fast. I'm halfway, on the central island, and the pedestrian crossing light is still red. Still no cars in sight. Still no one makes a move. I carry on. I want to get to the other side before the lights change but keep my speed natural. I can see their faces now.

Some of them look annoyed but one or two of them are smiling. It's still red. No cars. OK!

○

It's seven o'clock in the evening. Another day, another dollar. I'm lying alone on a bed in a room in a big hotel. This is my life. Sometimes it's like a film and all the lives in all the rooms seem like the dream of a man in a room in a big hotel. Here on the tenth floor I can hardly hear the traffic. All those people out there and the loudest sound in the room is the travelling clock on the bedside table. It's time to call a friend.

○

It was great to see David again. I went to his office near the American Embassy. He gave me a good welcome. "OK! The team's together again," he said, and I laughed.

It's a long way from talking about Mao Tse-tung with David in the coffee room of the Oriental Institute in Oxford, to talking about information theory and stochastic analysis in the bar of Maggie's Revenge in Roppongi. It seemed almost like another lifetime when we came to Japan on the programme. He's been here ever since. Now he has a Japanese wife, and two children, a boy and a girl, a house in Tokyo and a *besso* in the country. He lives here and does all his business in Japanese.

He told me what some of the others in the programme are doing. Four are in banking, two are in universities, one's in publishing and another's in market research.

"Like it said on the application form," he grinned, "improving understanding at grass-roots level."

It's Saturday morning and the sun is shining and I feel good. I'm going to call Sachiko.

I called the only number I had for her, somewhere in Yotsuya. An elderly woman's voice answered in Japanese and hearing the way she spoke I knew I had to use *keigo* respect language, which always makes me nervous. I didn't know who I was talking to so I said I was a friend of Sachiko from England. The woman asked me to wait while her husband came to the telephone. He could speak English. I thanked her and waited.

It seemed like a long time. I imagined a very old man in a dark blue *kimono* shuffling across a floor of sunlit *tatami* with stiff, painful movements. It took so long I was about to put down the receiver, then I thought of the little old man again and I held on.

"Hallo," said a voice in English. He sounded old but not decrepit. I introduced myself as a friend of Sachiko from England.

"Ah yes." The tone of voice could have been warm or cold. His pronunciation was almost too precise, the way film and radio commentators spoke thirty or forty years ago. I asked if Sachiko was well. He thanked me and said she was very well.

"As you may know, she married last July."

He wondered if I might like her address and telephone number. I said yes. There was another long pause. While I was waiting I realised I didn't even know her married name; he told me when he read out her telephone number. I thanked him for all his trouble and put down the receiver.

I still don't feel as if I'm really here. I'm describing what happened as if it happened to me. Part of my life has passed to a stranger.

○

I'm on my way to work. The sky is bright and the air is cold. The early morning sunlight is shining in the breath of the people waiting for a bus.

The sunlit side of the street is a golden mirror alive with shadows hurrying into the light.

On the other side it's dark and cold as death.

Laroche is walking over the pedestrian crossing. He's got his head down and his shoulders are hunched against the cold.

○

It's eight-thirty in the evening and I got back from the office a few minutes ago. The hotel room's tidy and the bed's made. There's a copy of the *Japan Times* on the table by the window and a neatly folded cotton *kimono* on the bed. Apart from the newspaper and the *kimono* there's no sign that anyone's been here.

Tonight's my last night. Tomorrow I'm moving into a company house. Maria Santini gave me the keys this afternoon.

"You're lucky," she said and smiled like a model in a fashion photograph. "On the open market it would cost more." Her teeth were so white it was difficult to concentrate on what she was saying. I kept wondering how she managed to get them so white. She told me I had an allowance for furniture and household items which had to be bought from one particular department store. I thought she was joking and asked her why. Her smile went crooked and the look in her eyes was hard and ugly.

"It's none of your business," she said, then recomposed her expression. "That's the way the company organises things. It's an excellent store. It has everything."

"Yes," I said. "But why?" She smiled but her lips were closed.

"Nobody else has complained."

"I'm not complaining," I said. "I'm just curious." She was in control again. She gave another fashion-photograph smile. "It's Administration," she said, "it's nothing to do with you. If you want, you can ask Laroche but I advise you not to."

"Oh," I said.

"Don't make problems," she said, "he doesn't like people who are difficult."

"Am I difficult?" I asked.

"We haven't decided yet."

I asked her what she meant by "we." The fashion-photograph smile came back and she raised her eyebrows. She didn't look very sincere.

"What do I mean?" The smile had a life of its own. "Oh, people here. The office. How do you say in English? You're not the only stone on the beach."

"Pebble," I said.

"Thank you," she blinked her eyelashes and her eyes were very blue, "pebble."

○

It's late on Saturday morning and the sun's shining and I'm not feeling so good.

Last night I met Joe in the lobby of the Imperial Hotel. I was sitting in an armchair drinking tonic and bitters, watching all the people in suits. The lobby of the Imperial Hotel in Tokyo must be one of the best places in the world to look at people in suits: every style from the sleek technocrat to the almost invisible aristocrat and every colour from cobalt blue to charcoal grey. There are Savile Row imitations from Hong Kong and designer originals that look like jumble from second-hand clothes shops. Loose, tight, baggy, crumpled, creased, shiny and immaculate: they're all there.

I didn't see Joe. Someone in a suit said *"Hisashiburi"* and there he was grinning and looking pleased with himself.

"Spooked you, huh?" he said.

"The real thing," I replied.

The last time I saw Joe he was sitting cross-legged in shorts and a Madonna T-shirt with a Kretek cigarette smouldering between his fingers under the maple tree in his garden. But there he was an urban *ninja* in a grey business suit, the model of a young American businessman, flirting gently with the people bringing drinks, in fluent Japanese.

He's still with the company, importing components for man-ufacturing semi-conductors. He was in his hi-tech company persona: using words like "synergy" and talking about hori-zons and goals and motivation. I didn't mind. Sometimes it takes a while to get back on the wavelength. I wasn't really listening to what he was saying. I was just thinking how good it was to see him. He's a hero. He's one of the few foreigners I know who understands Japan in a Japanese way.

With a father in the American foreign service, a mother from England and a childhood in American embassies all over South-East Asia I can more or less understand why he decided to live in Japan and study at Sofia university. But at some point there must have been a leap in the dark, or an act of faith or intuition. Like the man visiting the Zen master for tea and enlightenment who was told the full cup cannot be filled, Joe had to lose some of his American nature to become Japanese. But working in a Japanese company, living in a Japanese house with a series of Japanese boyfriends, Joe had stopped being a conventional American some time ago.

On the surface, he seems to enjoy being normal. He presents himself as a company man, whose life is the company, who can only talk about his work in the company. It's a role a lot of people understand, and the more he tells them about his work the less they want to ask. Sometimes, when the role takes over, he needs reminding that he's not a blue-eyed *salariman*.

I asked about life outside work and he said it was OK but the beginning of the year was tough when he split up with Keiji. They'd been together for five years. One day an Austra-lian appeared with a case full of money. A week later Keiji moved out, and now he's running a bar in Shinjuku with back-ing from a company in Sydney.

Joe said he didn't feel bitter or sad, just puzzled.

"We were very close," he shrugged. "At least I thought we were. Maybe it was all my imagination." I said I was sorry and told him about Sachiko. He said he was sorry too and suggested another round of drinks. I could see it was going to be one of those evenings in Tokyo which end up in a small room with low lighting and smiling hostesses lighting cigarettes and filling glasses of ice with Napoleon brandy.

I said yes and it was one of those evenings.

After the drinks at the Imperial, Joe and I are walking along the street near Roppongi crossing, it's a kaleidoscope of red and blue and yellow neon lights and car headlights and traffic lights and Joe's saying, "This is my home, goddammit." Then we're in Maggie's Revenge where I'm sitting next to a man with gold wire spectacles who says he's interested in understanding foreigners. He keeps on asking questions. He wants to know what I do and where I come from and what I think of Japan and why some foreigners smoke Kretek cigarettes. There's a lot of noise and people laughing and shouting but the man is different, as if he's enclosed in an invisible aura which protects him from the chaos and cross-currents of noise and energy. I feel he's examining me and for some reason he's pretending to be drunk.

I ask why he isn't drinking and he says he isn't thirsty. Neither of us says anything for a while. He looks at his watch and says it's getting late and he has to be getting home. I say it was a pleasure talking to him and he smiles and we bow to each other and he disappears, leaving his drink on the bar.

Joe and I are on the street again and Joe's saying, "Just imagine, will you just imagine for God's sake, we have machines with the ability to reproduce themselves, did you ever hear of someone called von Neumann?"

There's a man with a black moustache and his hair tied back like a *samurai* knight selling luminous rings and glowing bracelets of blue and green and orange light, and a woman fortune-teller sitting beside a paper lantern painted with astrological signs, shining a flashlight into the palm of someone's hand, and a man in a tuxedo handing out pink invitation cards, and a girl with long black hair and a white overcoat, and an old man wearing a top hat who calls out to us in English. "Good evening boys! Are you looking for a good time?" Joe says, "Yes, but not with you," and the old man smiles. Joe says it's a rip-off but we follow the old man under an archway of flashing lights into a lift which is just big enough for three people and the doors close behind us.

I look at the old man's face. There are a lot of lines and I wonder what sort of person reaches his age earning a living by inviting men off the streets to meet pretty ladies.

We're sitting at two sides of a low table with a mirrored surface and a woman with a dead smile is introducing some girls in cocktail dresses. Joe makes a joke and the woman's smile becomes human.

It's the time of night when I wonder why I'm alive and I want to go to sleep and dream of angels. A girl in a pink chiffon dress is sitting with her knees pressed close against mine. I ask what kind of music she likes and while she answers I find myself thinking of Tanya. One of the girls suggests some *karaoke*. She gives Joe the song book and the girls are pleased with the title he chooses. A video flashes up on a screen about a woman beside a grey sea: the close-ups of her face are in soft focus; her expression is supposed to be sad but I'm out of practice with Japanese faces and to me she just looks absent-minded.

It's my turn, the girls want me to sing in English and the choice is between "My Way" and "The House of the Rising Sun." I sing "The House of the Rising Sun."

Joe asks if anyone knows how to make an *origami* peacock out of a ten-thousand-yen note. While he's making the peacock a girl sings another song with an upbeat rhythm. It sounds like "time-to-go" music. Joe finishes the peacock. Its eyes are made out of zeros and by pulling its beak its tail feathers spread a little. The girls love it and cry "*Kawaii! Kawaii!*" One of them runs to fetch the *mama-san* who's counting the receipts. She comes over and tries to look uninterested but when she sees it she's impressed and asks Joe if she can have it for a *kiipuseiku*. He says it costs ten thousand yen. She pretends to be shocked he won't even give her a paper peacock but at last she hands over a ten-thousand-yen note and carefully balancing the little paper bird in the palm of her hand she smiles and says he's welcome any time.

As we're putting on our coats a man in a tuxedo appears. He asks if we had a good evening; if we like any of the girls it's possible to include everything on the bill. He insists on giving us the name card of the bar.

I have the card in front of me. The Topaz Club: "Happy life and amusing friends."

○

It's eleven o'clock in the evening. I'm just back from an office party.

This morning everyone in the bonds and international equities section received a photocopy map of the Ginza with the position of a restaurant marked in green ink. I asked Yamaguchi if the party was a celebration. He smiled and said it was to welcome me and a secretary called Kaoru to the office. Takahashi, Yamaguchi's drinking companion, added that the restaurant was famous for its "mountain atmosphere."

People started towards the restaurant around six-thirty. I went with Noguchi. He's a strange man who has difficulty looking people in the eye when he talks to them. He worked for Nomura for fifteen years until last spring when the bank made him an offer he couldn't refuse. He spends all day watching half a dozen screens arranged in a flickering wall of different coloured numbers and charts. His eyes are oddly focused, as if the after-images of all those numbers are dancing on his retina.

Having a conversation with him was like defrosting the ice in a freezer. I asked how the Treasury market was and he gave a one-sentence answer which would've been true any day in the last three months. I asked if the US trade figures would be better or worse and he said they'd be about the same. For a minute or so we walked along without saying anything.

I told myself that Japanese are happy to be silent together and feeling uncomfortable with silence was a Western reaction. It didn't make any difference. I still felt uneasy. I asked how it was working for a foreign company after Nomura. He made a sound halfway between a laugh and a sniff. Every time I asked a question he made the same sound. I guessed it might be a nervous tic.

"I like it," he said. For a few seconds it seemed that was all he was going to say. Then he said the size of Nomura's capitalisation in billions of dollars. He paused after he said that as if it was the answer to my question. He was working for a big Japanese company. Now he works for a small foreign company. He earns more money and has more freedom and he telephones his old colleagues several times a day so he doesn't miss them.

He talked about things that could be measured, like the capitalisation of companies and the numbers of employees. I didn't want to push him into talking about himself because talking about oneself can be difficult. It's *wagamama, jibun-kata*. It's taboo: it separates one from the group. Instead I asked if he liked working for the company. He gave another little snort and said, "*Tsuki desu yo*—sure I like it" and we walked along together in silence for another minute or so. Then he cleared his throat and said, "Do you like raw fish?" I said, "Yes, very much indeed," and after that we were silent until we reached the restaurant.

As we were taking off our shoes at the entrance other people from the office joined us. A maid drew back a sliding door and showed us into the room reserved for our party. There were two low tables made of wood: the surfaces were polished but the sides had been left irregular, preserving the shape of the tree. The floor was *tatami* matting, the walls were sand coloured and two bright fluorescent lights hung from the ceiling. There were no windows. Everyone stood around uncertainly until someone asked Noguchi, as the senior person present, to arrange the seating. There were polite smiles and formal expressions. It was more like a religious ceremony than a party.

More people arrived in twos and threes until there were about twenty of us, but the atmosphere was still hesitant and artificial, like a scene in which the actors weren't quite sure of their lines. On the other side of the sliding doors there were sounds of noisy conversation and laughter. The party next door were having a good time. I looked at faces and wondered how long the evening was going to last.

I sat next to Kaoru, who joined the company the same day I began work in the Tokyo office. She's twenty-six and pretty in a curiously un-Japanese way. Her lips are full and slightly open. When she smiles she's beautiful. Her English wasn't so good so we spoke in Japanese. At university she studied American literature. She specialised in the works of J. D. Salinger. Her favourite book was *The Catcher in the Rye*. I asked her why.

"Because the hero was easy for me to recognise." She smiled. "I felt I understood him." I thought of an imaginary teenage rebel in America in the 1950s and a young Japanese woman at a Catholic university in Tokyo in the 1980s and wondered what they had in common. I smiled and nodded.

Rex Matsumoto arrived and sat down opposite. For the first time I was close enough to see what kind of person he is. He's in his early forties. His voice is deep and strong and has an authority which almost compensates for his below-average size. Even for a Japanese he's small, but we were both sitting cross-legged at a low, wooden table so there was no problem. We were on a level.

His face is lean and ascetic and behind the lenses of his spectacles, his eyes glitter with intelligence. His style reminds me of a university lecturer with a private income, an academic with money. He grew up in the States but his parents spoke Japanese at home. He has a D.Phil. in sociology and anthropology from the University of California.

"I guess it may not be much of a surprise for you to hear that I was particularly interested in cross-cultural comparisons between the United States and Japan," he said. He chose his words with precision, enunciating them in a way which was more English than Californian. There was nothing Japanese about the way he spoke except for a trace of un-American formality.

I asked if he'd developed any general theory during his studies and he smiled, like a professor asked an elementary question.

"Let's say there are two different kinds of people," he said. "I call them 'stayers' and 'leavers.' " Some Westerners would have defined the categories further but Rex left the sentence as it was. I assumed Americans were "leavers" and Japanese were "stayers." We were speaking in English but our communication was Japanese. It was coming back to me: how people in Japan leave their sentence unfinished and the meaning shifts in the silence between one person talking and another person answering. Aposiopesis.

I waited for Rex to say something but he was lighting a cigarette and, as he exhaled, the door behind him rattled and slid back and Yamaguchi stepped into the room.

"Eh? Nanda?" he shouted. "What's happening? Why isn't everyone drinking?"

Rex called out in English, "We were waiting for you." Yamaguchi's face was mottled. He might have had a few drinks already.

"Ah! Matsumoto. What's that you said?" Yamaguchi looked at Rex as if he was surprised to see him. "It sounded a bit foreign." Yamaguchi spoke in Japanese. I thought there was an uneasy feeling among the people around me, but perhaps I imagined it. Yamaguchi gave a saccharine smile. He could have been referring to Rex's American background. I wasn't sure. He nodded to a secretary, who gave him a glass and filled it with beer. It was the signal for everyone to fill their neighbour's glass.

Kaoru took the bottle of beer on the table in front of us, and filled my glass. She held the bottle in both hands and poured slowly and carefully, almost to the brim but not so full that we risked pouring beer in our laps when we raised our glasses. Then she did the same for Rex Matsumoto and one of the bond dealers. We all stood up and Yamaguchi checked that everyone was ready.

"*Sore de wa, mina-san,*" he spoke in a sharp, military tone of voice, "OK then everyone, *kampai shimasho!*" We raised our glasses together and with one voice shouted "*Kampai!*"

The beer had been too long on the tables and it was luke-warm. Behind us, the doors slid open and a maid came in carrying trays of *sashimi*, slices of raw fish, boiled octopus and prawns, arranged around a miniature plastic pine tree on a glistening green island of seaweed. She was in a hurry and had no time for formality. The way she took orders for beer and *sake* made everyone relax.

We kept filling each other's glasses and the conversation got louder and the room got smokier. Several men took off their jackets and loosened their ties. Someone with a fat, shiny face leaned towards me and asked if I was strong.

"We Japanese are weak drinkers," he said.

"Ah," I said.

I'd heard it too many times before; almost every Japanese man says the same thing when he has a drink with a foreigner. I couldn't even pretend to be interested.

"Foreigners are very strong," he added. I agreed with him. "Japanese people have red faces when they drink." I nodded encouragingly. "Enzymes," he said, "we Japanese are allergic to certain enzymes in alcohol." He grinned and pointed at one of the foreign-exchange dealers whose face was already a dangerous-looking shade of crimson.

"Biologically we are different from other people." The conversation was following a familiar pattern. I asked him for an example.

"For your information," he picked up a piece of boiled octopus between his chopsticks and a pink tentacle trembled at the corner of his mouth as he spoke, "we Japanese have different guts from foreigners. It has been proved scientifically. And our centre of gravity is in a different place. And our brains are different. That is why we Japanese are so close to nature."

"There aren't many trees in Tokyo," I said.

"Yes," he smiled, "but our brains are different. For example, when you hear the voice of a cicada perhaps you do not think it is musical." I wasn't sure if he was asking a question so I just grunted, Japanese style.

"*So desho*, I think so," he said. "But when we Japanese hear the voice of certain insects we are much moved in our hearts." He blinked several times. "Frogs also." He sniffed and blinked again. "Excuse me. I am thinking of my *furusato*, the place where I was born. It is a deep emotion for me. Every summer when I was a boy we hunted frogs in the paddy fields. Even small frogs the size of a little finger make a big sound."

I remembered living in the country in the north of Japan, how the racket of the frogs, clattering in the moonlight, kept me awake at night and I wondered what kind of connection there was between their raucous croaking and the unique quality of Japanese brains. The man with the fat face was happy to explain.

"You see, our brains function in a different way. When we hear the voice of insects and other creatures, we listen with the same part of the brain that we use for language. Although the sound has no words it has great meaning for us." He gestured towards a selection of red slices of *maguro*.

"*Dozo*—please challenge this raw fish." I thanked him and there was a pause in the conversation while I watched him pluck a sprig of flower with his chopsticks from the base of the miniature plastic pine tree and strip its leaves into a saucer of soy vinegar.

"Such leaves have a delicious taste," he said. "I am a country boy. That is why I know these things." I asked what part of

Japan he was from and he told me about the village in Gifu where he lived until he went to university in Tokyo.

"At first it was difficult for me. I had to endure many things. My life was *gaman*—endurance. I missed the colours of the rice fields in summer, and the snow in winter. In Tokyo the snow is nothing in a few hours. Tokyo was like another country for me." I said I had the same feeling when I first arrived.

"Then perhaps you understand," he said. "My heart is in the country. There are many people like me: in Tokyo, in Nagoya, in Osaka. We live and work in the big cities, *but* our true home is in the country. Our heart is in the country. Every year at Obon, the Festival of the Dead, I go back to my village, my *furusato*, to show respect to the graves of my ancestors. We wash the stones, and give flowers and food and drink to the spirits of our ancestors." He laughed nervously. "Perhaps this custom seems primitive to you? Is it a shock for you?"

I said no it wasn't. I said Christians believe they eat the body of God and drink his blood. For a moment he looked incredulous and then burst into a fit of giggles. When he'd recovered himself he asked how it was possible. I described the ritual of bread and wine and said it was called communion.

"*Naruhodo*—I see." He smiled and filled my glass. "Now let us make Japanese communion." He raised his glass which was still full to the brim and grinned. "*Kampai!*"

The tables were littered with the debris of the meal; the miniature plastic pine tree had tumbled into a mound of seaweed; the barbecued pork and onions and gingko nuts and chicken livers had been eaten, and only the smoke-blackened wooden skewers remained; the rice bowls had been filled and emptied and the men were drinking *sake*.

Rex was talking to Kaoru. He asked whether she had a long journey home and did she have time for a *sushi*, or maybe she'd like to go dancing. She was holding her hand in front of her mouth to hide a smile of embarrassment. The man with the fat face was sitting with his arms folded and his head sunk on his chest, asleep. Yamaguchi stood up and steadied himself against the wall. His tie was loose and his eyes were bloodshot. The conversation died away. He licked his lips and smiled at no one in particular. After thanking everyone for making the evening a success he hiccoughed and smiled again.

"So," he said, and for several seconds it seemed as if he was thinking about someone or something very far away. *"Mina-san, kampai shimasho."* We raised our glasses obediently and there was a ragged chorus of *"Kampai!"* It was time to go.

People filed towards the door to put on their shoes and collect their coats. I wasn't sure what was supposed to happen next. Rex was still asking Kaoru if she wanted to go on somewhere else and she was still refusing but her resistance was weakening. Noguchi tapped the fat man gently on the shoulder and he woke with a start.

For a while I was part of the group, but the party was over. They were going back to their families and friends and I was on my own, a foreigner in Tokyo.

In the street outside the restaurant Yamaguchi, Takahashi, the fat man and a few others were standing in a small group. The fat man smiled at me and beckoned me to join them. They were discussing which bar to go to next. Someone suggested a place called Pépé le Moko and we set off. There were five of us. Yamaguchi, Takahashi and one of the bond dealers walked in front, the fat man and I followed them.

The street was like a video game of flashing signs with hazards suddenly appearing out of doorways like *salarimen* and office girls and traffic lights and car and pedestrian crossings. I let my body find a way through while I listened to the fat man beside me talking about the price of housing in Tokyo. We were approaching the road crossing by the Ginza station just as the lights signalled they were about to change. Yamaguchi and the others hesitated. The fat man called out to them to wait.

Yamaguchi turned round and I saw his face in the red and yellow light of a neon sign. He was leaning on Takahashi's shoulder.

"*Da-me*," he shouted in Japanese. "No way. I've had enough *gaijin* for today." He looked at Takahashi, who smirked. Then they put their arms over each other's shoulders, like a three-legged race, and lurched across the road in front of a line of cars sounding their horns. The lights changed as they reached the pavement where the other man was waiting for them. They didn't look back and I lost sight of them among the moving shadows on the other side of the river of lights rushing between us.

The fat man put his head to one side and sucked the air in through his teeth. He avoided looking at me.

"*Chotto muzukashi desu ne*," he said, "it's a bit difficult, isn't it?" I didn't say anything. "Well, anyway," he said at last, "it's getting late. This is my station. I must be going home now. See you in the morning."

"Yes," I said, "see you in the morning." The lights changed. We bowed to each other and I watched him walk into the silhouettes of people surging across the road.

○

It's eleven-thirty on Saturday morning, the sun is shining and the windows are open. The neighbour's cats are rolling over each other in the sunlight.

A couple of days ago a man from the Amsterdam office arrived in Tokyo on a round-the-world trip, telling people about the Dutch market. His name was Norman and he came from California. He was in his forties with the sort of face it's easy to trust; untidy hair, big nose, thick eyebrows, brown eyes with a tired humour. He kept saying it was his first time in Asia and he wanted to experience the real Japan. Not the tourist stuff. The real thing. He'd had enough high life and he wanted some low life. I said I'd take him to Shinjuku.

We finished work around seven-thirty and took a taxi north. The traffic was heavy and it was almost eight o'clock when we got to Shinjuku and the lights and signs and colours of the neon palaces and castles were flashing like giant pinball machines. We got out near the north exit of Shinjuku station, in the square with the big television screens. Norman liked it. It was like Las Vegas on acid with Japanese subtitles.

We started the evening in the area some foreigners call Piss Alley. The narrow lanes are still there, and the ramshackle little stalls and wooden cabins like brightly lit cupboards, with the smoke from grilled chicken livers and steam pouring out of them, and hardly enough space for six or seven men to sit in a line at the counter watching the master or his wife turn the scallops and pour the *sake*.

Every time I go to Piss Alley I think "this is the old Japan." It's how I imagine the shanty town of wood and paper and oil drums that was Tokyo in the months after Japan's surrender to America. Sometimes, in the light of a disintegrating paper lantern, there's even a ghost of Edo about the place. The smell of boiled rice and miso soup and fried vegetables and the sound of laughter and the movements of chopsticks and people's faces are the same as they always were, except the men drinking *sake* are in business suits and they wear electric watches.

We found a shack lit by a couple of bare light bulbs with some spaces free at the counter. There was a smell of charcoal and fat sizzling and the man behind the counter shouted a friendly *Irashai!* Welcome!

I ordered a couple of beers and some grilled fish and vegetables and Norman wanted some *sake*, to taste the real Japan, so I ordered hot *sake* and we said *Kampai!* to each other and talked about Buddhism and the Wheel of Suffering.

The master of the shop asked where Norman came from. I told him Los Angeles and he smiled and took a postcard from a ledge to show us. It was a picture of the hotel in Los Angeles where he goes every year for a holiday. Norman stretched out his hand and said, "Gimme five, man!" The man smiled and wiped his hands on a cloth and they shook hands.

We walked along a street that was bright with pink and green and blue signs, past the sound of recorded machine-gun fire from games arcades, and flashing lights, and marching music, and the rattle and clatter and roar of *pachinko* parlours, till we came to an area full of sex video shops and massage parlours.

There were several *chienpira* walking around with stiff movements and tough expressions, smoking cigarettes like fifties' wild boys. One wearing a long white tweed coat came towards us. His hair was greased into a curl on his forehead and he was wearing dark glasses. Norman said he looked like he'd forgotten to take the coat hanger out of his jacket.

The boy with the curl on his forehead fluttered his hand. "Sex show," he hissed. He led us to a doorway where a man in a suit with a black shirt was talking to another man in a loud pinstripe suit. Both of them were wearing women's slip-on shoes. I told Norman they were *yakuza* gangsters. He laughed and asked if they had a gender problem. Our guide gestured through the doorway and we went inside, down some stairs, and came to a man sitting on a chair under a red light bulb. The man held up his hand with the fingers apart and asked for five thousand yen. The top of the little finger on his left hand was missing. I paid and he waved us through a black painted door.

The room was dark except for a spotlight shining on to a small circular stage where a naked couple were embracing. I stood by the door while my eyes adjusted to the darkness and looked at the faces of the audience in the light reflected from the stage. Most were men, but there were two old ladies who could have been in their seventies, and several younger women; one was sitting with her head pillowed on the shoulder of a young man in a rugger shirt.

There were no seats free and we stood with our backs to the wall facing the stage. The couple on the stage were about twenty feet away. The man looked in his early forties, the woman in her mid-thirties. They weren't in time with the music but they seemed to have some kind of routine. They had a serious attitude to their work. It reminded me of a display by members of a keep-fit club. He carried her with her legs round his waist and her arms round his neck. Still together, he lay down and she turned round. He stood up and held on to her while she did a handstand. They were always together. Norman said they must have put in a lot of practice. They didn't say anything to each other.

The people in the audience could have been watching a film. I wondered what the old ladies were thinking, if they were thinking anything at all, or if they'd simply come for warmth and companionship. Perhaps it was more interesting than television. Once or twice they whispered to each other, leaning their heads together, but they kept looking at the stage.

On stage the woman had her legs round the man's waist, facing the audience with her arms stretched out like wings. An old man wearing spectacles in the front row was asleep.

I thought about the couple on stage, if they were paid by the minute or a flat rate for each performance, and what they said when someone asked what they did for a living.

The man was conscientious, the woman was accommodating. It was hard to know which would end first, the couple or the music: I'd been standing for a long time. At last the rhythm changed and the couple were still. The audience was silent for several seconds before giving a round of light applause.

The man grinned and bowed towards the spotlight. The woman threw a light *kimono* over her shoulder and bowed without looking at the audience. Norman said he'd had enough of the real Japan and suggested a beer back at the hotel. I got back here just before midnight.

The cats next door have disappeared and a woman is hanging out clothes on a washing line.

○

It's eleven o'clock on Sunday morning.

Last night I dreamed of Tanya: we were walking by a river

in the country. There was a white horse in a green field. She asked me a question which I can't remember, a voice said, "This is the way of all flesh," and I woke up here in Nakameguro.

From the window I can see over a tall wooden fence into the property of one of my neighbours. The house looks as if it was built sometime in the 1960s. The land attached to it is about the size of a tennis court. Nakameguro is a good residential area and the real estate value of the land, even without the house, must be worth more than the average Japanese worker earns in a lifetime. The house is a two-storey construction of white metal and concrete with a blue-tiled roof. The old man who lives in it has planted the garden with vegetables and made a scarecrow to watch over them. The scarecrow is wearing a Hankyu Lions' baseball hat and a tweed jacket. The old man's wearing a brown tracksuit top and dungarees, hoeing between a row of seedlings, trailing a scarf of breath that keeps unravelling in the sunlight.

He must be in his late seventies. I wonder if he was born in the country or in Tokyo. It's good to think of him doing the kind of work he did in the country. But maybe it's a habit left over from the days after the war, when the townspeople were starving and they cultivated their gardens because they were hungry. We haven't spoken to one another and I know nothing about him except his name which is written on the entrance gateway to his property: Uehara.

Next door, on the other side of the thick azalea hedge, is a larger, more modern house, made of concrete with picture windows and a flat roof. The walls are covered with ivy. The wind blows and the red leaves flicker in the sunlight. The house stands in a garden planted with dwarf pine trees and cherry trees through which a path of square paving stones winds its way across a dusty lawn. There are two cats, a tortoiseshell and a tailless Japanese tabby cat prowling through the dead leaves under the azalea hedge.

The tortoiseshell cat is moving towards the middle of the

hedge where there's a bamboo gate and sliding through into the old man's garden. The old man strokes the cat.

Through the other bedroom window I can just see into another neighbouring property. The house is old: it's made of weathered wood and it's roofed with grey tiles. In the garden there's a stone pagoda and a path leading to an ornamental pool under a leafless willow tree. It's a traditional Japanese house and a traditional Japanese garden. The windows are shuttered and the garden looks neglected: the stone path is covered with moss and the water in the pool is overgrown with weeds. Beside the house there's a persimmon tree and the ground is littered with golden fruit which has fallen and not been collected.

○

It's ten o'clock on Thursday night and I'm just back from a party at Roger Cranbrook's. The first person I saw as I came into the room was Charlie Pound from Goldman Sachs. He was wearing a crumpled white seersucker suit, talking to a Japanese woman in a pink Chanel dress. He looked bored and she looked pretty. A waiter offered a glass of champagne and I went over to join them. Charlie smiled. He tried to introduce the Japanese woman but he'd forgotten her name so she introduced herself: Yoshida, bond dealer with Merrill Lynch. Her hair was cut in a sharp, model-girl style that didn't suit her face which was soft and smiling. Charlie said bonds were boring, she said equities were risky. He turned to me. "Bonds are boring, right? The economy goes up and down, so do interest rates, so do bond prices—bond dealers make money. End of story."

The Japanese woman put her head to one side and pouted.

"Maybe when you are older, Charlie, you will like bonds. Young people like risk, old people like security."

Charlie shook his head. "No way," he smiled, "it's biological. They've done studies in the States. Some people need more risk. Their bodies need the adrenaline. It's genetic, like a big nose." Yoshida-san shook her head and smiled sweetly.

"Bullshit," she smiled. It was strange to hear the word "bullshit" from the orange lips of a pretty Japanese woman. I thought of all those Merrill Lynch bond dealers, raising the corners of their mouths and shouting into telephones—"bullshit" from the thundering herd. Suddenly she wasn't there.

"Merrill Lynch," said Charlie, "what do you expect?" I said she was better-looking than the Merrill Lynch bond dealers in London in shirts with button-down collars and brown brogue shoes and big meaty handshakes.

Charlie said he'd just seen the price of a stock he recommended go up by twenty per cent.

"Can you imagine what it feels like?" he asked. "Orgasmic," he said. "Absolutely incredible. It's better than sex. It's power. The feeling of power: moving the market. It's beautiful." I congratulated him. I asked what was happening on the Tokyo market.

"Money, money, more money," said Charlie, "the Japanese have won the semi-conductor wars, they feel more confident and they're going international. The most advanced technology rules the world. Pax Britannica, Pax Americana, now it's Pax Nipponica. The Japanese call it a 'borderless economy.' " I asked what he thought they meant by "borderless economy."

Charlie grinned, "Who knows? Maybe 'global market' sounds aggressive, or expansionist, or something. 'Borderless economy' sounds neutral. Japan lends money to the world to buy Japanese products and people pay twice; first when they borrow the money, then when they buy the product. Tokyo's a money machine, the capital of a twenty-first-century empire."

He asked how Tokyo was after London. It's a question I ask other people, it's a symptom of living abroad. Expatriate uncertainty; is where you are better than where you came from? I said I was still arriving.

"Each time I come back, it seems more like coming home," he said. "Maybe I'm forgetting what the rest of the world is like." He grinned as if he didn't really believe what he was saying.

"Maybe you're turning Japanese," I said.

"*So desu ne*," he smiled. I looked around at the other people. I recognised several faces; the round, pink face of Christopher Purvis (I hadn't seen him since we had the talk about post-traumatic stress syndrome), the smiling face of George Nimmo, Anthony and Claudia Cragg, and "Wily" Willoughby talking to a small man with a tightly pursed mouth and a mottled complexion who looked vaguely familiar, and might have been Philip Ramsend who used to work at Warburgs.

Roger introduced me to a young Japanese woman. Her hair was long, *o-jo-sama*—princess style, her face was smooth and open, and her eyes were clear and bright. She lived with her parents in Yotsuya and was studying earth science at the International Christian University. She liked travelling in Europe and playing tennis. She was a Baptist. Did I know that only one per cent of the population in Japan was Christian? She invited me to her younger brother's baptism. I thanked her and a waiter came and filled our glasses.

A Japanese man in his early forties joined us. His *meishi* showed he worked for Mitsubishi. He was wearing a Hermès tie. He began talking about the US–Japan trade deficit and the *o-jo-sama* princess melted away.

"The problem of the US–Japan trade deficit will not disappear," the man from Mitsubishi said, "until Japan changes its distribution system. It will take time. Our distribution system is part of the fabric of our society. Someone, X, sells, what shall I say?" he looked up at the ceiling for inspiration, "a bottle of whisky!" He checked our faces to see we appreciated his sense of humour. We nodded and smiled. "X sells a bottle of whisky to Y who sells it to Z who sells it to the customer. Or perhaps he sells it to A, who sells it to B, who sells it to C. Every sale makes the whisky more expensive. There are many small shops in Japan. We call these shops Mom-and-Pop stores. They employ many people. I think Napoleon said England was a nation of shopkeepers." He beamed with pleasure as he delivered the punchline. "Now we Japanese are also a nation of shop-keepers."

The room was crowded and the conversation was reaching the level of noise which happens when people at a party are into their third glass and beginning to realise how interesting they are. It was time to go.

I looked for Roger and his wife but I couldn't see either of them. I went towards the room where the coats were. I was putting on my coat when I heard the sound of a woman crying and a man saying, "For God's sake pull yourself together."

The air outside was cold on my face and there were flecks of snow scintillating in the brightness of a street lamp like tiny stars drifting into the dark beyond the light.

○

It's Monday morning and it's snowing. I'm looking out of the window into the garden of the old house next door and the snow is falling out of a grey sky, covering the darkness of the pine trees and softening the shape of the stone lantern. The paths are hidden and the snow has drifted into a frozen white wave against the door of the house. There are no footprints. It's like a picture in one of those books about Japanese architecture, full of beautiful photographs of houses and gardens with nobody there. I can just imagine someone taking a photograph of the snowflakes against a background of dark weathered wood and calling it "Winter in Tokyo." Or it could be a *haiku*: the silence of snow, the stillness of the trees, in the empty garden.

The streets are different. The snow's piled on either side of the road covering the curb, and instead of the pavement there's a track of ice and slush. People under umbrellas move through the falling snow. Things which were white look grey. Everything's white and grey except for the umbrellas. It's like a wood block print by Hiroshige: anonymous figures under umbrellas, Japan a hundred years ago in the falling snow.

○

It's lunchtime and I'm sitting in McDonald's.

I got paid this morning. It was the same as my London pay— no adjustment for living in Tokyo. I thought it was a mistake so I called Maria Santini but she said it was nothing to do with her. I had to talk to Laroche. His secretary said he was busy. I tried again and she said she would call me back. A couple of hours later I called again and she said he would be free for a few minutes if I came to his office immediately.

Same as last time, he was wearing his light-sensitive spectacles. The desk was clear except for a copy of *The Economist*, an empty coffee cup and a leather spectacle case.

"What can I do for you?" he said. I said I thought there was a mistake with my salary.

"What makes you think that?" he said. I told him. He looked at his fingernails and when I finished he sighed and said nothing was possible until the next salary review ten months from now. It should have been sorted out in London.

"I don't like money," he said, "I get nervous when I talk about it." I wondered what his problem was. My arrival in the office is an invasion of company territory. He wasn't consulted. Maybe he thinks it's a threat to his authority; someone in head office testing him, perhaps one of the old men on the fifth floor challenging his position. Perhaps sending me to Tokyo was just another move in some game I didn't know about. I told him I'd talk to Bob. He shrugged and said I could do what I liked, it wouldn't make any difference.

A couple of girls are giggling at me, seeing me talking into the recorder.

I don't think I want another hamburger for a long time.

I'd forgotten the strange, parallel universe of McDonald's in Japan, *Makudonarudo*. This is where to hear the beginning of global language. The waitresses at the counter sound like they're speaking English and Japanese at the same time. They smile a lot. They look as if they're having fun. Maybe working in McDonald's they feel *intanashionaru*. The piped music is bright and cheerful and the chorus is in English: "Happy life, Hap—Hap—Happy life, Happy life, Hap—Hap—Happy life."

I'd like to buy the world a Coke but sometimes I think I understand why people go wild with shotguns in crowded shopping malls.

○

I'm in the back of a taxi on my way home to Nakameguro.

It's raining and the street lights and neon signs are scattering across the windows in red and green and yellow stars.

I telephoned Bob an hour ago. He said it was a difficult situation and he understood my position but there was nothing he could do since technically I'm employed by the Tokyo office.

He told me a story. A little bird was in a snowstorm. It was very cold and the little bird was very weak. Its strength was failing, it couldn't fly any further and it fell out of the sky into the snow. It was dead to the world but still just alive. Then a cow, walking by, decided to stop, raised its tail, and dropped a mound of shit on the little bird. The heat of the shit revived the little bird: its little heart began to beat, it felt better. The heat reminded the little bird of the sun and it sang a song of delight at the memory of summer and the joy of being alive. On the other side of a hedge the farm yard cat was patrolling the farm for rats and mice. The cat heard the song of the little bird, crept up to where the song was coming from and ate the little bird.

The moral of the story is in three parts. Not all the ones who put you in the shit are your enemies. When you're in the shit, don't sing about it. Not all the ones who take you out of the shit are your friends. I asked Bob where he heard the story and he said he got it from a friend on the other side of the water.

While we were talking, Yamaguchi pretended to telephone someone. He picked up his receiver a few moments after he heard me mention Bob's name and pressed some numbers on his telephone pad as if he were dialling an outside line, but there weren't enough numbers, so I guess it was the combination for the conference-call connection, allowing him to listen to a conversation on my line. I watched him carefully. During the conversation with Bob, Yamaguchi didn't say a word; he just looked out of the window with a blank expression as if he were listening to a dialling tone. I wanted to see if he was listening to the conversation so after Bob told me the story I asked how the Invisible Man and the Queen of Hearts were doing. I saw Yamaguchi's eyebrows twitch. I guessed he wouldn't know the names of Bob's horses. A couple of seconds after I said goodbye to Bob, Yamaguchi put down his receiver with a look of irritation, as if he'd dialled the wrong number or the person he was calling wasn't answering the phone.

I could be imagining things, but I'm not.

○

The taxi driver was an amusing character. He came from the country, somewhere in Nagano prefecture and he thought Tokyo was a terrible place.

"Nobody has time for anything except making money. People don't care about each other. Some people would sell their wives if they could get a good price." He looked at me in the mirror and his eyes were smiling. He told me he tried to sell his wife but no one was interested so he was still driving a taxi.

"Eighteen hours a day," he said. "I've forgotten what my wife looks like. She's always asleep when I get back. I don't turn on the light. That way it suits both of us."

It's eight o'clock in the evening and I'm back in Nakameguro.

The house feels empty. Out there everyone is Japanese. In here I'm a foreigner. I live here but it's not home.

The room's decorated in bland, intercontinental colours. The walls are off-white and the carpets are a sensible shade of grey. The curtains are sepia and white. There are no pictures on the wall. The day after tomorrow someone from the office is delivering a sofa and two armchairs. Maybe it'll improve the place.

○

It's one o'clock in the afternoon and I'm on basement level three sitting at a table in The Café Human.

This morning I met the man who's delivering the furniture. His name is Matsuzaki. His *meishi* card describes him as Section Chief in charge of information technology. It seems odd for the person in charge of information technology to be driving round Tokyo in a van delivering furniture. I asked if he was sure he could spare the time. He smiled and said it was no problem. He smiled a lot, but his eyes were the same all the time. He said he needed to borrow the keys to the house to deliver the furniture. I drew a ground plan of the house and marked the room where I needed the sofa and chairs. He's going to deliver the furniture tomorrow morning.

○

I'm thinking about Matsuzaki coming to the house. When I met him there was a moment which made me think of the stillness in the *dojo* hall, practising *kendo*, in the seconds before a contest; the silent measuring of the strength and speed and willpower of the person standing opposite and the sense of a sudden attack about to happen. I had the same feeling looking at Matsuzaki. We could almost have been in a *dojo*, instead of Administration.

Sometimes the body remembers what the mind forgets.

Maybe his attitude reminded me of someone I fought in the *dojo*. Maybe it was chemical.

I didn't trust him. I don't know why.

But, suspicion without a cause is paranoia. Does he suspect me because I'm a foreigner or do I suspect him because he's Japanese?

○

I've made an experiment, nothing complicated. I collected some dust and fluff from the carpet and made three small marker pellets and wedged one in between each of the door frames and the doors leading into the room where I work and the two bedrooms. If anyone opens the door the dust falls to the ground. I marked the positions of the pellets against patterns in the wood. I've left the door of the living room open, so Matsuzaki shouldn't have any difficulty finding where to put the furniture.

○

I gave the keys to Matsuzaki this morning and he said he'd return them after lunch. I explained that the living room was the door on the left after the entrance hall and he said it was OK, he understood where it was. I thanked him for his trouble. He promised to call me when he arrived back in the office.

I'm sitting in The Café Human talking into this machine and he's in the house at Nakameguro.

○

When I came out of The Café Human it was raining. I'd left my umbrella in the office and I was standing at the pedestrian crossing opposite the station, waiting for the lights to change, when a man of seventy or so came up beside me and without saying anything held his umbrella over me. I looked at him and he smiled and we walked together across the road. When we reached the other side I thanked him again, we bowed to each other and went in opposite directions.

○

It's eight o'clock in the evening. The sofa and chairs are in the living room; they're a light beige colour which goes with the carpet. I sat on the sofa and it felt OK.

I checked the doors. All the dust pellets were on the floor.

○

It's good to be here. When I finished work yesterday I needed a break so I called Conrad and he invited me out here to his place in the country. It's good to see him and Fumiko again. It's been a long time. The children are taller and the wistaria by the front door has twined itself on to the roof tiles.

I took the evening train. I opened the carriage window as the train approached the station and caught the scent of pine trees in the darkness. A car pulled up in the station car park and flashed its headlights. I opened the door and there was music by Erik Satie on the car sound system and a smell of Kretek cigarettes.

Conrad hasn't really changed. He's still living in the old wooden house in the mountains on the edge of the forest when he's not somewhere in Asia taking photographs. He still does an hour of meditation before a vegetarian breakfast and he still smokes Kretek cigarettes. Fumiko is beautiful and silent as always.

Nobody mentions the long bond yield. There are no Reuters screens. When someone talks about the market they mean a collection of stalls with people selling smoking chunks of grilled octopus and piles of vegetables and pickles.

I'm writing this while my feet warm on the *kotatsu*. Conrad's sitting on the other side of the table reading a book. Fumiko is preparing supper. There's harpsichord music playing and a smell of rice and vegetables cooking. The children are upstairs in the bedroom doing their homework. The *tatami* is worn and polished with use. In the *shoji* sliding doors there are squares where the original paper has been torn and repaired. In several of the squares there are silhouettes of maple leaves which have been inserted between the layers of paper.

I remember the scroll painting hanging in the *tokonoma*; a winter painting of a snow-covered willow tree beside a dark grey river and the tracks of a bear in the snow. Last time I was here the painting in the *tokonoma* was of a dragonfly on a blade of grass, the sliding doors were pushed back, the *tatami* was warm with sunlight and the room was fizzing with the sound of cicadas.

This room is full of memories. I remember sitting here by candlelight smoking a Kretek with the *shoji* open, talking to Fumiko about *iroha* and listening to her tell the story of the Herder and the Weaver Girl. Another time with Conrad we drank tea through the night, watching the mountains on the other side of the valley emerging from the mist in the early morning light, like the mysterious original of a landscape in a Chinese ink painting. We counted seven tones of shadows, from the dark outline of the nearest hilltop, to the taller mountains becoming paler and fainter towards the horizon, and Conrad said once he'd counted eleven.

○

It's four o'clock in the afternoon and it's raining. I'm looking out of the window across the valley towards the mountains which are obscured by clouds. The rain's different from the rain at home. It has a different character. I look at the rain and think of what it was like to live in this valley a hundred years ago. No cars. No railway. Only a road for pack animals along the bank of a winding mountain river.

Thinking of the past and looking at the rain is like travelling in time: something changes, something remains the same.

This morning I was woken by the boys who wanted me to go with them for a walk in the forest. They wanted to show me where they had seen a *tanuki*. Kazu is eleven and Tomo is eight. They both look Japanese but Kazu has grey eyes. I followed them up the path that leads past the ancestral graves to the pine forest. The air was cool and the sky was grey. Kazu went in front but when we came to a fork in the path he checked with his younger brother before taking the right-hand path. We walked for several hundred yards in silence. Then Tomo said, "*Wah kusai!* bad smell!" and Kazu laughed and told him it was the smell of foxes.

A little way further on Kazu stopped and pointed between the trees to a small clearing.

"That's where the *tanuki* dance," he said. "We saw one of them in the moonlight." I asked what he was doing in the forest at night. Sometimes Conrad takes them for walks in the dark. "He teaches us how to be shadows," he said. "*Tanuki* are naughty, they change their shape and make people forget who they are." I asked if he liked *tanuki* and he looked doubtful.

"Not really, because they can do magic," Tomo said. Kazu laughed and teased him for being afraid of animals.

The forest was very quiet. It was my first time in the country for a while and I wanted to be alone. As if he heard my thoughts, Kazu turned to his brother and said they should be getting back to the house in case their mother was worried where they were. I thanked them for showing me where the *tanuki* danced in the moonlight and Kazu said, "You're welcome," exactly like a polite American boy except he bowed when he spoke.

I watched them disappear into the trees below and I walked on up the path. I wanted to reach the crest of one of the hills overlooking the valley.

As the path climbed higher it became more tangled and overgrown until it was difficult to see if there was a path at all. I was thinking I'd lost the path altogether when I came into another clearing and saw a small wooden shrine. The top of its roof was the height of my shoulder. The wood was weatherbeaten. Across the entrance was a string of ragged paper flags: inside there was a *sake* bottle, a saucer on a ledge, another saucer tumbled on the ground and a porcelain figure of Inari-samma the Fox God. Someone had come with offerings of rice cakes and *sake* and dressed the shrine with paper flags but the path was almost overgrown. Probably only one or two people a year made their way through the forest to where I was, in front of the shrine.

The trees were a thick wall around the shrine, hiding and protecting it from the rest of the world: making a secret place for Inari-samma. I closed my eyes and clapped my hands to attract the attention of the *kami*, then opened my eyes and as I walked away I caught the smell of foxes.

There seemed to be a path on the other side of the clearing leading further up the mountain so I followed it but it disappeared in a tangle of branches and dead leaves. Perhaps it was a track made by foxes coming to eat the rice-cake offerings. Perhaps it was only my imagination. I decided to carry on. The undergrowth wasn't so thick and the trees were less close together. I guessed I was getting near the top of the hill. Some of the trees were very tall, maybe two or three hundred years old; several were scarred by lightning.

Almost at the top of the hill I thought I saw a *torii* spirit bridge, but coming closer I found a tree struck by lightning smashed into the shape of an "H." Suddenly, I saw why the written characters for *kami* (god) and *jinja* (shrine) both used the radical for lightning: fire from heaven carving the tree into a spirit bridge. I closed my eyes and clapped my hands again. I looked up at the sky. It was dark grey and I felt a spot of rain on my forehead. It was time to go back.

I made my way down the hill until I found the path and by the time I reached the house, the shrine in the forest and the tree struck by lightning could have been almost as far away as Tokyo.

○

It's seven-thirty and I'm standing on the platform of the village station waiting for the train to Tokyo. It's stopped raining but there's still heavy clouds and mist. Beyond the lights of the station the village is invisible. A couple of eleven-year-old boys are standing some way further up the platform.

This afternoon Fumiko told me that Kazu and Tomo had been bullied at school and I'm looking at the two bristle-headed boys in tracksuits and thinking maybe they could have been the bullies. They look docile but a blankness in their faces suggests they might bully someone if they were told to by a gang leader now or sometime in the future.

○

The train's coming. I just heard the klaxon and now I can see the light of the carriages and the rails are hissing and pinging as the train gets closer. Clattering through the silent darkness of the country: the noise and lights of Tokyo.

○

It's Monday lunchtime and I'm sitting in front of the remains of a curry in an imitation Indian restaurant and I've just been served a cup of coffee by a Japanese girl in a turban.

This morning I asked Yamaguchi again when he was going to introduce me to some clients. He still hasn't introduced me to anyone. He said the market was dead and most clients weren't interested in business. Everybody's sitting on their hands waiting. He says it's better to begin a relationship with a deal that makes the customer feel happy. It's true. But it still doesn't explain why he's taking so long to introduce me to clients.

He doesn't like to push himself. He's not a typical Japanese: perhaps he's spent too long with foreigners. Somewhere along the line he discovered that working in a foreign company is an easy number. No one knows the language so there's always a smoke-screen available and he's a hero if he manages to do any business at all.

Laroche has to rely on people like Yamaguchi to tell him what's happening. But he can't check what Yamaguchi tells him because he can't speak the language.

I told Conrad the head of the office couldn't speak Japanese and he said it was an example of white people's arrogance towards yellow people: the white man assuming the yellow man has to learn the white man's language.

The operation is a mess, I'm in the middle of it and I don't see a way out of it. I can't go direct to the clients. I have to go through Yamaguchi. But if he doesn't do anything I'm stuck and he knows it. He says he's busy making a list. He said the same last week. Maybe it's not laziness. Maybe he just doesn't want me to do any business. But if not, why not?

The waitresses here don't seem to mind wearing their Indian costumes but the manager is a Japanese man in his forties wearing a turban with an ostrich feather. He smiles like the Japanese I saw in the Disneyland Park outside Tokyo, who were dressed as eighteenth-century French aristocrats, in ruffs, cuffs, and powdered wigs, grinning as if their shoes were too small for them.

○

Today I got a telephone call from Sachiko. Her parents told her I was in Tokyo and she telephoned the bank. It was strange to hear her voice after so long. She said she was disappointed I hadn't tried to contact her and asked me to dinner on Wednesday. She wants me to meet her husband. I thanked her and said I was looking forward to seeing them both.

We might never have been lovers but I knew what she meant

when she said perhaps some letters from abroad hadn't reached her. Apart from that it was like any other conversation.

◯

It's eight o'clock in the morning and I'm standing on the platform at Nakameguro waiting for a train. During the rush hour there's a train every five minutes and they're always on time. The next one should be here in three minutes. I'm in a block of thirty or forty people waiting in silence inside two white parallel lines painted on the platform. There are a dozen blocks of people like this at regular intervals along the length of the platform. The train will stop at exactly the same point as every other train, so the doors can open precisely opposite the parallel lines on the platform. A few people will get off, and then this block and all the other blocks along the platform will push through the doors and on to the train.

No one says anything.

I'm the only person talking and I'm talking into this. I look at people's faces and try to imagine who they are and what sort of lives they lead but with some it's hard to believe anyone's there, behind the eyelids. It's as if everyone's thinking of nothing because it's the only way human beings can endure this kind of existence.

This is Japan. It's the same everywhere. A sameness. Nothing, nothing, nothing. Jesus. The breath is rising above our heads and disappearing in the light. I have to believe there's a mystery, otherwise there's nothing.

The train's coming.

It's hard to see into the carriages. It looks as if it's raining inside. All the condensation. The train's stopped and the doors are opening, just a couple of people get off and now we're moving, OK. I'm holding the recorder to my chest with both hands. If I had my arms by my sides I couldn't lift them because of the crush. It's warm. All these people pressed together breathing the same air over and over: last night's *sushi* and beer and *sake*, this morning's grilled fish and raw eggs, scent, aftershave, tobacco and soap. The smell has a slightly metallic taste.

The platform attendants are pushing the last people into the carriage. Everyone's wearing overcoats so it's a squeeze. The attendants push and a muffled wave of movement reaches me through the layers of clothes and bodies. The doors are shut. OK. I can't smell the atmosphere any more. The train's moving. A jolt. Another slow-motion wave goes through the carriage. It's impossible to stand against it. Human waves. Our bodies move like one body. The *salariman* next to me has folded his newspaper so that it's not much wider than a pack of cigarettes. There's a man in front of me—his head's on the same level as my chest. Beside him there's a shop assistant with a red ribbon in her hair. I can hardly hear what I'm saying because of the sound of the train. This is where it's good to be calm, everyone pressed together, no facial expressions, no sign of the individual, no reaction, no movement, just being, waiting for the next stop, people getting off, less pressure, people getting on, more pressure, going through a tunnel, watching the condensation trickling down the glass against the blackness and trying not to think about earthquakes or the hands of the girl holding her handbag in front of her brushing against me, not quite in rhythm with the movement of the train, pressed close together, showing no emotion, a conspiracy of straight faces. She's looking at my tie as if it were a religious text. Sometimes I can only think of one thing at a time, like now. The long body of the Buddha is short. The short body of the Buddha is long. It's hard to think further than the next station. The doors open, more get out, fewer get in. It's easier to breathe but it's like the end of a massage. The contact isn't there. We've become separate people. We don't know each other. We have no feelings for each other, we do not wish to harm each other. We simply wish to live in peace, in harmony with one another. We're passengers on the Chiyoda line, travelling in the same carriage. Except for this coincidence we have no obligations, just avoid eye contact and keep a straight face, and as Hakuin said: "Meditate in the midst of activity."

People. Moving in all directions. People move differently here. As if they know where they're going and they know they'll be on time. A crowd isn't a crowd when it's Japanese. It's a group. Everyone moves at more or less the same speed. Hurrying interrupts the harmony; whatever harmony it is with the metallic click of the ticket collector flicking the ticket puncher between his fingers like castanets.

Almost every time I climb these steps I think of mountains I could be climbing. It's five minutes' walk from here to the office. I have five minutes to think my way back into the goals, the ambitions, and the priorities of an investment banker. Five minutes of freedom.

It's cold.

The air is clear and bright and the buildings are shining and this moment like any other could be one of a sequence of moments leading to enlightenment.

o

It's after midnight. A few hours ago I was with Sachiko and her husband. There was also a ballerina and a designer and another British banker in Tokyo and his wife, and we were eating Chicken Kiev and talking about Japan's trade surplus and avant-garde theatre.

I brought some flowers with me: roses and love-in-a-mist. She thanked me and kissed me and I kissed her. She introduced me to her husband: I recognised him from a photograph in a magazine. I bowed as he stretched out his hand to shake hands. Sachiko introduced me to the other guests. I still hadn't had a chance to look at her. She was smiling and talking to people and the banker's wife was describing to the Japanese ballerina how difficult it was to find women's shoes large enough for her in Tokyo. The ballerina sympathised and said she had to buy children's shoes when she was in London.

Sachiko's husband and I talked about England and Japan and the similarities between the two countries. We mentioned the usual things: *shima-guni konjo*, the island-country complex, and conservatism and respect for tradition. He said living on an island off the mainland of continental Europe was like living on an island off the mainland of continental Asia. I said the only thing between us was the Eurasian landmass. He didn't laugh. I looked at his face and wondered if Sachiko had told him about the past. I guessed not but I could have been wrong. It was strange to think of his face being close to her. Perhaps he was thinking the same thing about me, but the more we talked, the less likely it seemed that Sachiko had said anything. I liked him. We got on well together.

I didn't get much of a chance to talk with Sachiko, although towards the end of the evening she sat beside me and asked what it was like banking in Tokyo. She said she was surprised to hear I was in Tokyo but more surprised to hear I was a banker. Why banking? I said it was a way to come back to Japan. She nodded.

Her face was different; it belonged to someone else. The way she smiled was different. I remember the flicker of her eyebrows when she tried to stop herself laughing. I was looking for someone who wasn't there; the person I loved had become someone else.

But what was I expecting? That she'd drop the flowers I gave her and throw her arms around me? Or an almost invisible sign with her eyes that she remembered the things I remembered? Why should she? Besides, she was always a wonderful actress. She hid the way she felt from everyone. No one knew. No one.

Perhaps the music she chose after dinner, by Couperin, meant something. She used to play it in London. I hadn't heard it since we were together. For a second I had a clear memory of us together. Then it was just music from the past which I remembered. I looked at her once or twice while it was playing but she was talking to someone else. Probably it was a coincidence.

She was the reason I came to Japan, not the only reason, but my own secret reason for coming here, and now I'm here, watching the voice-activated light signal on the recorder flickering as I speak; talking to myself.

○

The traffic's not moving. It's stretching all the way up to Roppongi crossing. Better get out and walk.

There's a policeman standing inside a telephone booth removing labels advertising girls for sex. Silhouettes of people pass through the headlights of cars and red lights flashing in clouds of exhaust smoke, and there, just visible through the glare of the city, over towards Tokyo Tower, there's a moon, like a ghost from the past that's slipped into the present.

Off the main road it's quieter. It's like stepping into a ramshackle village strung together with telephone wires. Lanes. Cats. The smell of vegetables frying and the sound of people laughing through the half-open door of a *yakitori* bar.

○

It's one o'clock and I'm back in Nakameguro. I said goodbye to Tony half an hour ago in a club where he was talking to a Filipino girl about a place called Porto Galeria. They'd just discovered it was her home town and Tony was smiling like someone watching his stock rising on a Reuters screen.

The evening started when I went round to Tony's place. He was in good form. Apart from the usual problems with customs, business is going well and he has a lot of clients. The laughter lines around his eyes are deeper. He loves women and they love him judging by the messages they leave on his answer phone and he still has a *futon* in the cupboard in his office just in case, although since the trouble with his back the *futon*'s stayed in the cupboard. But he likes to go out in the evenings. We had a couple of San Miguel beers, ice cold, and

Tony told me about his trip to the Philippines. Several Westerners were attacked while he was there and people were talking
about a drug called ice hitting the market. He stayed with Sean
and then with a girlfriend. After a couple of weeks he'd had
enough. He said he was getting too old for it. We finished the
beers and Tony put on his shoes to go out. Talking about the
Philippines had made him restless. He wanted to see what was
happening in Roppongi.

"All the girls," he said, "it's cruel out there. It hurts. Some
of them are gorgeous. They know it. It drives me crazy." He
suggested visiting a few bars and I said OK.

We started the evening at Henry Africa's. It's one of those
bars where foreign men who've just arrived in Tokyo sit and
drink Budweisers and try to flirt with the waitresses and wonder where all the women are. It was bright and empty. God
knows why Tony likes going there. Maybe it's habit. Ten years
ago it used to be a bar where Japanese women went to pick up
foreign men. Not any more.

We drank a couple of Budweisers and Tony had a conversation with one of the waitresses. I wanted to be somewhere
different. Sitting in Henry Africa's was a bad experience. I
suggested another place. Tony said he knew a nice little restaurant near Satin Doll.

Outside the streets were getting crowded. Everyone looked
as if they were going somewhere exciting. Tony groaned whenever he saw a pretty girl or an attractive woman. It was like
walking with someone who's sprained his ankle. It took almost
a quarter of an hour to reach the restaurant, but we could have
made it in half the time.

The restaurant was the sort of place where young women go
after work if they haven't got a date with someone. It was clean
and bright. We sat at a curved marble and chrome counter next
to a couple of young women who looked like secretaries. Tony
smiled and said he liked the atmosphere. The decor was between a *fin de siècle* Viennese café and a new-age snack bar.
There were a lot of gilt mirrors and glass tables with roses on

them and one wall was covered with a Klimt-style mural of an almost naked woman in a gold headdress stroking a pink horse with wings. The music was Vivaldi's "The Four Seasons." The ambience was nice. "Nice," Japanese style.

A waiter came to take our order and Tony spoke to him in Japanese. The young women near us stopped eating and looked at each other. Tony made a joke about something on the menu and the waiter laughed. The young women leaned towards each other and started whispering. The waiter took our orders. They were almost silent with their heads close together as if they were sharing a secret. Tony looked at me and raised his eyebrows. He asked me to say something in Japanese.

"It's been a long time," I said. *"Hisashiburi desu."*

Tony replied in Japanese. He said he wished he could find a nice Japanese girl to marry.

There was a stillness over his shoulder. The one nearest to Tony asked her friend if she'd like another coffee. Tony started speaking in Japanese again, telling me about a woman he'd loved, who lived in Nagoya, whom he'd hoped to marry, who'd been killed in a car crash.

The waiter brought our drinks. The young women were still whispering. The one next to Tony ordered two more coffees. Tony winked and turned to her and asked, in the politest Japanese, if she could possibly recommend any of the wines on the wine list. She looked at her friend and they both started giggling. Tony repeated the question and her expression softened into the beginnings of a smile. Her friend asked Tony in broken English if he could speak Japanese. Tony said yes and they giggled again.

They were in their mid-twenties and worked as receptionists for Mitsubishi. They liked their work but they wanted to get married soon.

"We are like Christmas cake," said the one next to Tony, "twenty-three, twenty-four is a good time. So is twenty-five. After twenty-five no Japanese man wants us." Tony looked sympathetic and asked if she had a boyfriend. He hoped she wasn't lonely. They were laughing and smiling and flicking their hair over their shoulders.

I was thinking of Tanya. Maybe she'd like to come out to Tokyo for a while. The more I thought about her the less I wanted to be where I was. I didn't want to talk to people who described themselves as Christmas cakes or listen to polite questions about what Japanese food I liked. I wanted to be with Tanya.

Tony asked if he could buy them drinks and they seemed puzzled, as if he'd just asked them the distance from the moon to the sun. They thanked him and the one next to Tony said her friend was tired. Tony asked for her telephone number and she wrote it down on a card while her friend checked the bill.

They stood up to go and we stood up and bowed. Tony promised to telephone and the one who liked him smiled. Then they bowed, waved their hands like little wings and said "bye bye" and were gone.

Tony was in a good mood. He had a new telephone number. He ordered a bottle of wine and told me about some recent girlfriends. Perhaps the wine was colouring his memory when he told me about three sisters in Osaka. He talked about business in Japan: he said the Japanese treat business like a game of go; they think strategically and give up short-term gains for long-term advantages. Then he grinned and said, "It's all go in Japan."

He was still wanting to meet some girls so we went to a bar where a lot of foreigners and Japanese were standing close together smoking and drinking and comparing each other's style. The place was decorated with sheets of luminous plastic and Day-Glo ropes and netting and Christmas-tree lights. There was a lifesize inflatable doll hanging over the bar with a handful of yellow feathers instead of a fig leaf. The music coming out of the speakers was inner-space music with the bass turned up so loud I could feel the drum beat in my rib cage. There were a lot of Japanese fashion victims trying to look casual and relaxed, with unlit cigarettes between their fingers and absent-minded expressions on their faces.

It was somewhere to be seen, not heard. Tony's clothes were OK; he could have been someone rich trying to look poor or a fashion photographer. I was a chameleon in a pinstripe suit. I bought a couple of beers at the bar and we drank them next to some women wearing leather jackets and jeans. One of them had a picture of Ayatollah Khomeini embossed on to the back of her jacket. Tony tried talking to her but she wasn't impressed and the conversation was over in a couple of minutes. We finished our beers and made for the door.

I thought of the Japanese proverb, "It's a hard thing to be born a woman." It was good to see Tony but looking for girls in bars wasn't what I wanted to do. I told Tony I was tired and came back here.

I've tried telephoning Tanya several times but the line's always engaged.

○

Yesterday I had lunch with a friend of a friend, Harry Sasaki. He is a well-preserved man in his late sixties, with a straight back, silvery hair and a gentle manner. I wouldn't have guessed he was a war criminal.

Christina told me he was the most unlikely war criminal she knew, and I laughed. When I met him I knew what she meant. He spoke with a perfect American accent. He wore a dark brown tweed jacket, dark grey trousers, a thick cotton shirt and a wool tie. We sat down for lunch in a room at the top of the Imperial Hotel, overlooking the Imperial Palace, and he ordered a couple of beers and asked after Christina. He said he was looking forward to seeing her when she was next in Tokyo. I could see he wasn't sure how much Christina had told me.

"I hear you were a convicted war criminal" didn't sound right. "Would you like to talk about some of your war experiences in the Philippines?" didn't sound much better. I wasn't sure what to say. War crimes aren't the easiest topic of conversation with a convicted war criminal. Not five minutes into a first meeting.

I explained that I was in Japan on business, and he relaxed a bit. I asked how he had acquired such good American pronunciation. He smiled and began his story. His father had a small silk business in Niigata in the late 1920s. When the silk market collapsed, he decided to sell up and take his wife and two sons to a new life in America. Harry was eight years old and his younger brother was three.

"It was a whole new world for me," he said. After the mountains of Niigata, California was big and strange and exciting. The people were friendly and Harry was soon speaking English at school, although at home his parents spoke Japanese. His father worked in a canning factory. His mother stayed home and continued her previous way of life: she cooked Japanese food, made Japanese pickles and kept the old festivals. The boys were expected to observe the traditions of their homeland.

By the time Harry went to high school he was bilingual in English and Japanese. After graduating he decided to visit Japan and took a ship to Yokohama. It was 1939. He returned to the village where he was born. "I was coming home." Harry smiled, then frowned. "It started so beautiful and ended so ugly." Like snow, I thought, but I didn't say anything. I wasn't sure if he was talking about the war or Japan or himself.

I said I thought it was difficult to judge the actions of war in peacetime because war and peace are different worlds. He suddenly looked very old and tired and said that he lived with the memory of the war every day. It wasn't exactly a confession but I thought I understood what he was saying.

"It's not possible to judge the past," he said, "but people remember." I was about to ask him which people when, as if he heard what I was thinking, he said, "I remember."

A few months before, he had been in a bookshop and seen a book about the war in the Philippines written by his commanding officer. He'd read a few pages and realised it was all lies. As he told me this his expression reminded me of the face of a demon guardian at the gate of a temple.

"Whatever happened during the war, it's wrong to lie about the past," he said. "It's shameful." We agreed that people who forget the mistakes of the past are condemned to repeat them. The waiter came and asked if we wanted sandwiches.

While we waited for our order to arrive, Harry told me about his time in prison. The food was better than anything he'd had during the war—sometimes there was so much he couldn't eat all of it. Meanwhile, outside the prison, people in Japan were starving. He got on well with the American guards and was put in charge of the prison library. He decided to read the Bible. When he was growing up in the States the only English books he read were the ones his teachers told him to read: facts and figures. If he read for pleasure, he read Japanese books which his father recommended. I asked why he chose to read the Bible and he smiled. "Because I was feeling bad and I remembered people in the States calling it 'the good book.' Reading it didn't make me feel any better, but it helped me understand a lot of things about the Americans and the British."

After he finished the Bible he made a reading plan for the thirty years of his sentence. He kept to it methodically and read his way through the complete works of Shakespeare and Dickens and several other authors, before he was released, his sentence shortened to ten years. I thought of him sitting in his cell, making his way through *Dombey and Son* and *The Pickwick Papers*.

Did it occur to him that he might have been a traitor to America? Did he search in desperation for some way to return to life as it was before everything went wrong? Had he simply adopted the taboos, shibboleths and customs of the conquerors? I wanted to ask him, but the sandwiches arrived and instead we talked more about food, about Kobe beef, Texas beef and clam chowder.

I looked for a sign, something in his eyes or face which might explain why he was tried and found guilty of war crimes. I saw nothing. He didn't defend the past; he didn't deny it; he seemed to accept it. If he felt guilt he showed no sign of it. He had spent time in prison and had been released. He had paid his dues and he was a free man.

He told me that he worries about his wife who suffers from arthritis and that he's proud of his son who works for one of the big securities companies. He enjoys his work in the travel business and likes going to the United States. "It's a great place to visit," he joked, "but I wouldn't want to live there." We finished our meal and Harry insisted on paying. As we shook hands and said goodbye to each other in the hotel lobby, Harry said he hoped we'd meet again. "Any friend of Christina's is a friend of mine."

I thanked him and said I hoped we'd meet soon. He turned to walk away. I glanced behind me at an electronic map of the world, covering the wall of the lobby, that showed the different times in the major cities. It was two o'clock in the afternoon in Tokyo, six in the morning in London and ten the night before in Los Angeles. I turned back and looked for Harry Sasaki. There were several men like him in the lobby, wearing raincoats, with silvery hair. But no Harry.

○

It's almost lunchtime. I'm writing in this notebook which is a diary and a way of looking busy at the same time.

Yamamoto is sitting at her desk looking at a screen. So is Nakamura. So is Sakamoto. So is Terasawa. All the people in rows, looking at screens, hypnotised by their machines. Sometimes it seems like we're all turning into machines. Yamaguchi's reading the company handbook. Yesterday he finally got around to making a list of clients and he's going to introduce me to the first of them next Monday. Hallo Mitsubishi.

Laroche is wandering around talking to people. When he doesn't know what to say to someone he winks at them. He winks a lot. Maria Santini says he was a student radical at university in 1968. Now when he's not winking at people he spends his time taking people out to lunch and dinner.

Writing is a mask of activity.

I can watch the people around me like Takahashi sitting at his desk in front of his screen. He's probably waiting for details of the long bond issue, but he could be thinking of his wife or practising green-screen Zen: thinking of nothing while the machine's working, like Daruma sitting in front of the wall waiting for enlightenment. He's sitting in a chair looking at information. Eventually a bit of information will make him lift his telephone, press a button and talk to someone. A number will change and Takahashi will move into action. Perhaps. He's just adjusted his spectacles on the bridge of his nose and licked his lips. That's all. He's still looking at the screen, perhaps he's thinking about last night, or tomorrow night. Takahashi is picking his teeth and running his tongue under his upper lip and blinking.

Yamamoto is sitting next to him. She has a strong intelligent face. She lived in London for three years with an English boy-friend. Then they split up and she came back to Japan and went into banking. She's in her late twenties. She doesn't want to get married, it's too much hassle. She just wants enough money to be free to do what she likes. She thinks more like a foreigner than a Japanese. She's not afraid to argue with people in the morning meeting which horrifies and amuses her Japanese colleagues. Secretly they admire her. She says what they'd like to say. She doesn't play the Japanese game. She plays the *gaijin* game and she knows how to be rude to foreigners. Just this morning she shouted at Clather who told her she'd forgotten to do something. She pointed at him and said, "I'm nobody's fucking secretary, fuck off!" Clather didn't say anything. He couldn't think of a come-back. She's one of the few Japanese women I know who have frown lines. Maybe her screen's too bright.

Uchida is sitting beside Yamamoto and looking over her

shoulder at her screen. He doesn't have a screen of his own because he's one of the new trainees. He's twenty-two years old and he has a big honest face with sticking-out ears. He's looking at the screen as if it was a cardiogram of his own heartbeat. He's still on probation and he wants to show he has the right attitude and takes his work seriously. He probably doesn't understand what he's looking at but he's reluctant to ask, because this is Japan and the student doesn't ask questions but waits to be told by the teacher.

I can only see the back of Terasawa's head. Her hair is black and beautiful. It's thick enough for her to let it grow longer, over her shoulders, but she keeps it short, late 1950s' style, just over her collar, every hair cut to exactly the same length. She's wearing a lime-green jacket with wide shoulders and her Chanel handbag is on the desk beside her. There's something sad about her. She wanted to be a ballet dancer. She still walks with her feet pointing out and moves in an oddly precise way which makes her actions seem self-conscious and artificial. She speaks Russian and English and French. Terasawa is about the same age as Yamamoto. She's pretty and intelligent but Yamamoto is more popular, even though she's less Japanese. They sit opposite each other, separated by their dealing screens, and hardly ever talk to each other.

There's an empty desk next to Terasawa and then there's Sakamoto, who's in his late twenties and still unmarried. He's talking on the telephone and swivelling in his chair as he looks from one screen to another. Sakamoto is a normal, regular, Japanese bond dealer. He's always at his desk before eight-thirty, he has no enemies, never says anything at the morning meeting, smiles at other people's jokes and never tells any jokes of his own. People in the office call him "Phantom." I asked Kaoru why he was called "Phantom." She laughed and asked if I thought he had a very strong personality.

Yamaguchi's not at his desk. He's my immediate superior and I'm the only other person in his department so I have some idea of what he's doing. He knows that I know. While he was a one-man department he could do what he liked. Now he's lost that freedom. I've moved into his space and taken some of his freedom.

A few nights ago we had a drink together after work. It was a drinking ritual to get to know each other, to discover each other's *honne*, true feeling. We both drank a lot. We ended up in a red-lit bar with couples at tables and men sitting on stools at the bar. Yamaguchi said it was one of his favorite drinking places.

The girl behind the bar didn't recognise him but there was a *kiipu* bottle with his name on it, in a cupboard behind the bar next to a life-size reproduction of Manet's *The Bar at the Folies-Bergère*. French accordion music was playing and there was a smell of Gitanes and Disque Bleu cigarettes. The atmosphere was like a party where everyone was waiting for a special guest who hadn't arrived. I asked Yamaguchi why he liked the bar. He smiled and said, *"La nostalgie."*

I asked what it was like coming back to Japan after so long abroad. "Sometimes it's like living in a prison," he said. I thought that was all he was going to say. Then he added, "But it's where I was born and it's where I want to die." In a Japanese way, the answer to my question was in what he didn't say. It had taken a while to get used to the Japanese mentality. After three years in France, his friends and family appeared *majime*—serious. He laughed but he didn't look happy. I recognised the irony of coming back. It's supposed to be happy but sometimes it's sad: the present is different from the past, people change.

The bar was beginning to empty. We'd finished a bottle of brandy but my head still felt clear and bright. I had just enough control to worry I might be losing control. For a while Yamaguchi didn't say anything. He just licked his lips and stared somewhere in the middle distance. He was smiling and nodding to himself. Then he asked a series of questions. Did I like Laroche? I said I didn't know him well enough to say. Did I know a book called *The Narrow Road to the Deep North* by Basho?

I said it was one of my favorite books. Had I heard that Basho was a spy? I said no and Yamaguchi told me a theory that Basho encoded information in the *haiku* which he wrote about the places he visited.

I was tired and I didn't want to talk about spying to anyone. I wanted to go to bed and read a good book and Yamaguchi wanted to tell me how Basho was a spy. He'd drunk a lot. Perhaps he was miscalculating the meaning of what he was saying in English. It's difficult to be subtle in another language. He was smiling but what he was saying sounded more like an accusation than a conversation.

I offered something towards the drinks but Yamaguchi insisted on paying. I didn't make any resistance: it wouldn't have been correct for a *kohai* (junior) to pay for his *senpai* (senior).

After the ritual of getting drunk together Yamaguchi has been more friendly. But it's only surface. His face is smiling but his voice is impersonal. It's as if he's retreated behind an invisible screen that conceals his thoughts from me. Not a good working relationship.

◯

It's midnight Tokyo time and I've just been talking to Tanya in London. She's booked a ticket and she's arriving in a fortnight's time.

Living in Tokyo can be heavy on the heart, like a one-sided love affair. It's better with someone.

I'm glad she's coming.

◯

I'm standing on the platform at Nakameguro and the sunlight is shining on the railway lines like silver and the sky is blue. I can feel the heat of the sun on my forehead. People have left their coats at home and instead of the blacks and browns of the last few months there are greens and blues and whites and yellows. The man next to me is looking at the pigeons strutting after each other on the platform.

○

I'm walking along one of the little streets near the station. Bunches of Day-Glo plastic cherry blossoms are waving from the lampposts and telegraph poles. The apron of a woman selling vegetables is very white in the sunlight. There's a smell of *don-buri* cooking which reminds me of Kashima. I'm trying to imagine this sort of day in London but it could only be Japan. The light is strong enough for me to see the different colours of black in people's hair. There's a middle-aged woman in a smart suit beside a pug dog which is squeezing a turd on the pavement. She's taken some tissue paper from a carrier bag, picked up the turd, wrapped it in paper and put it in her bag.

There's nothing between me and the sky and there are things to look at like the plates of plastic imitation food in restaurant windows. The red slices of steak have faded because they've been in the light of the window too long and the beefburgers and fried eggs need dusting. There's a stall selling man-size inflatable Godzilla monsters and T-shirts with slogans in Japanese English like "Let's snatch! for beautiful human life," "A is for Apple Pie" and "The meaning of our future is happiness," and shopping bags decorated with cartoon kittens smiling and the message, in English, "Max—the best little cat house in town, accessories and something good."

I remember this sort of weather in the country: the sky reflected in the water of the rice fields and, over the reeds, the estuary with the white square sails of fishing boats in the distance like details in the background of a landscape by Hiroshige. This could almost be a street in a small town in Ibaraki instead of the middle of Tokyo. A woman is looking at me from the other side of a pile of giant radishes. She's like the women I used to see working in the fields: twinkling brown eyes, strong cheek bones and protruding teeth.

I smile at her and her eyes almost disappear in the lines of a smile gleaming with gold fillings and for a moment I'm back in the country.

○

This morning Yamaguchi and I went to a major client or, to be exact, an institution which was a major client before the crash. Since then, they've bought no shares in any European market.

We took a taxi to their offices near the Imperial Palace. On the way Yamaguchi rehearsed the meeting one more time. After introducing me he would give a brief overview of the European economies, repeating the London office's view; the strength of the Deutschmark and the weakness of sterling in relation to the dollar and the yen. Then I would talk about a few companies, the ones recommended by the analysts back in London and Zurich.

We arrived five minutes early. Yamaguchi straightened his tie, patted his hair and licked his lips. I began to feel nervous. We came to a door with a sign outside it in Japanese and English which said "Securities, Trading and Investment" and went into a room the size of several tennis courts, lit by strips of neon lighting. Both ends of the room were covered with electronic information boards of share prices. Hundreds of people were sitting at desks in rows. All the men were wearing white shirts and all the women were wearing pale blue uniforms like supermarket attendants. There was a desk with a plastic sign in Japanese and English which told visitors to ring for attention. Yamaguchi pushed a button and a woman in a pale blue uniform was with us bowing and smiling and asking who we wanted.

She went over to a desk in the middle of a maze of men in white shirts and talked to someone, then hurried back and asked us to follow her. She took us along a corridor and opened a door into a room overlooking the sloping stone walls and the moat of the Imperial Palace. The sky was blue. The sun was sparkling on the water. The view was like a Japanese Tourist Board poster.

The woman closed the door and Yamaguchi said that at current values the area of the Imperial Palace was worth the same as the State of California, maybe a little bit more. He suggested calculating how much the floor space of the room in which we were sitting was worth. We sat down side by side on a beige sofa, facing the door. It didn't look like a room in an office block on prime real estate. It had a mid-sixties look: it might have been smart and fashionable around the time of the Tokyo Olympics. The sofa and chairs could have come from a second-hand furniture shop, although the white anti-macassars on the headrests were clean and pressed. At one end of the low wooden table was a model car made of silvery metal: the glass sunroof of the car was the lid of a box of cigarettes. At the other end of the table was an ashtray set in a lump of pale green malachite. The walls were bare except for a gilt clock with a pendulum motion that looked like a consolation prize on a quiz show and a small oil painting.

There was a knock at the door, and two men came in. They were in their mid-thirties. We exchanged *meishi* name cards and sat down. Yamaguchi talked and one of the men made notes while the other with spectacles listened. They both looked tired, but alert, like people working on will-power. They were both wearing Hermès ties. I wondered how many times a week they listened to descriptions of the European economy: all the American, European and Asian institutions telephoning and visiting to tell them more or less the same thing while they sat there, nodding their heads and taking notes, at the centre of a network of information from around the world. They could compare what we had to say with a hundred other top-level sources. They have a lot of money so they get a lot of information. Mr Reed of Citicorp says, "Information is money on the move." Sometimes it seems like the only spoke in the wheel is human error.

Yamaguchi finished what he had to say and the man with

spectacles grunted softly as if he'd just eaten a big meal. He turned to the man who'd been taking notes and asked if he had any questions. Neither of them had any questions. Yamaguchi said he would ask me to give them some company recommendations.

It was my first business conversation in Japanese for some time but I was finding the words, until I needed the phrase for "long-term strategy." My mind went blank. I couldn't remember the words in Japanese. The man with the spectacles nodded and said "long-term strategy" in English. His accent was New York Jewish. After that I spoke English. I guess he had been a research analyst in the States: he asked the same sort of questions about the companies as I asked when I was a research analyst working on Japanese companies.

The meeting lasted about forty-five minutes. It ended with an appropriate pause, and Yamaguchi murmuring that we'd taken a lot of their time. They thanked us for a useful and interesting visit.

As we were leaving I had a closer look at the small oil painting: a landscape of dusty blues and greys with a line of willow trees and a spot of red. The signature in the corner looked like Corot.

The man with spectacles said the company directors had been interested in art for some time. He laughed. Was it a good time to sell Impressionist paintings?

In the taxi on the way back to the office, Yamaguchi assessed the meeting. The age of the men sent to meet us wasn't encouraging—if they'd been slightly older it would have been better. But the one with the spectacles asked for a selection of company reports. All in all the feeling was good, *kimochi yokatta*, the feeling was good.

○

I didn't ask why such important clients weren't already receiving reports.

I was having a slow-motion flash on the whole situation. I saw how Yamaguchi has been stalling me for months. Who knows why. Perhaps he wants to see how I react to being in free space with nothing to do. Or perhaps it has something to do with Laroche.

○

Last night I met Tony. We arranged to meet at Shibuya near the station. He was waiting by the bronze statue of the faithful dog Hachiko which sits on a concrete plinth and stares myopically at the giant television screen on the opposite side of the road.

There were crowds of twenty-year-olds in clean T-shirts and laundered denims milling around, trying to look like James Dean. We crossed the road and went down a side street. The pavements were full of people: businessmen bowing to one another outside *karaoke* bars; solemn and self-conscious couples holding hands, or smiling and laughing with their arms around each other's waists; a man with a glistening cloud of shining helium-filled balloons jostling at the end of a web of strings rising from between his fingers; young men with bands of white cloth tied neatly around their foreheads clapping their hands at the entrance to *yakitoriya* from which conversation spilled in waves into the electric brilliance of lights from a *pachinko* parlour.

Down another side street, which wasn't so bright, along an alleyway, and we stopped in front of a plate-glass window surrounded by pink flashing lights. Inside there were posters of young women wearing swimsuits. A man was standing in the pink, neon-lit doorway. He had a humourless face. Tony greeted him in English. The man ignored him and turned his head slowly in the opposite direction. Tony took another step forward. For several seconds neither of them moved. At last the doorman turned to face Tony with a bored expression.

"*Dame!*" he said, "*gaijin dame!*" and turned away again. Tony began to speak in Japanese. He asked if the owner of the club was about and told the man to give him his best regards. There was a moment of stillness, then the man switched personality and began hissing through his teeth like a steam engine starting up and went into a routine of bowing at every other word.

We passed through the doorway down a short spiral staircase and came to a ticket booth where the man selling tickets recognised Tony and showed him a big smile glowing with gold teeth. The room was smaller than I'd expected, with a low ceiling. A dim spotlight glowed over a tiny, semi-circular platform, which projected several feet into the first few rows of the audience. Only the front half of the room had any seating; the rest was filled with men standing in groups or alone smoking cigarettes and talking excitedly. Those sitting close to the stage were gazing at the curtains behind the spotlights. Some of the men in the front row were leaning against the stage.

I followed Tony as we made our way to the far side of the room. There were no seats available, so we positioned ourselves against a wall. It was crowded; more than a hundred men pressed into the cramped space. Tokyo rents are expensive. I made a quick calculation; half a million yen for a couple of hours' basement space, three or four times an evening. It was a respectable return per square foot—probably a lot better than the return on the floor space at the office.

In the front of us, two men who looked like construction workers were talking in Korean. The music disappeared into the babble of the audience's conversation. The spotlight grew brighter, there was a movement behind the curtains, and a dwarf with a painted clown's face stepped into the circle of light.

"Welcome, honoured customers and friends." He bowed deeply. "It's my pleasure to introduce the evening's entertainment. We trust the girls who dance for you will be to your satisfaction. We have Mariko-chan with us again: we hope she will meet with the approval of regular customers who have asked to see her while Mariko-chan was on holiday with her family in Osaka . . ."

"Why didn't you tell me?" someone called from the audience. "I was there last Wednesday!"

"Then we have something different, America girl Suzi-chan." The dwarf began to move to one side of the stage; his walk was clumsy and disjointed. His shoes were uneven; one was much larger than the other and looked like a surgical boot. He stopped in mid-stride and, for an instant or two, the spotlight lost him and wandered over the empty corner of the stage.

"Excuse me, dear customers," the dwarf's voice called out of the darkness. "This evening we have a special performance, it is a privilege to welcome graduates from a college of dramatic arts; these talented young actors will perform a mime dance of the love affair and horrible tragedy which was made into a film called *Ai No Corrida*. They will mime to traditional Japanese music. Please enjoy yourselves."

A Japanese song, a slow, old-fashioned, slightly wistful melody, pre-prosperity music from the 1950s, came from the amplifier above our heads and the dwarf hobbled out of the spotlight. The bright circle of light remained. There was a movement in the folds of the curtains, then another, and with a jerk the sparkling material began to open before our eyes.

A woman in a brightly coloured *kimono* stepped into the light and advanced towards the front of the stage. The light penetrated the white cosmetic covering her face, and revealed the set of her eyes and the contours of her cheeks and the shape of her mouth under the vermilion of her painted lips. The dwarf said it was a pleasure to present a very special friend, Mariko-chan, there was polite applause and someone in the audience called out, "It's good to see you again, Mariko-chan." The woman in the brightly coloured *kimono* bowed. She stood for a moment waiting for an appropriate interval to enter the music and dance. The spotlight was unrelenting; it showed a woman in an imitation of *geisha* finery, with a face of worn beauty and corruption.

She began to dance. The central spotlight dimmed and other lights at the front of the stage glowed into life, no brighter than paper lanterns. The music turned into a song, and Mariko-chan danced an interpretation of the words. It was a simple story about a girl in a mountain village waiting for her lover to return from far away. Thirty or forty years ago, when it was written, the song would have had a particular poignancy, when the last men were coming home from the war and the bombed towns and cities were drawing in labour from the country to help rebuild Japan.

Mariko-chan's movements were cramped with grief and desire. It was midsummer in the village. Mariko-chan was on her knees. The upper part of her *kimono* was loose and as she lowered her fan from her face the silk material slipped from her shoulder. With a gesture of self-conscious modesty, Mariko-chan rearranged her *kimono*, casually revealing as much as she concealed. Her breasts were small, but even in the softened light it was possible to see they were not the breasts of a young woman.

The girl in the village was lying awake at night, thinking of her lover; Mariko-chan was half kneeling, half reclining in the middle of the platform, supporting her body with her right hand while her left hand moved under the folds of her *kimono*. One of the Koreans whispered to his companion and they both laughed. The girl was describing the gentleness of her lover. Mariko-chan moved her legs slightly, deepening the shadow that was just visible under the border of her *kimono*, in between the whiteness of her knees.

Some of the men in the front row were leaning against the stage, their faces no more than a few inches from Mariko-chan's feet, which were neatly enclosed in white cotton *tabi* socks. Mariko-chan did not register their presence; instead she turned her head, very slowly, to the left and to the right. Then like a time-lapse film of a flower in the final stages of disintegration, she unravelled the last length of her *obi* at her waist and lay back. For a while she remained still, almost rigid.

The rhythm of the music changed. A young man in the front row was gazing reverently between Mariko-chan's knees towards a dark triangle which was more shadow than revelation. Another man took off his spectacles, wiped the lenses with his tie, adjusted them to the bridge of his nose and leaned forward again. Mariko-chan rolled on to her back, reached her right hand under her right thigh and raised it until her knee touched her shoulder. The left half of her body hardly moved.

A man wearing a baseball hat in the second row leaned his head to one shoulder, like a prospective customer in a used-car showroom looking into the engine of a car. With a quick, show-girl flick of her legs, Mariko-chan offered her body to another section of the audience, and the man in the baseball hat cocked his head to the other shoulder.

Once the audience had examined her, Mariko-chan took a more formal kneeling position. She was still wearing her *kimono* loose and untied. She reached into the left-hand sleeve and drew out a dark silk wallet from which she took half a dozen or so rubber contraceptives.

The dwarf, who was still standing in the semi-darkness at the edge of the stage, made another announcement. "Unfortunately, due to recent legislation, it is no longer possible for Mariko-chan to get to know her playfellows as closely as she would like. But anyone in the audience who is curious to know Mariko-chan better is most welcome."

Mariko-chan made a formal bow, with the delicacy of a maid welcoming a customer to a traditional tea house. The man in the baseball hat lifted his index finger. Mariko-chan made an arch expression and said something which I could not hear. Several other men close to the stage raised their index fingers.

Mariko-chan bowed to each customer before rolling a contraceptive on to his upraised finger. After distributing three or four contraceptives, Mariko-chan knelt down at the edge of the stage, spread her legs and leaned back on one hand, with the other she guided the rubber-encased index finger of a man in the front row into her body. For a minute or so she balanced on the balls of her feet, supporting herself with her hands, and watched the probing of the man between her legs. "Careful, sir!" She gripped the man's wrist. There was an edge to her voice, "I'm not a man." She drew his hand away from her body and took a tissue from the silk wallet which she folded round the contraceptive before removing it. Then she bowed, smiled and moved on.

It was the turn of the man in the baseball hat and Mariko-chan guided his finger into her. The man bent forward, and Mariko-chan adjusted herself to his curiosity. The man didn't look at her face, but Mariko-chan kept a constant eye on him and just when it seemed as if his attention might become too familiar, she drew back her hips, leaving him bending forward, staring at the tip of his finger wrapped in a glistening condom. Like mica on *shunga*.

As the laughter subsided, another customer raised his hand this time with two fingers inserted into the contraceptive. "*Dame!*" Mariko-chan pretended to smack the man's wrist. "Certainly not. You've only paid for one finger, not two. Don't be unfair."

For the last inspection Mariko-chan chose a young man in the front row watching her with a religious intensity. He was less confident than the others. When she rolled the condom on to his finger he bowed so deeply and so frequently she had difficulty in putting it on. Once again she opened her legs and drew his hand towards her. As she did so, the young man looked at her face and smiled apologetically. She nodded encouragement. He frowned with concentration like a small boy. After a minute or so, Mariko-chan nodded again and the young man, bowing, withdrew his finger. Mariko-chan took another tissue and deftly plucked the contraceptive from his finger. Then she bowed to him, smiled and rearranged her *kimono*.

Mariko-chan slipped her arms through the sleeves of her

*kimono* and began to collect the discarded tissues in a neat pile, but some men in the front row were calling for more. "Come on, Mariko-chan, give us another look. Let's see what you've got, don't be shy."

Mariko-chan gave a mock frown. "Girls are supposed to be modest. Haven't you seen enough?"

"No!" they shouted. "Not yet! Show us everything!"

Mariko-chan pouted, walked to the front of the stage and lifted her leg over a particularly noisy customer, completely covering his head and shoulders with the hem of her *kimono*. There was a momentary pause, a muffled cry—"*Wah! Kusai!*"—and guffaws from the audience at the man's exclamation of disgust. I noticed a smile widening on Mariko-chan's face as she stepped back and drew her *kimono* about her.

"There now," the dwarf interrupted, "I hope Mariko-chan has satisfied your curiosity, sir. But don't worry, there is still another act to come!"

Mariko-chan placed the last of the tissues in a small square of red silk, which she tied loosely together to make a *furoshiki*. With the bundle in one hand and her *obi* in the other she gave a hurried, informal bow.

"Thank you, Mariko-chan," said the dwarf, his voice rising, "everyone please, a round of applause for Mariko-chan!" The spotlight settled on her unsteadily. Some of the audience were still clapping as Mariko-chan began to make another bow and the curtains closed unceremoniously in front of her.

A blue-green spotlight appeared over our heads, directed on to a small globe turning at the end of a short rod extending from the ceiling. The globe was covered with a mirror mosaic of squares, triangles and hexagons, which cast the light into corners of the room in a bewildering shoal of luminous flecks, momently revealing people's faces among the closely packed shadows: someone in mid-smile, another scratching his chin, a little man staring at the darkened stage.

The blue-green light faded and for several seconds there was darkness. Then a circle of light moved across the little stage and the sequinned curtains shimmered as the dwarf reappeared to announce the mime of Sada Abe's Passion.

I remembered the name. Sada Abe was famous or notorious: a woman who killed her lover. In Japan her name has the icy fascination of a *femme fatale*. She killed her lover by mistake: somehow in the heat of passion, she strangled him. When the police arrested her they found among her personal effects the penis of her dead lover, which she had cut from his body and wrapped in silk. After her release from prison she became a *mama-san* and ended her days in a bar in Inaricho.

The music faded and the lights dimmed and then, instead of the sounds of disco rock there was *koto* music. As we listened to the music's slow beginning, one string plucked at a time, the room, the dwarf, and the audience dissolved in shadow, until there was nothing but the sound of the *koto* in the dark. Gradually the stage emerged from darkness. There were two silhouettes of a man and a woman dressed in *kimonos*. As the light grew we saw their faces: they were both in their early twenties. They remained absolutely still, looking into each other's eyes until the stage lights reached a brilliant intensity. The young man slowly raised his arm and placed it on the woman's shoulder.

The way they moved reminded me of the slow, deliberate gestures of *nō* players, but as the rhythm of the music quickened, the precision and formality of their movements disintegrated. His hands moved over the surface of her body and the *kimono* slipped from her shoulders; her breasts were bare. She pulled at his *kimono* which fell open and as he lowered her gently to the ground, his *kimono* concealed her nakedness. He seemed unmoved by what he was doing, as if all his attention was concentrated on the movement of his body and the rhythm of the music. Her eyelids were half closed and her body was unresisting. They took off their *kimonos*. She was naked but he was still wearing a white cotton cloth tied round his waist and between his legs. The music accelerated. He had difficulty keeping time with the music. She whispered something; it was the first time their faces were close. He nodded but his face wore an expression of mask-like indifference. Her fingers gripped the red *obi* sash beside her. The music ended dramatically in a jangling collision of chords. The young man lay very still on top of the girl. Around his neck was the red *obi* sash. The girl's arms dropped to her sides.

A deep flute note sounded through the room. The girl ran her fingers through the young man's hair. He did not move. She pushed him. He rolled and lay on his back with his eyes closed and his mouth open. Another long low note reverberated around the room. I could hear the flute player's intake of breath. The girl was leaning over the young man with her back to the audience. A sharp, high-pitched note sounded on the flute and as it died away she lifted a white cloth splashed with scarlet about her head. She folded the cloth and placed it beside her, covered the young man's face and torso with his *kimono*, and then turned once more to face the audience. For several seconds she knelt without moving: Sada Abe, staring into the oblivion of life without her lover.

Then she began to caress her body as if her hands belonged to someone else, as if she was surrendering her own, individual identity to the group identity of the audience watching her. Her eyelids closed and her head leaned gently to one side. The audience's attention was focused on her, aroused by her, willing her towards some kind of ecstasy: group sex, Japanese style, uncomplicated by physical or emotional attachment.

The woman lay bathed in her own sweat: with her head and shoulders towards the back of the stage and her legs wide apart she displayed herself with the fingers of her left hand and began to masturbate with her right hand.

The man directly opposite her, in the front row, remained seated, but those on either side and in the row behind him got to their feet and looked over his shoulder with the same concentration as men looking over the shoulder of a player at a critical moment in a game of Mah-Jongg.

The music changed and became like peasant dancing music; staccato breaths hurrying the rhythm on. The woman on the stage was arching her body. Her eyes were shut tight and her teeth were clenched in an expression of physical effort. The men watching her were silent, tense with anticipation, waiting for her to bring herself to the point of climax.

The woman shook her head from side to side. The movement of her hand was almost invisible: a semi-controlled trembling of the wrist. Then she opened her mouth in a sharp intake of breath that was audible through the sound of the flute, slowly lowered her hips and her legs with a brief, involuntary tremor and lay still except for the rise and fall of her body as she breathed in and out.

She knew the music. A few seconds later it came to an end. There was silence. She was still in the circle of light. The stage went dark.

Then the spotlight came on again, and there she was tying the *obi* of her cotton *kimono* and smiling nervously. She seemed a stranger in her own body, bowing clumsily and avoiding the spotlight with her eyes as if it was the glare of some implacable authority.

Out of the shadows behind her, the young man appeared in his *kimono* and she withdrew into the half darkness so he could occupy the centre of the circle of light.

The man bowed again. I looked for signs of affection between them, the man and woman facing us, but there was nothing I could recognise as tenderness. It was just a professional relationship: a double act.

"OK," said Tony, "let's get some *sushi*."

○

This morning I took a taxi to Roppongi. I'd arranged to go over some pictures with Michiko at her studio at the top of a block of flats, just a few minutes from Roppongi crossing. The elevator only went as far as the seventh floor, then there was a metal staircase on to the roof, which had a tubular balustrade.

Michiko wasn't about, but the weather was fine and I wasn't in a hurry. I walked over to the railing. A slight breeze was blowing, carrying the smell of noodles. There was a steady thunder from an overhead expressway a few blocks away and the tops of cars and lorries were visible through a gap between the buildings.

The horizon was made of office blocks in different colours: pink and white and brown and yellow. Tokyo Tower was just visible over a sign advertising Mitsubishi. The office blocks enclosed an area of smaller buildings. A few were two or three storeys tall but most were traditional, single-storey houses, roofed with tiles in blue-green or reddish brown glazes. From where I was I could see into the backyards and gardens. In one yard there was a mass of rusting corrugated iron sheeting and disintegrating machinery; another was a patch of thorns and weeds littered with Sprite cans and beer bottles. Between them, protected by a tall wooden fence, was a garden of carefully arranged stones planted with delicate bamboos. Beside a dilapidated house like a shack was a small patch of waste land with a cherry tree rising from a tangle of undergrowth and two white chickens pecking at the ground.

At the base of the building, a narrow alley led to the garden gate of a clapboard house, with sun-beaten timbers and a tin roof painted with red lead. An old man and a young boy were pushing a bicycle up the alley. They opened the gate and wheeled the bicycle inside. The old man shuffled towards the house while the boy leaned the bicycle against the shed. On the other side of the house was the cemetery of a Buddhist temple.

The rows of memorial stones were laid out on a grid pattern, crossed at intervals by paths of rectangular flagstones. Here and there among the graves were pinewood staves, painted with the characters of the names of the recent dead in black ink brush strokes. One group of staves was almost white in the bright sunlight but the surface of the others had already darkened, and the ink was faded.

In the shade of an ilex tree, an old man in a dark suit and a woman in a silver-grey dress were standing in front of a grave. The old man gestured towards a pillar of stone on a square plinth; on either side were two metal vases containing the remains of chrysanthemums. The woman put down the shopping bag she was carrying, picked up the two vases and walked away.

The old man leaned forward to examine the inscription on the stone and ran his fingers along the carved characters. Then he took off his jacket, folded it and placed it carefully on a low stone wall around the grave. The woman returned with a bucket of water. The old man rolled up his sleeves and the woman gave him a scrubbing brush from her shopping bag. She squeezed some soap into the bucket and the old man set to work scrubbing the stone pillar until it was covered with a mass of white foam dripping to the ground.

The woman reappeared with another bucket of water and the two metal vases which she filled with laurels from her shopping bag.

The old man rinsed the soap from the stone, examined the plinth and began scrubbing again. The woman went to fetch another bucket of water.

The stone was rinsed again and the woman placed the two vases of laurels on either side of the plinth. Between them she placed a rice cake and some cigarettes. The old man took something from his pocket, lit it with a lighter and placed it a little distance away from the rice cake and cigarettes. Then he rolled down his shirtsleeves, straightened his tie and put on his jacket. The woman smoothed her dress and stood a few steps behind him. First the old man put his hands together, then the woman, and they both lowered their heads in prayer. The old man's hair shone like spun glass in the sunlight.

There was a smoky, bitter-sweet fragrance of incense in the spring air.

The old man raised his head and said something to the woman. Then he picked up the empty bucket, she picked up her shopping bag and they walked back slowly along the path together.

I wrote a message on a scrap of envelope and pushed it under the door of Michiko's studio. "In the cemetery—back in a while."

It was simple enough to find my way. There was nobody about. Some graves were memorials to the vulgarity of the dead: big black slabs of basalt so highly polished it was possible to see one's reflection in the surface of the stone. Other graves were older and plainer: rough cubes of weathered stone and artfully natural-looking rocks, relics of the philosophy of other, vanished generations.

Several graves had been damaged and repaired. The surface of a few stones was strangely dark and in places it seemed as if the stone had vitrified in some intense heat. I wondered what kind of inferno had swept the cemetery, blazing with an intensity so fierce that its heat had cast a permanent shadow where the fire made the stone burn.

I came to the grave which the old man and the woman had been tending. The stone was still wet but the same shadow was there, burned into the rock. I remembered a similar shadow on another stone, where a man was sitting on the steps of a bank on 6 August 1945, preserved in the atomic bomb museum in Hiroshima.

I looked at the date of the gravestone; the third year of the *Showa* era, 1929, the year of the Wall Street Crash. Minoru Yasakawa was seventy-nine years old when he died. He was born when Tokyo was still called Edo and the country had been in seclusion from the rest of the world for more than two hundred years. He was a small boy when the American Commodore Perry's black ship sailed into Edo Bay, demanding that

Japan end its self-imposed isolation from the world by opening itself to foreign trade.

It was Easter Sunday and Minoru Yasakawa, who smoked cigarettes, had been dead for almost sixty years. The old man was probably his grandson.

The heat of the sun on the back of my head was making me drowsy. It was too hot to think about ancestor worship and reincarnation, survival in the memory of one's grandchildren and resurrection.

I thought of the old man washing the grave of his grandfather.

The wind rustled the branches of the ilex tree and the shadows of the leaves danced over the shadow in the wet stone and the sunlight in the water was a mirror of fire.

Someone was calling my name.

○

Last night I had dinner at Christopher Forbes'. I like Christopher, but I don't understand him. Sometimes I think I can see who he is, other times it's as if there's nobody there at all. He's married since I last saw him. His wife's name is Sarah and they met in Mandalay. Like Christopher, she's slightly unreal, as if part of her is somewhere else.

The other guests were Japanese and foreigners. At dinner I sat next to a woman called Odette Lançon. Her father was a French merchant who came to Japan in the 1890s. She was born in Yokohama and lived in Japan until she left for Europe in 1940. I asked what it was like in Japan just before the Second World War.

"Arrogance and greed and fear," she said, "now the cycle has come full circle and we have arrogance and greed again, but at least the fear is missing." I asked about the arrogance and greed. She said it wasn't the Japanese people's fault, it was the fault of their rulers.

In the 1930s the Japanese were educated into believing they

were a superior race. State Shinto imposed a sacred duty on Japan to free the countries of the yellow people from the rule of the white people.

"They were yellow, we were white. They wanted an Empire for their Emperor, the Son of Heaven. It was all rather beautiful in a way, and that made it more frightening. The future was a better place than the present: everyone believed it was and so it began to come true. It was called the Great Far Eastern Co-Prosperity Sphere, now it's the borderless economy. *Plus ça change—plus c'est la même chose.*"

She drew air in through her teeth like someone Japanese.

"*C'est difficile,*" she said and shook her head.

I would have liked to know what kind of fear had the power of silence after fifty years but she didn't want to talk about it. Suddenly she seemed more Japanese than French. I asked her, if the past was a mirror, what she saw in the future.

"My departure," she gave a weary smile. "I am leaving Japan," she shrugged.

It sounded like a confession of failure. She thinks modern Japan is devouring itself, it is "autophagist." It's destroying itself in order to become a global power. At heart, Japan is a civilised country, but it's going the way of America and selling its soul for materialism. She recognises the feeling, it's like the thirties; something wrong with the national psyche, a sort of spiritual malaise which blinds the Japanese to faults which the rest of the world sees at a glance. Once was enough, she said, she doesn't want to see it happen again.

A Japanese man in his sixties on the other side of the table leaned forward and said, "Forgive me." He hesitated. "I couldn't help overhearing your conversation, I agree with you whole-heartedly." His English had a slightly old-fashioned formality. His face was different from that of most Japanese of his age; it was gentle and his eyes had a sense of humour.

"When I was in Inner Mongolia I saw how selfish the Japanese could be." He cleared his throat and described how he went to Inner Mongolia in 1940 as part of a programme known as the *Zenrin Kyokai*—the Good Neighbour Association. But instead of helping the local people, the Japanese exploited them.

"All we wanted was as much meat and wool as we could get from the nomads." He shook his head. "We didn't treat them like human beings."

Christopher said it sounded like the British in India. The man apologised for contradicting him and said he was also in India in 1946 and what the British did in India was nothing like what the Japanese did in Mongolia. Odette asked what he thought was wrong with Japan. She addressed him as Kimura-sensei.

"Compassion," he said. "Japan seems to have forgotten the Buddhist virtue of *ninjo* compassion. We have forgotten the meaning of *bushido*." After saying the word "*bushido*" he looked at us to see our reaction. "Not the *bushido* of popular fiction," he smiled. "*Bushido* the way of the *bushi*: the code of knights living in the country. The heart of *bushido* is Buddhism. The heart of Buddhism is *ninjo* compassion." Kimura-sensei described how, during the 1920s and 1930s, politicians and generals misused the culture of Japan for their own purpose and gave *bushido* another, false meaning. They used the religion of the Japanese people for their own ambitions.

"If Japan is to be a great country, the Japanese must see themselves clearly. When we see our own faults we will have compassion for others. Until then we will continue to be selfish Japanese."

I could see Odette was about to ask another question, just as Sarah appeared with a raspberry soufflé. For a while the conversation was about fruit, and puddings, and whether or not the Japanese like sweet things as much as the English or the French. Kimura-sensei confessed he liked the taste of fermented mare's milk.

Over coffee I talked with the young Japanese woman who was sitting between Christopher and Kimura-sensei. All through dinner I'd been wondering if I knew her and when she mentioned Johnny Tallis I recognised her: Fujiko. The last time I'd seen her was after a party at Johnny's flat in Akasaka. There was a lot of *sake* and it was three years ago. She wanted to talk about Johnny.

She was there when he went over the edge. She'd just gone into the kitchen to get some ice when she heard a girl scream. She ran back into the room. The window onto the balcony was open, she saw someone looking over the railings—the girl was huddled on the sofa with her face in the cushion sobbing.

"I felt very cold," she said, "everything went grey. I thought my heart would come out of my mouth." By the time she got to the balcony and looked over the railings, down to the street below, Johnny was already trying to get to his feet. Her hands were trembling. It was like an awful secret she needed to share with me, because I was a friend of Johnny.

Her version of what happened was different from what Roddy had told me. The man with Johnny wasn't American, but Australian and he wasn't an old friend, just someone Johnny met by chance in Indonesia. He left Japan soon after and she hadn't heard of him since; nor had anyone else. I asked about the other Japanese girl and something happened in her eyes, like a shadow passing over water. For a while, she didn't say anything, almost as if she hadn't heard me. Then she gave a little sigh and said, "Saaaaaah," which meant she didn't know or didn't want to say or she couldn't remember or she was deciding what to say in reply.

Then she blinked and said the girl's name, Michiko. Michiko Takayama was nice, polite, easy to get along with. Her description of the girl was a polite formula. She wasn't thinking about what she was saying. She was in the past. I was only half listening. I was remembering Johnny's flat.

From the doorway between the kitchen and the living room it was possible to see someone on the balcony. In my imagination I could see the figure of the Australian from Indonesia, but I couldn't see his face. The Japanese girl, Michiko, was huddled on the sofa. Her face was hidden among the cushions. But what were they talking about when she left the room?

Where were they standing? What did they say when she came back into the room? And how did the Australian react? The look in Fujiko's eyes said it was better to leave it all in the past.

I asked if she saw much of Johnny's friends. She said Christopher and Sarah were the only people she'd seen for a while.

Kimura-sensei apologised for leaving so early. The train journey back to his home took an hour and a half and his wife was waiting for him. We all stood up and bowed and Christopher went with him to hail a taxi. When he came back he told us more about Kimura-sensei.

Hisao Kimura was now Professor of Mongolian Studies at Asia University, Tokyo. In 1940 he had been contacted by Japanese intelligence, who wanted information on the movement of arms and ammunition into China from Russia. Several men had already set out on the same mission. None of them returned. Kimura-sensei volunteered. He was eighteen years old. He went as a Mongolian Buddhist monk and spent many months working his way through the lines of the communists and the *Kuo Min Tang*. Then a Muslim warlord arrested him and held him prisoner for a year. On his release he travelled south towards Tibet, but by the time he reached Lhasa Japan had lost the war. He decided to go on towards India. In Kalimpong he met a British intelligence officer. He was recruited and went on another mission into Tibet to report on a possible Chinese invasion. He kept his cover; British intelligence still thought he was Mongolian. After he had spent some time in Lhasa the Tibetan authorities became suspicious of his contacts with social reform groups and he was expelled from the country. It was the end of the mission. In Calcutta he turned over his cards to the British authorities and was given a ticket home.

I thought of the mountains and rivers and snow and stars that Kimura-sensei must have seen and the loneliness of the long-distance spy. I wondered what it was like coming back to Japan and living in Tokyo.

We talked about spying and Sarah asked Christopher to describe his meeting with the man from M.I.6. Christopher smiled as if she'd said he was good in bed and told us about the day he received a telephone call from someone suggesting he might like to discuss a possible career move. Christopher assumed it was just another headhunter but the man mentioned a couple of things which suggested more research on his background than usual, so he agreed to a meeting. The rendezvous was the Tartan Bar in the Okura Hotel. The man said he would be carrying a copy of the *Financial Times*.

"When I got there, what do you think?" Christopher grinned. "At least three blokes reading the *FT*. Just what you'd expect. Typical M.I.6—couldn't organise a piss-up in a brewery."

A man in a suit came up with a copy of the *Wall Street Journal* and apologised for the confusion. He'd tried the hotel bookstall but the *FT* was sold out. Over a whisky, he suggested meeting someone on an informal basis who could help set up a business. I looked at Christopher and wondered why he was telling us the story.

"All these blokes looking over the tops of their newspapers," he said. "It was a bloody laugh, I tell you."

I asked if the man in the suit was successful and Christopher grinned.

"Denial is confirmation," I said.

"I like to be my own boss," he said, "run my own business. Number one for number one is my motto." Odette said his single-mindedness was the reason he was so successful in Japan. Christopher looked modest and Sarah said she sometimes wished he wasn't quite so single-minded and they gazed at each other like a couple in a TV commercial for life insurance. We all said what a wonderful evening it had been and how much we'd enjoyed ourselves.

I took Fujiko home by taxi. We didn't speak much. It was Japanese silence and it felt good. I remembered the last time we saw each other, after Johnny's party.

We were together. We understood each other without saying

anything. I kissed her goodnight and she said thank-you and I thought of Tanya.

○

The market's a stuffed dodo.

Yamaguchi has gone for an early lunch with an old university friend from Mitsubishi and the sky is blue and bright over towards Tokyo Bay.

This morning Yamashita, head of the swaps team, came to me and said I owed him money. This puzzled me since we haven't said more than a couple of sentences to each other while I've been here. Yamashita has all the humour and charm of last week's *Wall Street Journal* but I noticed a thin little smile at the corners of his mouth so I thought perhaps he was joking. But he wasn't. He unfolded a piece of paper in his hands: it was the bill for my telephone with every number I'd called and how long each call had lasted. It was all there. Itemised.

I didn't see why the head of swaps should be asking me for money to pay my telephone bill and I said so. He gave another thin little smile and said that as well as head of swaps he was also one of the directors in Administration. I asked if it gave him the right to receive my telephone bills and he made a noise like a sheep sneezing. Since it was a company apartment, in the interests of efficiency and convenience the telephone was in his name. The itemisation of calls was an optional service and could be discontinued if it was unnecessary. I said I'd give him the money after lunch.

I had to admire the way it was done: no-mask Zen, clear and simple. I liked the style; a hint that it was all a long and complicated practical joke. Sometimes Japanese humour is like a shaggy-dog story—it's difficult knowing when to laugh.

○

Last night our company gave a party for people from Mitsubishi. It was meant to be a *sakura* party but the blossoms are late this year and the weather was cold and windy. The party was held indoors, on the second floor of a hotel overlooking a small park of cherry trees. Kit said the price of the room increased the more blossom there was on the trees. The branches of the cherry trees were almost bare and dripping with rain.

The people from Mitsubishi arrived in a group. Everyone was wearing a badge saying who he was and what he did. In the middle of the room was a table spread with *sushi* and canapés and bottles of beer. Clather greeted a couple of Mitsubishi men like long-lost friends and they grinned at him uncertainly. As he went to get drinks for them I heard one of them whisper that all foreigners looked the same. Yamaguchi was laughing and joking with Yamamoto and an older man from Mitsubishi. A lot of the people from Mitsubishi remained in little groups of their own talking among themselves. So did we. It wasn't individuals meeting but the companies, like two big creatures sniffing each other: a corporate date.

○

Tanya's next door sleeping off her jet-lag and I'm sitting here with an ice-cold, low-alcohol beer and the sun is shining.

She was almost the only person on the flight who wasn't Japanese. Coming out of customs she was surrounded by *salarimen* in suits and Japanese tourists back from shopping in London, all wearing Aquascutum raincoats, Austin Reed jackets and Hermès ties. She was wearing a white T-shirt, white jeans and white shoes. She didn't see me. I wanted to laugh because she was there and we were going to be together. She saw me and smiled. For a second she was like a stranger. Then I kissed her.

I'd remembered the colour of her eyes but I'd forgotten what it was like to be together.

◯

The cherry trees in my neighbour's garden have little pink buds, the colour of sugar mice. The buds are pink and the sky is blue. If I was in England I'd look at the cherry blossom and think, "It's pretty." Here in the land of cherry blossom, it's different. In spring the religion of the people is *sakura*, the sacred flower of the Emperor.

The blossom next door is *ichi-buzaki*.

A *haiku* by Basho. *Sama zama no koto omoidasu sakura kana*— How many things they call to mind these cherry blossoms.

If I were to wake Tanya and ask her to look at the cherry blossoms there'd be a distance between us. She'd say, "Yes, they're good," and I'd be thinking that she was looking at them like trees in a garden or a park in England. Not *sakura*.

Perhaps I've fooled myself into believing I can see a tree in Japanese.

*Sakura*. Mention the word to people here and it's like giving them a whiff of amyl nitrate. *Sakura!* Is it late? Is it early? How far north is it today?

It was *sakura* in Kyushu last weekend. *Ichi-buzaki, nibuzaki*, through the successive degrees of the cherry blossom sweeping across the country like a *tsunami*, a Hokusai wave of flowers, until the final explosion of *man-buzaki*, total blossom.

*Sakura* makes the heart beat faster.

It's spring. And Tanya is here.

◯

Outside the sky is bright and the water surrounding the Imperial Palace is flashing like a sword in the sunlight and the jet planes on the horizon taking off from Haneda make me think of other places and things I could be doing.

Yamaguchi is drinking from a little brown bottle. It's a health drink for middle-aged executives with stress problems. They drink it and they feel happy and strong according to the television commercial which has an image of a man climbing a waterfall. When I imagine what it's like to be a *salariman* I think of the man climbing the waterfall.

Yamaguchi is finishing the drink. Even though it's a small bottle he puts his head back to finish it, like the man in the commercial, and then he licks his lips and makes a sound between a gasp and a sigh like a *samurai* draining a cup of *sake* in an old-fashioned, sword-slashing *chanbara* film on television.

When Yamaguchi taps a cigarette from his Mild Seven packet he looks distant or philosophical. Like the man in the commercial for Johnny Walker whisky, it's difficult to know what he's thinking.

If he's thinking.

○

The sky's grey and so's the market.

I have three clients now. I talk to them every day about European markets. Usually they've heard the stories before I tell them because information from the London office arrives late. By the time it gets here most Japanese investors have already talked with our competitors and decided the day's investments. Some people in the London office still think the world is on Greenwich Mean Time. I know the problem. Watching the sun set over the Imperial Palace, it's difficult to imagine what it's like in London.

In the morning, coming in to work, seeing the square shapes of the office blocks in a golden haze like giant screens unfolding and the birds circling over the trees of the Imperial Palace, and the sunlight flashing on the windscreens of the cars, Tokyo is where the sun rises and the rest of the world is still asleep. Or so it seems.

○

It's seven-thirty in the evening and I'm standing in a carriage of an underground train on the way to Nakameguro.

I'm by the door, looking out of the window at the darkness of the tunnel. I can see the reflection of a Japanese woman opposite me. She's looking at me. She's curious. She's noticed me talking into this recorder but she doesn't want to look too obviously in my direction. We're going through a tunnel and the sound of the train is too loud for her to hear what I'm saying. She's pretty. The shape of her mouth suggests a sense of humour. I turn my head slowly and look at her, as if by accident. She blinks and turns her head slightly. We're both looking out of the window at the blackness. I can see her reflection but her eyes are in shadow.

I bow to her reflection in the darkened glass of the carriage window and her reflection bows in return.

○

Last night Tanya and I had an argument, our first argument in Japan, in the local supermarket. We were at the fish counter. Tanya asked what something was and without thinking I said *kaibashira*. She asked what it was in English. The tone of her voice made the attendant at the fish counter look up. I saw Tanya's face reflected in a mirror, at another angle, perhaps as she appeared to the Japanese girl serving at the counter: a foreign woman raising her voice at a foreign man, arguing about scallops. It would have been funny somewhere else, but in my local supermarket, here in Tokyo, it was loss of face and I said so. Tanya put the basket she was carrying on to the counter, said, "I'm not Japanese," and walked out of sight behind a wall of tinned octopus. I told the girl at the counter my friend was new in Japan.

I found Tanya behind some tinned tuna looking at a display of dried jellyfish and fish bonbons.

She didn't want to behave in a Japanese way. Why did she have to change the way she was to suit Japanese people? What was this Japanese way of doing things? She wasn't going to be turned into a Japanese girl. And what was so special about Japanese girls anyway?

○

Yesterday we went cherry blossom viewing. For some people cherry blossom viewing is like a religious duty. For other people it's singing songs and getting drunk and being sick in cardboard boxes. Either way, it has to be done.

We took a taxi to the cemetery at Aoyama Bochi. The air was mild and there were people everywhere. Some were sitting on sheets of plastic; others had covered the ground with flattened cardboard like *tatami* mats, with their shoes in neat rows on the edge, and were sitting or kneeling *seiza* style in circles. There were company groups and family groups and groups of individuals, laughing, drinking, smiling, shouting, clapping hands, singing, dancing, eating, snoring, fanning themselves and slapping each other on the back, all together under the silent thunder of a great wave of flowers above their heads in a spray of petals. A man with a crown made of Sapporo beer cans taped together called out to us in English. "We Japanese love *sakura*, we Japanese love *sake*, please enjoy yourselves."

He smiled at us as if we were strangely shaped balloons floating in front of him. His face was copper-pink. I said I liked his hat in Japanese and he invited us to drink some *sake*.

A dozen people were sitting on a mat of plastic imitation reeds singing a song about making typewriters. We took off our shoes and the man with the crown of beer cans made a space for us between Toyama of sales and Nakamura of accounts. The man with the beer cans introduced himself as

Hashimoto, founder and president of the Hashimoto Type-writer Company. He said Tanya looked like an American film actress. I translated and Tanya thanked him.

"Have a good time," he said, "foreigners think we Japanese only work. But we have a good time, don't we?" He grinned at the blossom above our heads.

"*Intanashionaru shimasho.*" He raised his cup of *sake*, "Let's be international." Nakamura leaned towards us and asked if we were enjoying ourselves. I said the feeling was good. Toyama asked if Tanya was happy. I said she was happy.

Hashimoto waved the employees of Hashimoto Typewriter Company into another chorus while Nakamura gave us cups of *sake* and Toyama asked which country we came from, what we were doing in Tokyo and how we liked Japan. I asked about Hashimoto Typewriters. We talked a lot about typewriters: mechanical typewriters, automatic typewriters and voice-activated typewriters. In the old days, when there were ten thousand characters or more a good typist could manage fifteen or twenty words per minute. We discussed the merits of certain kinds of typewriters in great detail. I looked at Tanya. She didn't say anything. I thanked Nakamura and Toyama for their hospitality and they smiled with relief.

A man with a sallow face was singing a song about the joys of spring and Hashimoto was clapping his hands in rhythm and smiling as if it was a song he remembered from his childhood. I bowed to him. He nodded, and waved, and continued clapping.

We put on our shoes, bowed to Toyama and Nakamura and joined the sightseers walking along, looking at the people singing and drinking under the trees. We passed some old men singing a song that was popular with the army during the war. I looked at the ancient warriors under the cherry blossom, like a band of strange-looking sages in a Chinese scroll painting, and thought of the massacre at Nanking and the sweet smell of the hot *sake* under the white flowers waving in the sunlight.

Tanya said she'd had enough blossom.

Her eyes were almost the same colour as the sky and her lips were slightly open as if she was about to say something and I kissed her because we were foreigners in a cemetery full of Japanese and it was springtime in Tokyo.

○

It's after midnight and Tanya's in bed.

I'm just back from a visit to Ueno Park with Roger. We wanted to see the *sakura* parties at night, but we were late and by the time we arrived most of the people had gone. Some were in sleeping-bags, others had wrapped themselves in sheets of air-bubble plastic. A few lay sprawled on the bare earth like poison-gas victims under the smoky lilac glow of the night sky. There were drifts of rubbish, piled in knee-high mounds by the side of the road.

"The end of the party," said Roger, "tomorrow's the hang-over."

I didn't say anything. The sky over the trees was the colour of the sky in a bad dream. We were walking towards the light of a fire between the trees. There were figures moving around the flames. Something was happening on the edge of the light. A shadow came towards us dragging something. I thought it was someone with a sack of rubbish but then another shadow ran forward and kicked the sack of rubbish. A cry of pain was broken by the sound of another kick. Whoever was lying on the ground needed help. I went towards the shadows. It seemed the sort of fight where there might be knives. I remembered the man with the knife under the stars on the beach in Morocco. I remembered the lesson. Keep away from knives at night. It's not like a film, with the moonlight flashing white on metal. In the dark a knife is invisible.

Some people were kicking a man lying on the ground. I shouted in English to confuse them and asked what they were doing. One of them turned towards me. I measured the distance between us.

"*Gaijin!*" said a shadow.

"Stop it," I said. "*Yamete kudasai! Dame desu!*" I hoped a foreigner speaking Japanese would distract them. I felt like a character in a black comedy. I was a stranger, an outsider. That was my protection.

One of them had a flashlight.

"Hello," I said, "*Konnichiwa.*" I hoped it was as strange for them as it was for me. I didn't want them taking me too seriously. I told them to stop kicking the man on the ground. I couldn't see their faces. The shadow with the flashlight made a half-hearted attempt to stop the kicking. The man on the ground was pulled by his hair into a sitting position and a voice called him a nobody, a nothing. The flashlight caught the man's face which was smeared with blood. The man's head jerked forward like a puppet with loose strings. I heard Roger telling me to leave it alone. The man was trying to get to his feet. The shadow with the flashlight kicked him in the back and the man stumbled forward.

I said it was enough. I spoke in Japanese. Someone muttered at me, using the word *o-mae*. It wasn't my business. To prove it, one of the shadows aimed another kick at the man. Roger said he was going. As I turned away one of them lunged at me but the others held him back. It was like a fight scene in a TV soap series: he shouted and waved his arms but somehow it wasn't convincing. I walked away, not too quick, not too slow, and found Roger on the other side of the light by a street lamp.

"We Japanese are a peace-loving people," he said. His voice was a parody of a self-satisfied Japanese describing Japan to a foreigner. "For us *wa*—harmony—is most important. We Japanese understand each other's feelings. We know each other's mind."

My mouth was dry. I took a deep breath. I wanted to sound normal and relaxed. I was annoyed with myself for reacting as if I was frightened. I told myself it was adrenaline. I took another deep breath. Roger was talking about violence. It was the first time in ten years he'd seen violence in the street.

"It's what happens when people discover they can break the rules," he said. "Géricault was right. Civilisation is a raft. *Après nous le déluge. Sauve qui peut.*"

Ahead of us people were dancing under strings of electric light bulbs to the music of an accordion. It was traditional, *enka* music with an odd, pre-war rhythm. Some were in evening dress, others in everyday clothes, one or two in tracksuits and a few in *kimonos*. There was a fat man in a straw hat with a cigar and a woman in a pink and gold lamé cocktail dress. Several old men with red faces were drinking *sake* and some old women were sitting, talking together. The accordion player was in white tie and tails and his hair was parted in the middle. At a glance he was in his forties but the brilliantined hair had an artificial blackness and his face was the face of a man of sixty. The music was pre-war and the people dancing in front of us were doing something like a slow quick step which could have been an old-fashioned Tokyo dance, but perhaps they couldn't dance any faster. I looked at the faces of the men and wondered what they did during the war: in some of the older women's faces there were lines of sorrow and endurance, but most of them were smiling.

We watched the dancing for a while in the light of the flickering light bulbs under the cherry blossom and listened to the music which was hardly changed from the music of fifty years ago.

Then the accordionist stopped playing to make an announcement. He thanked everyone for their company: he'd enjoyed playing but it was getting late and everyone had to work tomorrow, didn't they?

We stepped into the darkness of the path between the luminous branches of the blossoming trees with the sound of "Auld Lang Syne" echoing over our shoulders.

There was a smell of burning plastic in the air and the blossom had something of the glow of the lilac orange sky. I thought of walking under the cherry trees in Kashima and going north, in the footsteps of Basho, seeing the wild cherry trees in the mountains like miniature white waterfalls and the wind scattering their petals like snow in the moonlight.

○

It's lunchtime and it's a beautiful day: Tokyo Bay is blue and sparkling and the sky is full of light.

I've finished updating the stock indices, I've checked the Reuters news pages and the latest market reports. I've made two cups of coffee and read the *Asian Wall Street Journal*, called three clients and counted seven cigarette ends in Yamaguchi's ashtray.

Yesterday Tanya asked me what I do every day in the office. I told her about reading economic articles and telephoning clients, recommending a buy or a sell of shares in some company because a research analyst in Paris or London thinks it's a good idea. I mentioned company visits and lunches with fund managers and after-work drinks, and meetings and presentations, and meetings to plan meetings and discussions about sales strategies and corporate policy and office politics. Tanya asked why I was working in the company. Wasn't it just a lot of men in suits, talking about numbers and thinking about money, feeling important because they'd managed to persuade themselves and everybody else that they were important when really they were just a lot of men in suits talking about numbers?

○

Tokyo: a high-speed *nō* play, on the dark side of science-fiction comedy, where *samurai* in robot-manufactured business suits read comics about schoolgirl sex. New product. *Shinhatsubai*.

○

The sky is the colour of a switched-off television screen and the city is a sprawl of concrete covered with wires and aerials.

From where I am I can see several Tokyos. It doesn't look like a city where people matter. The office blocks are machines for working in: the architecture of materialism, on a geological fault, at the wrong end of an earthquake cycle.

Down on the ground, at the entrance to the station, there are little old ladies in white bonnets polishing the Gucci shoes of *salarimen*, there are *rāmen* stalls, and *yakitori* bars by the railway lines full of men in suits and women in dresses. From here they're invisible.

○

The life expectancy in Afghanistan is the lowest in the world at forty-two years and in Japan it's the highest, at seventy-eight years. After these few months in Tokyo I've earned more than most Afghans earn in a lifetime.

○

It's my lunch hour and I'm on my way to the Kyobashi Kaikan where I swim most days.

It's good to get away from the office and walk along the street in the open air looking at people.

An old man in his sixties has seen me using the recorder. He's pretending to ignore me but he's looking from under his eyelids. I nod at him and smile and he turns his head, just a little, as if he'd seen something over my shoulder.

The faces of older Japanese change when they see a foreigner. Sometimes their faces go dead. It's something about the past, how it was just after the war, concealing the shame of defeat by a show of indifference. All those foreigners with their red faces and blue eyes and loud voices and chewing gum and cigarettes buying girls with bars of chocolate. Nowadays, only a *salariman* from out of Tokyo looks twice at a foreigner.

There's an old man pushing a barrow stacked with newspapers and folded cardboard boxes. His hair is over his collar and his face is unshaven. I've seen him before. He has a shelter made of polythene under the bridge I pass on the way to the swimming pool. He doesn't see me. He's somewhere else.

The man reminds me of a sequence of film taken at Hiroshima a few weeks after the atom bomb was dropped. The film's in black and white: the camera sweeps across a landscape of charred rubbish and there's nothing except a grey road between piles of ash and then, in the distance a small dark figure appears jerkily pushing a cart along the grey road.

Every time I see the man I think of the shadow pushing the cart through the waste land and wonder if the old man is somewhere like that in his mind, living in a landscape of the past.

○

It's one-forty-five and I should be back at the office by two o'clock.

The pool wasn't too crowded, just a few old ladies and a couple of overweight men in their fifties. I prefer it when there are *obaachan* in the pool. It's like getting into a big bath in an *onsen*. They smile and bow and I smile and bow. When there's only an attendant it's more like entering a *dojo*—no smiling, just a bow. On Thursdays half the pool is roped off and a group of men in tiny swimming costumes do warm-up exercises and steam up and down the pool kicking water in people's faces.

I like swimming. I'm less of a stranger when I'm in the pool. I think the other people feel the same way: we're all in the water together. *Hadaka ii kimochi*, a simple kind of friendship, no words—very Japanese.

I'm walking along the pavement in the sunlight and the wind is fluttering the green plastic leaves of artificial willow strands waving from the concrete lamp posts. There are shop assistants from a department store in blue and grey below-the-knee uniforms, silver-green eyeshadow and pink and purple lipsticks and 1940s' peek-a-boo hairstyles, and schoolboys in dark blue nineteenth-century Prussian-style school uniforms, tailored to look like heroes in schoolboy *manga* comics: extra-wide padded shoulders, trousers with three-inch turnups, and brass buttons everywhere.

There's the office.

If I were a *salariman* I'd look at the line of windows with white Venetian blinds and think "That's where I belong" *uchi desu*, the place where I am. I think of Yamaguchi and Nakamura and Hiroguchi and Laroche and Clather: comparing each other's suits and pens and watches and cufflinks, and smiling and smiling and smiling as if they're having the time of their lives.

○

It's Saturday afternoon.

A musical-box melody from the loudspeaker on the other side of the road telling school children that it's four o'clock has just died away. Tanya's in the bedroom and I'm sitting here, looking out of the window at old man Uehara weeding his vegetables. It's a typical Tokyo afternoon. The sky is grey and the air is very still.

The rooks in the trees are making a lot of noise. The windows are wide open but there's no breeze. Tanya says its going to thunder. If I concentrate I can hear the sound of the trucks on the main road. Yesterday I asked Yamaguchi what people in Tokyo do at weekends and he said, "Eat, drink, shop, sleep and go to love hotel."

I could read a book or have a cold beer and watch some television or I could wake Tanya and we could go to Harajuku and listen to the bands and see the kids dancing, or go shopping, or practise golf swings in a multi-storey golf range or eat a *bifubaaga* at *Makudonarudo* or go fishing for carp in a square concrete pool with a few hundred other people in a line together.

It's the Tokyo feeling—nothing happening and nothing to do but wait for something to happen.

Tanya doesn't like me using the recorder when we're together. She says it interrupts the flow. This morning we were having a coffee in a *kissaten* when I saw a shopping bag with a slogan in English—something like "New Aspects of Revolution in Fashion and Ideas"—and I'd just got the recorder out of my pocket when Tanya said either we talked or she'd go and I could talk to the recorder. I put it away and we had an argument about priorities. Why waste time in a bank in Tokyo? What about the rainforests? All the trees disappearing because the Japanese use throwaway wooden chopsticks. All the dolphins. All the whales. All the child prostitutes in Thailand and the Philippines. Japanese money. Japanese world.

"Japan's OK," she said, "the problem is the Japanese."

I asked if she was having delayed culture shock, but no, it wasn't culture shock, it was the Japanese, so clean and polite and boring, like well-behaved schoolchildren.

I said she might see things differently if she learned the language.

"What's the point?" she said. "I don't want to be Japanese."

We sat with our coffee in front of us not saying anything. I thought about my first few months in Kashima and the feeling as Japan closed in, day by day, and the pain as I learned the subliminal mantra "Do as we do or die." I thought about how places can become part of people.

Tanya was staring out of the window as if the street was a film she'd seen several times before. I said there wasn't much danger of her becoming Japanese. That suited her fine, she said, but I'd better be careful; I might turn Japanese. It could happen, like the wind blowing and my face changing, and I wouldn't even realise what had happened.

I almost told her about this diary, how it reminds me of the distance between what I see and who I am. But instead I said, "Coming to Japan isn't necessarily a beautiful experience." We took a taxi back and by the time we arrived things were better between us.

Sometimes it's me, sometimes it's Tokyo, sometimes it's just Japan. But it's OK. We can do it.

○

Friday.

Yesterday one of the old men from the fifth floor in London visited the office. I recognised the bags under his eyes from the photograph in the company magazine. He didn't look much better in real life. We were across the table from each other at lunch. He had a brandy-and-cigars voice and a laugh-with-everyone manner. He was enjoying himself, he wasn't used to the respect people were showing him. He thought it was from the heart.

Laroche was sitting next to him, smiling and nodding at everything the old man said. It was strange. He was behaving exactly like a Japanese. The old man probably didn't notice or perhaps he thought Laroche was trying to ingratiate himself. Laroche doesn't speak Japanese; on the surface Japan hasn't touched him, but it's got inside him.

In the evening there was a party for the old man at Laroche's house. It was compulsory. I called Tanya. I thought she might be interested to see the people I work with. She said she'd come if it was a matter of life or death. We arranged to meet at the Imperial Hotel at seven o'clock in the lobby. She appeared at seven-fifteen wearing a black velvet dress and a rock-crystal crucifix at her neck tied with a pale blue ribbon. She said she wasn't sure what to wear to a party of Japanese bankers.

We arrived at the house in Azabu a few minutes before eight o'clock. A Filipino maid opened the door and asked us to follow her into a room where twenty or thirty people were standing around with glasses in their hands. Everyone was at the one-drink stage except for Taniguchi who'd taken off his jacket and loosened his tie. There were two groups, some standing around the old man from London, the others around Laroche. There wasn't much to choose between them. All the Japanese were looking attentive and respectful. Clather was with the old man, nodding his head and smiling a smile that was going at the edges and Klaus was beside Laroche with a second-in-command expression on his face.

An *obaachan* in a *kimono* asked what we'd like to drink. She turned to me first. Tanya said she'd like a whisky and soda, no ice. I asked for a glass of champagne. The woman in the *kimono* whispered to a waiter and made an elegant, ancient, *geisha*-style shuffle towards Laroche to let him know we'd arrived.

He nodded and carried on talking. He wasn't wearing his spectacles. His eyes were small and brown. He didn't notice us until we were on the edge of the circle. Then he saw Tanya and gave us a big welcome; he was glad I could make it, had I got a drink and who was the lovely lady with me? He understood why I left the office early. Everyone laughed obediently.

The waiter came with the whisky and soda and the champagne. He was confused because Tanya was having the whisky and soda. He thought it was a man's drink. Laroche asked how long Tanya was staying in Tokyo. Klaus's smile slipped like a spoiled adolescent's because Laroche wasn't talking to him. I left Tanya and joined the old man's group. Everyone was silent and looking at the old man except for Yamaguchi who was standing on the other side of a pillar with a cigarette hanging out of his mouth.

The old man had reached a no-man's-land where he'd told all his best stories and he wasn't getting any response; just a polite silence and Clather smiling as if he'd eaten too many cream cakes.

The old man launched into a story about a foreign business-man who came to Tokyo to give a presentation. The business-man couldn't speak Japanese so a woman interpreter stood beside him translating. The businessman started his speech with a joke. The interpreter translated it and the audience shouted with laughter. The businessman was pleasantly sur-prised. It wasn't even particularly funny. He told another joke and the same thing happened. It was the best speech he'd ever given—every joke got a laugh. After he finished, he thanked the interpreter and asked how she'd translated his jokes so successfully. It was easy, she said. Each time he told a joke she warned the audience he was telling a joke, apologised for being unable to translate it and asked the audience to laugh.

Clather wasn't sure if the old man was telling a joke. He looked at the old man. The old man smiled. Clather grinned and everyone laughed and the waiter came and filled our drinks.

It was the first time I'd seen Laroche's house. The room could have been an illustration in a lifestyle magazine; a lot of chrome and black leather and white surfaces. Everything was new ex-cept for a Korean medicine chest with gleaming brass handles and a nineteenth-century print of foreigners in Yokohama be-side an old-fashioned steam engine. On top of the medicine chest was an empty glass bowl and a silver-framed photograph of a woman with big bones and blonde hair holding a cat. There was another photograph in a clear plastic mount of the same woman in a white garden chair with a small boy standing beside her frowning.

I was next to Yamamoto. I asked how the bond business was doing and she said it was OK, there was a lot of interest from the pension funds. She hesitated. I could see she wasn't sure whether to ask how it was on my side of the business. I liked her tact. She didn't want to ask a question which might make me feel uncomfortable. She said how sad it was that *sakura* was over so quickly and we got into a conversation about *mono-no-aware*, transience, mass-production and built-in obsolescence.

In the taxi back Tanya told me it was the last time she wanted to go to a party of bankers. All those men in suits pretending to be interesting—trying to remember the titles of the latest films and books—using words like "downside" for "disadvantage" and "bullish" for "enthusiastic" and slipping into numbers and statistics, after a couple of glasses of champagne. Laroche gave her a name card and told her to call him if she needed anything.

"The man's a creep," she said, "why do you work for him?"

○

This morning I opened the mailbox at Nakameguro and among the letters there was one addressed to Sarah at her flat in Bunkyoku. I called her when I got into the office. She wasn't surprised that I'd received a letter for her. Only last week she received a letter addressed to a friend of hers. She blamed the sorting office: with so many foreigners in Tokyo, keeping track of them all was stretching their resources. She didn't mind what happened to letters as long as they arrived. She laughed and said it was lucky we knew each other.

○

Today I was at a lunch organised by Yamaguchi for two clients from Mitsubishi: Hasegawa and Takeda. We went to a French restaurant called Madame Jojo's, which is supposed to be one of the best in Tokyo. It's decorated in a style most people would recognise as money: somewhere to take people to underline the company's desire for a closer relationship.

We sat at one of the tables at the far end of the restaurant. There was a small oil painting in a circle of light, showing a plump woman with blonde hair and red cheeks. In one corner of the picture there was a single letter "R." Hasegawa said "Kirei desu," which could have meant he liked the picture or the girl. Yamaguchi said she was too plump and Takeda giggled nervously. A waiter appeared silently at the edge of the table and said in a smooth voice that as we probably knew, it was painted by Renoir, the French Impressionist, which arched people's eyebrows and made their mouths go into little "O"'s of surprise. Ah! So it was a late Renoir! The girl's eyes were slightly crossed. The waiter gestured with an unassuming elegance to other spotlit pictures glowing in the semi-darkness on the other side of the room: Dubuffet, Chagall, Dufy. Yamaguchi pretended to be as surprised and interested as our guests from Mitsubishi who were showing how impressed they were by gasps and sighs of reverence.

Going to Madame Jojo's was a nice Japanese way for Yamaguchi to let them know how much our company valued their business. Choosing a French restaurant gave him a chance to speak French, which emphasised the international skills we could bring to any future business relationship.

The waiter presented the menu. Takeda glanced nervously at Hasegawa. Set menu, A or B or C or à la carte? As Head of International Securities he had to choose first. The menu was in French with Japanese subtitles. Hasegawa's expression reminded me of the face of a man going first into a minefield. He looked on the side of the set menu. A, B and C were progressively more expensive. A cost as much as the average Japanese workman earns in a week, C was almost double, B was in between. Choosing A might seem a bit cheap but on the other hand choosing C might seem too familiar. B was the obvious choice but it was lamb. Perhaps it was a clever marketing move by the management since most Japanese don't eat lamb.

Hasegawa's eye flickered over the à la carte side of the menu and the waiter appeared, smiling like a Khmer buddha, and asked if he might perhaps make a few suggestions. The caviar was Iranian and very good indeed, and the sea urchin was fresh. He also recommended the Pacific prawns in garlic and

Pernod. Hasegawa's eye glanced over the set menu again: he sucked in the air through his teeth, looked at Yamaguchi, looked at the menu again and let the air out in a long sigh, Saaaaaah! He gave up. What was Yamaguchi going to have?

Yamaguchi did what everyone was hoping and ordered the most expensive dish on the menu, something fishy with caviar. Hasegawa chose the same. Since Takeda was only a section chief in charge of German equities he went for Dover sole. I had sea urchin's eggs.

Yamaguchi asked what they would like to drink and Hasegawa said water; company policy, no alcohol at lunchtime. Yamaguchi chose a Chablis and when the bottle arrived he managed to persuade them both to have some.

Hasegawa had just come back from Europe. He enjoyed Versailles, it was much more beautiful than the Tower of London. Then he mentioned in an almost matter-of-fact way that Takeda also went abroad recently, to Hawaii.

Takeda was still on his first glass of wine but his face was already a delicate tint of salmon pink. When he heard the word "Hawaii" he grinned and blushed the colour of red tuna and mumbled that he'd just come back from his honeymoon.

Hasegawa was the go-between in an arranged marriage between Takeda and one of the secretaries in the strategic planning department. Hasegawa grinned with pleasure and nodded as Takeda described meeting his future wife for the first time and seeing how much more beautiful she was than the photograph which Hasegawa had shown him. It was love at first sight thanks to Hasegawa. We congratulated them both and everyone smiled.

After that the conversation was Tokyo business style: simple questions with easy answers and everyone laughing at each other's jokes. Nothing was controversial: everyone agreed with everyone. Yamaguchi suggested another bottle which made Hasegawa grimace at the pain of having to say no, one glass of wine was fine, he had to set a good example to Takeda. Yamaguchi ordered another bottle anyway. I watched their faces as Yamaguchi filled his glass. They were smiling. Perhaps they were wondering what it was like to work in a foreign company.

Takeda asked if I liked Japan. I said it was my second home. Yamaguchi said France was his second home at which the men from Mitsubishi went silent and then Hasegawa put his head on one side and gave a deep sigh, Saaaaaah!, and said the world was changing and everyone was becoming international, which gave us all a chance to say *So desu ne!*—and feel good because we all agreed with each other.

Another waiter appeared with a trolly full of cakes and tarts. Takeda licked his lips. Hasegawa looked at his watch with Roman numerals: there was only enough time for coffee.

Yamaguchi was paying the bill when I had a moment in slow motion when everything shifted focus. It wasn't the Chablis. I was thinking of a man who gave me a handful of dried mulberries when I was in Afghanistan. Hasegawa was looking at Yamaguchi and smiling a sort of leftover smile and Takeda was asking about the daily news sheet of market comments. The memory of the man in Afghanistan was like a ghost at the table. I could see him rubbing the bony flank of his horse with a rag. I remembered his thin, gentle face. I looked at my hands on the table in front of me and wondered what they were doing there.

Yamaguchi finished describing the company services to the men from Mitsubishi. They thanked us both for a very good meeting and Hasegawa said he was looking forward to receiving our daily information sheet. We said goodbye in the street outside the restaurant. Yamaguchi bowed lower than usual, so I did too but after the third bow, keeping the smile on my face was a test of mind over matter. The men from Mitsubishi disappeared into the subway and Yamaguchi said he thought the lunch went very well.

The street was echoing with the chorus of a marching song of the last war roaring from a loudspeaker on the back of a truck, hung with *hi-no-maru* Rising Sun flags and slogans against Russia. The traffic lights changed to red and the truck came to a halt beside us. The driver was wearing mirror-glass spectacles. In the back of the truck an old man in a dark, double-breasted suit was sitting on a chair holding a microphone. There was something wrong with the microphone. The old man was speaking into it but the marching song kept roaring out of the loudspeakers. He shook the microphone and tried to get the attention of the driver but the sound of men chanting their way to victory drowned his voice and the driver in dark glasses continued staring at the road in front of him.

We crossed over, the lights changed and I watched the lorry go past with the loudspeakers blaring warrior voices and the old man on his chair frowning and shaking the microphone. I pointed at the truck and said, "Japan" and Yamaguchi laughed.

○

Sunday morning and Tanya's packing a suitcase in the room next door. She's been wanting to go to a hot spring for weeks so we're going to a place called Takamatsu *onsen*. It'll be good to get out of Tokyo, away from the concrete and noise and people. Tanya says I'm bad-tempered and I need a holiday. It's Japan. Sometimes it gets between people. Like last night: we went to a restaurant where the only place to sit was on a *tatami* floor. Tanya said she didn't mind sitting on *tatami* since she was wearing jeans and she sat down cross-legged. I said women in Japan didn't usually sit cross-legged and Tanya looked at me as if I'd told her I didn't like the colour of her lipstick when she wasn't wearing any. She said she wasn't Japanese and she didn't want to kneel.

I said, "It's not me, it's Japan."

"Perhaps Japan isn't a free country," she said, "but it's a free world, and I'm not Japanese."

It's six o'clock in the evening and I'm sitting on warm *tatami* in a cotton *kimono*, with a cold beer on the table beside me. The paper shutters are pushed back and I'm looking out of the window at a little mountain river. Tanya's still in the hot plunge and for a few minutes it's good to be alone, looking at the sun through the leaves, listening to the sound of the water. Very natural. Very Japan. Or at least very close to the popular Japanese image of Japan: the real Japan, a peaceful place where people live in wooden houses in the country having deep and inexpressible relationships with nature.

The room overlooks a river. In the 1920s this was a fashionable hot spring. The *ryokan* guide description made it seem the perfect place for a weekend in the mountains: "Built 150 years ago beside a river in quiet beautiful surroundings, traditional-style bathing in hot springs in the open air. Close to nature." Perfect.

The outside was just like the photograph in the *ryokan* guide. Inside, in the entrance hall, we found ourselves in a crowd of *obaachan* grandmothers with gold teeth. A middle-aged woman in a *kimono* came to welcome us and showed us to our room.

We unpacked and changed into *kimonos* and followed the signs to the main bath. The passages were cold and silent except for the sound of plastic slippers on linoleum and a feeble coughing from one of the rooms. The dark green linoleum in the corridors was worn and a ghostly smell of boiled cabbage and cleaning fluid hung in the air.

In the main bath there were separate changing rooms for men and women but everyone shared the same pool. I undressed quickly so I would be waiting for Tanya when she came out of the women's changing room. The bath hall was a large room with walls covered in green tiles, except for the wall facing the door which was an illuminated fish tank. In the middle of the room was a square green pool of steaming water. Through the steam I could just see the head and shoulders of an old man and woman sitting in the water, very still.

We nodded to each other and I went over to wash at a little tap sticking out of a lump of volcanic rock built into the wall. I got a couple of washing bowls and waited for Tanya. I wanted to show her the Japanese way of doing things. She came out of the changing room and said hello in a whisper as if she was in a church. I reminded her about washing before getting into the pool and not getting soap in the water. She asked why and I said it was so everyone could bathe in clean water and maybe it had something to do with Shinto rules of purity.

We washed and rinsed and eased into the hot water nodding and smiling at the two old people who smiled back at us. A little later the old couple got up out of the pool and tottered to the changing rooms.

Tanya was moving to where I was when she started. She didn't say anything, she just pointed to a corner of the pool which was in shadow. At first it looked as if someone had left their sponge in the pool, only it wasn't a sponge. We got out and washed and rinsed in silence. As we were finishing, a couple of men came into the room. They looked as if they'd been drinking. One of them glanced at Tanya, muttered to the other, and they both giggled. Tanya whispered that she'd had enough and went into the women's changing room.

The men were on the opposite side of the room splashing and rinsing themselves. I could hear most of what they were saying. They were talking about the size of Japanese and foreign women's breasts, and one of them said, "*Yappari nippon sei ichiban de nai?*—of course made in Japan is best, isn't it?" The other man laughed and said he wasn't sure, all he knew was that a lot of foreigners had AIDS. I got up to go and then I thought of the thing at the bottom of the pool. I went over and said there was something in the pool. The man nearest to me grunted as if he'd bumped into someone, and turned to his friend and said, "This one speaks Japanese." They thought the thing like a sponge at the bottom of the pool was some kind of mineral deposit.

◯

The maid who brought us supper in our room said there was dancing downstairs from nine o'clock. So here we are, it's five-past-nine and at a guess the average age of everyone around us is seventy-five.

We're sitting on a *tatami* floor looking at a stage with cheap red curtains drawn across it waiting for something to happen. There's some old-fashioned, twinky-twanky folk dance music coming from a pair of ancient speakers like grey suitcases by the side of the stage.

The music's stopped.

Now it's started again and the curtains are opening and there's a woman in a red and gold silk *kimono* standing with her back towards us. She's moving her head from side to side in time with the music. Her hair is piled up on top of her head to show her neck, which is slender and beautiful. The way she moves makes me want to see her face. She's just turned round. Everyone's clapping. She's an old woman but she moves like a girl when she glances from side to side, and makes a movement with her fan, and looks at the empty stage in front of her as if a man was standing there, waiting for her to say "yes" or "maybe."

She probably learned to dance before the war and if her teacher was as old as she is now, she could be dancing the way they danced a hundred years ago. Her smile is the ghost of a *Meiji* smile. Watching her dance it's possible to see the past come to life again—like last summer in the wings of a butterfly that's survived the winter.

The *obaachan* beside us says everyone comes from Miyagi prefecture. Almost all of them are farmers or farmers' wives. They've been here a week and they'll be here another fortnight. She likes it here, the water's good for her rheumatism and it gives her children a rest from looking after her. Sitting here surrounded by a crowd of people in their seventies makes me think of all the articles about Japan's ageing population: everyone saving for their old age. We're in a room full of them. All those years and seasons gathered together, wearing identical blue and white cotton *kimonos* with an average life expectancy of seventy-eight and still going strong.

Most of them grew up believing the Emperor was a god. Their past is different from ours. An old man's looking at us. I've nodded to him and smiled. No reaction. He's smoking his cigarette as if he hates the taste of tobacco or the sight of us. Or perhaps he has indigestion.

○

Monday and it's almost lunchtime.

Laroche is wandering around the dealing floor, stopping every now and again to talk to someone like a commander reviewing the troops. The Japanese smile when they see him. He has a word with one or two of the secretaries who giggle and put their hands over their mouths and he scratches his stomach and strokes his tie and looks round the room with a pleased expression.

In six months he hasn't asked a single question about what I am doing. Maybe he thinks he gets enough information from Yamaguchi. I've told him several times about the communication problems with London, the need to translate market reports into Japanese and the delay before introductions to clients. Last time he said he was sorry, he didn't know anything about my side of the business, and if I had any problems I should talk to London. I talked to London and they said I should talk to him.

The weekend at the *onsen* didn't improve things with Tanya. She says Japan is OK but she doesn't like the Japanese and the only reason she's here is because I'm here. When we're alone together, I'm happy. She's young and pretty and she has a sense of humour which makes Tokyo fun. But when we're with

Japanese people I remember what she thinks of the Japanese and it's difficult.

Last night I told her I had to be here for another six months and she said she wasn't sure she could stay that long. She wants me to give up this assignment and become a person. I asked what she meant by "a person" and she said, "not a company clone, a person."

This morning at the meeting, the room was crowded because it was Monday. Clather had just finished talking about how important it was for everyone to telephone their clients. He was walking towards the door when Klaus came into the room. There wasn't enough room for them to pass each other. One of them had to step aside. They both missed the moment to let the other pass. Instead they stood their ground. Everyone was watching them. They must have known how they looked but neither of them wanted to move. Clather tried to turn it into a joke by smiling and saying "Excuse me." Klaus didn't smile, he just shook his head, then turned his shoulder as if he was going to shove Clather out of the way. Clather tried to do the same but it wasn't convincing and Klaus said "thank-you" in a loud voice as he pushed past him.

○

Last night we met up with Joe. We went to Shinjuku and had something to eat in a *yakitoriya*. I wasn't sure how Joe and Tanya would get on together but they liked each other. After dinner Joe offered to take us to a bar.

We arrived at one of those buildings covered in electric signs for clubs and *karaoke* bars with names like "Prince" and "Crystal" and climbed a narrow staircase to the fifth floor. Joe led us along a passage smelling of disinfectant and stopped in front of a grey metal door. There was music on the other side. Joe knocked on the door and a young man in his early twenties opened it. When he saw Joe he smiled and opened the door wider. He was dressed in a bright turquoise *happi* coat loosely tied at the waist. It didn't look as if he was wearing anything else. He glanced at Tanya and me and asked if we were friends. Joe nodded and the young man apologised; he didn't want to give a bad impression by being so untidy. Joe told him not to worry and we followed him into a place that was dimmer than a photographic dark room and sounded like a discotheque and smelt of cigarettes and aftershave with a trace of something like ammonia. The blue and orange lights were turned down low and it was difficult to see what was going on.

The young man led us to a table and Tanya and I sat down on a dark velour sofa with our backs to the wall. Joe and the young man sat opposite us. Joe put his arm round the young man and told him it was too long since they'd seen each other, then switched to English and introduced his friend as Maki-chan. Maki-chan bowed and apologised for being shy because he couldn't speak English. Joe said it didn't matter. Maki-chan ran his fingers through Joe's hair and told him it was thinning. Joe laughed and used a word I didn't understand. Maki-chan squeezed the lobe of Joe's ear and said too much sex made people's hair fall out.

A waiter in an even shorter *happi* coat appeared at our table and took our order for drinks. While Joe was checking the list of cocktails I asked Tanya if she was OK and she nodded.

Joe tried persuading the waiter to do some cabaret. The man giggled and put his hand to his mouth. He was tired, he said, but he'd do his best. He took our orders and came back with a tray of drinks and a pen torch and sat at the next table with his back to us. I asked what the pen torch was for and Maki-chan said *erebeta*. The waiter was nervous. He wasn't used to performing in front of foreigners, but he was going to do his best—*ganbarimasu*. I asked Joe what kind of cabaret it was going to be and he laughed and told me not to worry, the waiter wouldn't do it if he didn't enjoy it.

Something was happening at a table on the other side of the room. Another waiter in a *happi* coat was standing with his back to us in front of a man in a suit who was sitting at a table. The knees of the man's trousers were sticking out, either side of the waiter's bare legs and the man's arms were round the young man's waist. The waiter was having difficulty keeping his balance.

The waiter at the table next to us stood up, turned round and shouted *Hai!* and Maki-chan pointed the pen torch at his groin. Joe cheered and Tanya said, "So it's true what they say about the Japanese." Maki-chan gave the pen torch to the waiter standing in front of us and asked him to do the *erebeta*. The waiter nodded and brought the pen torch towards the tip of his penis which was uncircumcised. Then he eased the pen torch under his foreskin and a little pink glow descended down the shadowy outline of his semi-erect penis. Tanya said she hoped he wasn't doing himself any harm. The waiter laughed and the little pink glow went up and down several times, and appeared in the folds of his scrotum, silhouetting the oval shapes of his testicles through a little orange screen of flesh. Maki-chan asked what I thought of the performance and I said it was the first time I'd seen anything like it. Maki-chan told the waiter to do another trick.

The waiter took a potato chip from a bowl on the table, broke it in half, and inserted the two pieces into his foreskin and twisted his scrotum round his testicles. Last time "elevator" was the clue. This time we had to guess what the trick was called. Joe already knew the answer. Tanya and I were the only ones playing the game and neither of us had any suggestions. Tanya asked, "animal, vegetable or mineral?" and Joe said "animal." I tried to think of something like it, but it just looked like what it was: a penis with potato chips wedged under the foreskin. It turned out to be a snail. Maki-chan asked if there was anything similar to the game in England? I said charades, maybe. Maki-chan thanked the waiter for his efforts and the man bowed and smiled and wished us a pleasant evening.

After the waiter had gone, Maki-chan apologised for the

performance: the man wasn't strong enough for the finale so he would stand in for him. Joe hoped Tanya wasn't bored. She said potato chips wouldn't be the same again.

Maki-chan pulled the neighbouring table closer, took some chopsticks from the centre of the table and put them like a bridge across the two tables. He got up and stood in front of the bridge of chopsticks and switched on the pen torch. His other hand was holding his erect penis over the chopsticks.

"Like karate," said Maki-chan, "but not karate." He brought his hand down suddenly, there was a sharp cry and the pen torch fell on the floor. Maki-chan gasped through his clenched teeth that he was fine, just fine. He sounded like someone in pain. He picked up the torch and shone it onto the bridge of chopsticks. It was still intact.

I knew what was going to happen. He had lost face, and in spite of the pain he was going to try again. He did. The second time we said how brave he was, but the chopsticks were still intact.

We said third time lucky but it wasn't. Tanya said perhaps it would be better with just one chopstick. Maki-chan was reluctant. He couldn't understand what the matter was; maybe the wood was different quality, but at last we persuaded him. Just one chopstick. He stood there, concentrating, gathering his *ki*—energy. He tried again. There was a split of wood and he shouted something in Japanese and smiled and we all clapped. I didn't hear what he yelled at the moment of success. It sounded something like *hashi kowai* which would have meant he said he was afraid of chopsticks. I nodded and smiled but then Joe said it was the name of a film about prisoners of the Japanese blowing up a bridge in the jungle called *The Bridge Over the River Kwai*. Maki-chan explained it was a very popular film in Japan. I asked Maki-chan what he thought of the film. He smiled at Tanya. "Beautiful," he said. "Very beautiful."

○

It's nine o'clock in the evening and Tanya's working in a place called the Club Sapphire. She didn't want to teach English grammar to resentful children after they'd finished school, or make conversation with the bored wives of *salarimen* and she didn't want to work in an office. She thought working as a hostess in a bar would be more interesting.

She doesn't have to do anything except pour drinks and talk to people in English. The owners of the club want an international atmosphere because the more international *salarimen* have more money.

I'm not worried about her, because this is Japan. But I wish she was here. Being alone reminds me of the time before she came.

Living with someone it's possible to make a world and retreat into it. Tokyo solo is different. It's Japan and the individual; a feeling of being alone and surrounded at the same time, like the character for *komaru*, a tree with lines on all four sides around it, meaning to be in trouble.

○

I think the papers in my desk at the office have been disturbed so I've inserted a hair between the pages of my company note-book, to see what happens.

○

This evening Tanya and I had dinner with a Japanese-English couple. His name is Noboru and her name is Caroline and they met at Cambridge University. He works for Mitsubishi and she writes articles for foreign magazines about what it's like living in Japan. They have a daughter who goes to the International School in Tokyo. Next year they want to send her to boarding school in England.

The other guests were an Australian artist and his wife who were visiting Japan for the first time to study techniques of making *washi* paper. He was called Gary and she was called Noleen and they came from Sydney.

I asked Noleen what she thought of Japan and she said it was much nicer than she expected. The big towns and cities were ugly but the countryside was beautiful. Some of her family disapproved of her coming to Japan.

"The Japs gave my father a bad time during the war," she said and then she blushed and started talking about a meeting with an old man in Kyoto whose family had been making *washi* paper for three hundred years. She couldn't speak any Japanese and he couldn't speak English but somehow the old man communicated with his eyes. I asked what he communicated and she said a feeling which was peaceful and spiritual.

Noboru said perhaps she was describing a special Japanese feeling call *ishin-denshin* which was like telepathy only different. We talked about the way Japanese people understand each other without having to say anything.

It was one of those evenings when every conversation is *nihonjin-ron*, why are the Japanese so Japanese? Does a person have to be Japanese to understand the Japanese? Do the Japanese understand the Japanese? And is Japan different from the rest of the world or is the rest of the world different from Japan?

Noboru kept saying things like, "We Japanese must become more international," "Japan has to accept its global responsibility," and "Japan has no excuse for not opening its markets to the world." Caroline didn't say much but went in and out of the kitchen fetching bowls of pickles and *senbei*.

He's becoming English, using words like "absolutely" and "tremendous," frowning at the mention of the Prime Minister and smiling at a story about a dog. She's becoming Japanese; nodding and letting other people do the talking and arranging things on the table with a grace and attention to detail that seems more Japanese than a Japanese.

On the way back in the taxi Tanya said she couldn't understand an Englishwoman wanting to marry a Japanese man, even one like Noboru. I said that a friend called Lesley had told me Japanese men were the world's best-kept secrets and wonderful lovers. Tanya wasn't convinced. She'd seen a television documentary about prostitutes in Thailand who'd described their Japanese clients as cruel and vicious. A couple of days ago she was sitting next to a man on the train who was reading a *manga* comic and she noticed the pictures of the story. In one panel a group of Japanese men had captured a woman with blonde hair, in the next panel they'd stripped off her clothes and tied her with ropes, and in the next panel the men were pushing the woman head first into the back end of a cow. She didn't look any more. But she had a question for me. If Japanese men buy that sort of thing to look at on the train, what's their attitude towards sex?

○

It's Wednesday morning and the sun is bright. The sky is almost white and the sea is like a great green mirror.

The market is dull.

The new assistant who works part time filing research reports is standing on the other side of the desk by the window. Today she's wearing a yellow sailor shirt and dark blue tartan shorts with straps over her shoulders, white socks and shiny black plastic shoes. Her hair is braided in two short plaits on either side of her head and tied with yellow wool. She's pretty in a sexless sort of way. If someone asks her to do something she says *Hai!* in a high-pitched sing-song voice, the way children answer in school. She giggles a lot and sometimes when she's going between the filing units she gives a little skip.

A couple of days ago Sanno asked what I thought of the new part-time assistant. I said she worked hard. She asked how old I thought she was. She seems like an immature twenty-year-old so I said twenty-three but according to Sanno she's twenty-eight. Sanno said, "She's *buriko*. A pretend kid." Sanno is twenty-two.

I wonder why someone in their late twenties chooses to dress like a primary-school child. Maybe she's afraid of adult life and wants to be treated more gently by dressing like a child. Maybe she's afraid of time passing and wants to stop at a stage when her life was uncomplicated.

Sanno said most *buriko* girls weren't really as childish as they seemed. Some are very ambitious and dress like *buriko* to attract men—because Japanese men are shy with women of her age. Perhaps there was the suggestion of a smile in Sanno's face, I wasn't sure. "Maybe they like to dress so that Japanese men are not frightened," she said, "maybe Japanese men prefer young girls."

○

This morning I opened my company notebook and the hair which I left between the pages was still there but it had moved.

Whoever opened the book must have noticed the hair as they turned the pages and tried to replace it.

Trying to hide the evidence that the marker trap had sprung suggests they knew what it was—but noticed it too late.

They couldn't know if I'd memorised the page numbers and they took a chance and put it back anywhere.

It could be Matsuzaki. It's almost certain he looked into the rooms of the house when he delivered the furniture. He also has the keys to all the desks on the dealing room floor—a curious fact which I discovered when I mislaid the keys to my desk and asked Administration for a duplicate. But it could also be anyone who has the key to my desk, or some other way of getting into it.

They know I'm keeping a diary. They've read it several times; when they read it first, they found something which made them want to read more. They're curious. They want to know what I'm thinking. They want to know what I'm doing. Finding the marker trap may have made them suspicious. Otherwise they wouldn't have replaced the hair. They pay attention to detail. They've taken care not to alert me to what they've been doing. They don't want me to know they're spying on me.

○

It's Friday afternoon and it's raining. When the sky is grey Tokyo looks terrible, like the insides of a television dismantled and spread over the landscape. It's difficult to believe people live in it.

Last night Tanya got back at eleven-thirty. She was tired. She looked like someone who'd spent a long time hearing about computers and semi-conductors in Japanese and English. The guests from the computer conference were all between forty and fifty: middle management *salarimen* on the town. At first they were very shy. The *mama-san* told them Tanya came from England and spoke no Japanese so they had to speak English with her. No one said anything. At last, a man beside Tanya giggled and said, "Brooke Shields." Tanya said, "Charlie Chaplin." The man said, "London" and Tanya said, "Tokyo." The man pointed to her drink and said, "Coca-Cola" and Tanya pointed to his tie and said, "Hermès." The man nodded. Then someone else in the group said, "Hong Kong," and the man blushed.

The Club Sapphire is a place for up-market *salarimen* to have a drink after work. The *mama-san* who runs the bar is strict about customers' behaviour. What people do outside the club is their own affair, but favouritism is bad for business. The *mama-san* speaks little English. She wants the Club Sapphire to be a nice place; nice girls, nice customers. She's a small, plump woman in her late forties and she's a hard-headed woman. A hostess who is more than ten minutes late for work loses an hour's wages and there's no overtime.

There are three Japanese hostesses at the Club Sapphire and one other foreign hostess called Bella from Israel. Bella's been travelling for eighteen months in Asia and when there aren't any customers she tells Tanya about her adventures smuggling precision lenses and dental equipment from Japan to Korea.

So far Tanya hasn't talked much with the Japanese hostesses. Only one of them speaks any English. Her name is Junko. She's twenty years old and she's saving money to go to Europe. She dreams of meeting a romantic Swiss man who will ask her to marry him and she will say yes because Switzerland is the most beautiful country in the world and she wants to live there.

The hostesses at the Club Sapphire are paid to welcome customers and show them to their tables. They take orders, serve drinks, light cigarettes, look pretty and listen to whatever the men say. The *mama-san* tells the hostesses to remember their "charm points." Tanya's charm points are her long hair and the colour of her eyes.

The customers are all men. They all drink *mizuwari*—whisky and water with lots of ice, and few of them speak more than one or two sentences of English. Tanya says the most difficult part of being a hostess is not yawning in front of customers: a Japanese businessman talking about Princess Diana in pidgin English has a powerful narcotic effect, they always make the same joke, punning on the Japanese sound of her name. They also like talking about whisky, the Queen, golf, Scotland and the Prime Minister.

○

Yamaguchi is leaning back in his chair with his tie loose at the collar and his eyelids are half closed.

Is this the real Japan?

There are 120 Japanese here and six foreigners. It's a foreign company, but most of us speak Japanese and do things in a Japanese way. The foreigners aren't necessary but in return for being here, we provide information. We learn about them and they learn about us. In a company like this it's difficult to tell the difference between them and us.

What did she mean when she said I was getting a lot of

telephone calls? When he looks at me like that what is he thinking? Does she know more than she says? What is he wanting to know?

Everyone knows the rules of the game: don't trust anyone, don't get caught and don't give the game away.

○

Last night I went to dinner with Tiziano and Angela. I was late and everyone else was already sitting at the table. Edward Seidensticker was there and Yoshiko Wakayama with a Philippine poet and Tiziano's Japanese guide and interpreter, Otomo, in a cloud of French tobacco smoke and a Japanese couple who smiled and said nothing but "yes please," "no thank-you" and "it was delicious." Before we finished the pasta, the conversation turned to Japanese policy in the Philippines. The Philippine poet reminded us what the Japanese did during the war.

"I cannot forget," he said, "I cannot forgive. God can forgive, but I cannot." The Japanese couple nodded agreement. Otomo gazed at his empty wine glass and shook his head. He looked as if he'd already had a lot to drink and he might not have been listening to the conversation. The poet was angry, his eyebrows were drawn together in a frown and there were tears in his eyes. Yoshiko Wakayama enquired gently what it was that he could not forget, but he didn't want to talk about it. Tiziano hit his fist on the table and shouted there were some things that God, even if he existed, wouldn't forgive and shouldn't forgive, like war crimes and crimes against humanity. The Japanese couple nodded agreement. Otomo was gazing at his glass which had been refilled. I thought he'd lost track of the conversation but suddenly he said the massacre of the Chinese in Nanking was wrong and the killing and torture of civilians in the Philippines was wrong but what about the bombing of Hiroshima and Nagasaki, wasn't that wrong as well?

Edward Seidensticker said Otomo was missing the point.

Perhaps the bombing of Hiroshima and Nagasaki was necessary to end the war more quickly. Perhaps it was wrong, but even if it was wrong, the evil done by the Americans to the citizens of Hiroshima and Nagasaki did not cancel the evil done by the Japanese to the people of the Philippines and a whole lot of other countries in Asia. He smiled and said he still hadn't found a way of saying "two wrongs don't make a right" in Japanese. The Japanese couple smiled and nodded and Otomo lit a cigarette. Angela glanced at Tiziano and Tiziano smiled and shrugged his shoulders.

Otomo was like someone looking out to sea; he sighed and raised the glass to his lips but lowered it without drinking. There was something theatrical about him, as if he'd watched old men in French cafés, drinking wine and smoking cigarettes, and copied the way they sat and the way they spoke—even the way they were silent before making a reply. He was still more or less in control, but he was having difficulty translating his thoughts into English and several times he slipped into French. He asked Seidensticker what he did during the war. Seidensticker replied he was in the navy and Otomo said he'd heard it was something to do with naval intelligence. Seidensticker asked what difference it made. Otomo thought it made all the difference.

"An intelligence officer has to be loyal to his country," he said. "An intelligence officer has to be prejudiced in favour of his own country: if not there is a danger he might become too closely involved in the country from which he is supposed to collect intelligence." If Seidensticker was an intelligence officer, he couldn't be objective about the bombing of Hiroshima and Nagasaki, even though he understood Japanese culture very well. He would always be prejudiced in favour of America.

Tiziano put his arm around Otomo and told him not to be such a serious-minded old sod and asked why he had to smoke such filthy French cigarettes. Otomo immediately switched from the role of aggressive French intellectual to apologetic Japanese guest and began bowing to everyone with a pained expression on his face, saying how sorry he was until Tiziano stopped him with a question about a Soviet agent in Japan called Sorge. Asking about Sorge was a good way to sidetrack him because Otomo likes talking about communism. He tells everyone that he is a communist and some people still seem to believe what he says. I think it's a mask he wears to confuse people.

Wakayama and Seidensticker talked about the problem of translation, across time and culture, while Otomo gazed unsteadily across the table. He reminded me of a comedian imitating a drunk. He put his glass down heavily. "Professor Seidensticker," he said, "were you not in the American foreign service?"

Seidensticker frowned and smiled. "I was in the navy. Remember?" He folded his napkin into a good approximation of a seaman's hat. "A sailor, if you know what I mean." Angela asked if anyone would like coffee. The Japanese man with the Hermès tie thanked her. It was time to go home. His wife nodded and smiled like a schoolgirl hearing the bell for the end of a lesson. Seidensticker said he had to be getting along too.

By twelve o'clock, Otomo and I were the only guests. He was explaining how the Parcham and the Khalq factions in Afghanistan were examples of popular Marxism, Angela was looking tired and Tiziano had gone to bed. I was interested in what Otomo was saying but it was late. I thanked Angela and got up to go but Otomo wasn't letting me escape so easily. He hadn't finished telling me the real reason for the assassination of Ambassador Dobbs in Kabul. He invited me to his house so we could finish our conversation.

We went to his flat in Roppongi. He'd forgotten his keys and he had to ring the bell for his girlfriend to open the door. She wasn't dressed to meet a stranger but she didn't seem embarrassed. Her name was Kyoko. She apologised for being sleepy and asked if we wanted something to eat. I wasn't hungry but Otomo told her to bring some rice crackers and dried *ika*, cuttlefish.

The room was Japanese style with a *tatami* floor, covered in books and papers. In one corner there was a grey metal filing cabinet. Two televisions were stacked, one on top of the other, inside the *tokonoma*. The only other furniture was a low table, on which were more books, empty cups and glasses and a portable computer. Otomo told me to make myself comfortable while he went to the lavatory.

Kyoko was in the kitchen. I moved a few books and sat cross-legged beside the low table on the side facing the *tokonoma* with the two televisions inside it. Otomo could have followed tradition and hung a scroll painting in the *tokonoma*, maybe even arranged some flowers in an *ikebana* display, but instead he had filled it with a couple of televisions, old models, the sort people leave on the street corner to be taken away. Otomo came back with two glasses full of ice-cubes and a bottle of brandy.

After that I have only disconnected memories of our conversation.

I remember Otomo saying something about researching the backgrounds of students who met the Japanese crown prince while he was at Oxford; showing me a list of names of students at Merton College and asking if I knew any of them. I remember him telling me that I was a spy and looking into my eyes to see if my pupils dilated or contracted. I looked back at him and thought about the colour of his eyes, while he asked me why I was working in a bank in Tokyo when I was really a specialist on Iran and Afghanistan. I said that asking people to admit or deny being a spy was like asking if they'd stopped beating their wives, the question contained an accusation. He apologised, which made me feel I had to apologise for speaking so directly to him. It was just curiosity, he said, he didn't mean to embarrass me. The next thing I remember we're eating some fish cooked by Kyoko and Otomo is trying to teach me the words of an old song.

Then it's late and Otomo's standing on the pavement below

his flat swaying slightly and bowing to me as I get into a taxi and I'm telling the driver where to go in Nakameguro but the words don't come as quickly as they should and I'm wondering how I'll feel in the morning.

○

It's Saturday morning and the sun is shining. The leaves of the camellia bushes and the tiles on the roof of the house next door are glistening with little points of light. Everything seems extra bright today but maybe it's just the effect of last night. We went over to Joe's place in Shijo.

Joe opened the door in his underpants and a cat shot out between his legs with two dachshunds chasing it. The next second the cat was in a tree and the dogs were under it barking. Joe rushed after them shouting and somehow he managed to grab them, one under each arm, and ran back inside. He did it so fast I reckon he must have a lot of practice.

He was worried the dogs would disturb his neighbour, Madam Matsumoto, who lives on the other side of the hedge, and teaches traditional Japanese tea ceremony to young ladies. She had classes most evenings. Sometimes the dogs get excited and start barking and she telephones Joe and threatens to call the police unless he controls the dogs. Once she actually telephoned the police but luckily, by the time the officer arrived the dogs had eaten their dinner and they were slow and sleepy.

We went into a room full of potted plants. It was like a clearing in a forest with a dining table and chairs in the middle of it and a parrot hanging from a light fitting, making a noise like the sound track of a nature programme about the Amazon jungle. The parrot's a grey bird with a minimal vocabulary. He's called Bibi. For a while it made sounds like a cat meowing and dogs barking and then it swore a few times in Japanese and started making a deep groaning sound.

Joe went to put some more clothes on and Tanya and I sat

there listening to the parrot. The moans had an urgency that was almost human, like someone on the edge of pain or pleasure. I thought of Joe's boyfriends and looked at Tanya. I remembered Madam Matsumoto's tea ceremony class next door and wondered if the parrot's cries penetrated the azalea hedge. One or two cries hit a high note that was almost unbearable. I visualised Madam Matsumoto explaining the correct way to fold a silk scarf to three or four silent girls: this way and that way and then another blood-curdling shriek from the parrot. I imagined a woman in her early sixties with carefully painted lips, neatly plucked eyebrows and precise gestures explaining the sense of inner harmony necessary for a true appreciation of the tea ceremony, smiling sweetly as she looked into her students' faces to see if they understood what she was saying, as Bibi went into a series of sharp rhythmic cries. I wondered what was happening on the other side of the azalea hedge. The dogs were barking and Bibi was sounding like the climax of a snuff movie.

Joe came back into the room. He was wearing a blue and white cotton *kimono*. He put the parrot back in its cage, took a black cloth from the table and put it over the parrot's cage. There was a little leathery croak and then silence.

"It's like Walt Disney," said Joe, "when the dogs chase the cat it excites the parrot. The parrot shrieks which makes the dogs bark."

One of the dachshunds had caught the cat between its front paws. The cat was meowing but making no resistance and the dog was hugging it the way some dogs hug people's legs. The other dog was skittering to and fro and then it mounted its companion. The animals' progress across the *tatami* was slow and unsteady: like a fur-covered, clockwork train set, with a cat's head and dogs' tails and legs everywhere. I asked Joe if it took a long time to teach them and he said they taught themselves. He filled our glasses and lit a Kretek cigarette. It was some time since I'd had the spicy sweet smoke in my nostrils: a memory of another life, like a different kind of sunlight. The wine was suddenly warm and sharp tasting. I asked Joe for another ice-cube.

"*Suppai desu ka?*" said Joe.

"Yes," I said. "*Suppai desu.*"

Tanya asked what we were talking about and Joe apologised for speaking Japanese. Sometimes he forgets if he's speaking English or Japanese. Living in Japan, reading the *Nikkei-Shinbun* and watching Japanese television, it's easy to slip into Japanese. Joe smiled to himself and then tried to look serious but the smile kept returning to his lips. I asked what he was thinking about. He said something about the way Japanese people think in double meanings, like reflections, and then he cleared his throat and said we should help ourselves to everything, it was all in the kitchen; *sashimi*, another bottle of wine, whatever we wanted, and could the person who went to the kitchen bring the bottle of Tanqueray gin that was in the ice-box.

The ice-box was empty but a half bottle of Tanqueray gin was in the kitchen sink beside a plate of red and white fish. There was a bottle of wine in a plastic bag. I put everything on a tray and carried it into the room. Joe was standing up trying to do something with the sound system and as I put the tray down the room exploded into music. Joe said something. I asked him to speak up or turn the music down.

"Snoopy," he said. "You know Snoopy? And Charlie Brown? Music is my security blanket." He started talking about his childhood and the orang-utan given as a token of diplomatic friendship to his father. His friendship with the orang-utan was very deep: each knew how the other was feeling, it was communication without words, like telepathy.

We got into a *nihonjin-ron* discussion about the way Japanese communicate without saying anything and the difference between *ishin-denshin*, and *hara de* and *hadaka*. Joe said foreigners had difficulty understanding the Japanese because the Japanese communicate in a different way, in silence. For two or three hundred years Japan was a totalitarian state, where a man could be executed for the crime of unexpected behaviour and saying the wrong word could be fatal, so the Japanese became masters of non-verbal communication.

"Even in a police state, it's hard to convict a man for smiling too much," said Joe. "That's when the Japanese learned *inginburei*—the art of insolent politeness—how to give drop-dead smiles." Tanya asked Joe if he could read what Japanese people were thinking by looking at them.

"There's no mystery," he said. "It's just a different vocabulary. Ten years commuting on the Shijo line, seeing the faces, you get the basic grammar anyway."

I knew what he meant about the basic grammar, seeing the message in people's eyes, reading the character of a smile and interpreting the tone of a person's voice. But then he started talking about *ki* spirit and intuition, looking through people's defences.

I thought of his Japanese boyfriend, Keiji. They lived together for five years. One night they made love as usual before going to sleep. The next morning Keiji moved all his things out to go and live with an Australian businessman. Joe knows the Japanese, but he didn't know what was happening with Keiji, his lover. If it could happen to Joe, it could happen with anyone.

We got back late, which is maybe why the light outside seems so bright when I look at it, I can almost feel it at the back of my head.

○

This morning when I telephoned Joe there was a long silence and then a click before the dialling tone. This afternoon the telephone rang and when I answered it the line went dead.

I've been here before. Almost everyone on the programme experiences it. Little things become big things. There are coincidences. After a while there seems to be a pattern and it's time to ask if it's real or imaginary.

When I arrived Yamaguchi asked if I was a spy. Then a man came to deliver furniture and went into all the rooms in the house. Letters went to the wrong address. Someone opened my desk and looked through my papers. Last week Otomo asked if I was a spy. Today the telephone didn't work properly and there was a wrong number.

I'm a Japanese-speaking lawyer working for a bank in Tokyo.

I enjoy *haiku* and I'm collecting material for a book about Japan.

When someone like Yamaguchi or Otomo asks if I'm a spy it makes me feel like a traitor—as if I've betrayed their trust by pretending to be something I'm not—as if I'm hiding behind a mask. The problem is that if they believe there's a mask, there is a mask—even if there isn't.

Life looks different through the eyes of a mask. There's a shadow at the edge of things. What one can't see one has to imagine. Maybe there's something. Maybe there's nothing.

What sort of person asks someone if they're a spy? Yamaguchi, for example.

Yamaguchi's family own one of the largest ball bearing manufacturing companies in Japan and his father's a multimillionaire. He went to Waseda, a business school in Montrose and the London School of Economics. He speaks English, French and German. He could do almost anything he wants but instead he's chosen to work for a foreign company—a second-rate job by Japanese standards. Most Japanese who work for foreign companies do it because they earn more money and it gives them a chance to travel. But Yamaguchi doesn't need the money and he doesn't like travel. With his background and qualifications he could have gone into the Japanese foreign service, or the Ministry of Finance. I can see him working as a research analyst for a bank in Europe, something like commercial intelligence. Maybe that's what he was doing when he was in Frankfurt, working for Deutsche Bank.

Foreign companies in Japan could be seen as a risk. Having one or two people in each company is a simple precaution, nothing cloak-and-dagger, just an understanding that if anything happens which might be important they know whom to contact. While I was at Citicorp a team from the tax office came and made a company inspection. I heard them telling someone it was his duty as a Japanese to inform the authorities of any irregularities. It wasn't an obligation, but a duty; not as a citizen, or a tax payer, but as a Japanese; and that was just a man from the tax office talking to a filing clerk.

Otomo comes from a privileged background like Yamaguchi. He went to Keio, studied in Paris for a couple of years, then joined Mitsubishi and worked in the Middle East for five years. Now he's in Tokyo he calls himself a freelance journalist but he spends most of his time working as an interpreter and translator for foreign journalists. He says he's been a communist ever since university but companies like Mitsubishi make a thorough investigation before employing anyone. If they thought he was a communist he wouldn't have had a chance.

Some Japanese trading companies are used by Japanese intelligence for information gathering, particularly in third-world countries. For anyone wanting to monitor foreign journalists' activities in Japan, working as an interpreter is a perfect cover: find out what journalists want to know and control the information they receive.

For that matter, what was Otomo doing with a list of people who might have come into contact with the crown prince at Oxford?

But even if Yamaguchi or Otomo is working for Japanese intelligence, it's OK. We're allies. We all believe in democracy, free speech and the rights of the individual. This isn't Soviet Russia or Nazi Germany. Or some kind of brave new world.

Sometimes it all seems like a guessing game, or a game of make-believe. But it's there, in between guilt and fear, a feeling when I breathe; a heaviness that won't go away, like something I'm not supposed to know, or a secret that belongs to someone else, an invisible weight over my heart. Like Midas' servant weighed down by what I cannot tell, I have to say these things to this recorder.

○

I saw Harry again today. We arranged to meet outside the station at Shibuya, by the statue of Hachiko, at one o'clock. The sun was shining and the crowds outside the station were dressed in summer colours. I joined a group of people standing by the statue. I carried a newspaper, but I didn't read it.

It was almost one and I began to worry that Harry might not come. I was nervous. Our last meeting went well: there was an understanding between us. But perhaps I had imagined it. It was hard to see why an old man should travel across Tokyo to meet someone he hardly knew, to talk about things most people would be happy to forget.

Then I saw him. I was surprised at how old and frail he was. He was wearing a light-grey suit and was using a bamboo walking stick. We shook hands. The shape of his hand in mine was like an old friend's.

We had lunch in the Seibu department store. There was a lot of background noise and Harry's voice was not loud enough for the recorder, so I took notes. Harry asked if I'd heard from Christina. I told him that she sent her love and hoped to see him soon. He smiled and I thought what a nice grandfather he would be. I knew he was waiting for me to ask questions, but it didn't feel right to begin, so I said something about the weather and he said it would soon be the rainy season. He told me how important the seasons are to the Japanese.

"We Japanese are deeply affected by the seasons. Every *haiku* has its season-word. Scroll paintings in the tea room are changed according to the season, with cherry blossoms in spring and chrysanthemums in autumn." He asked if he was talking too fast for me. I thanked him and said no, I understood what he was saying; but wasn't the Japanese attitude to the passing of time Buddhist? The cycles of death and rebirth, the Wheel of the Law and the Wheel of Suffering, leading finally to Buddha, to the great enlightenment.

Harry said yes, but Japan's religion is Shinto. The week before he'd read in a newspaper a survey of Japan's religious beliefs: seventy-five per cent of Japanese described themselves as Buddhists, ninety per cent as Shinto. "The survey wasn't wrong," he said. "It showed the way we think of ourselves. We're Shinto when we go to the shrine for a festival or when someone is born or gets married; we're Buddhist when someone dies or when we think about the past and the future life."

I asked whether he thought of himself as a Buddhist or a Shinto believer.

"When I think about it, I'm Buddhist. But I feel Shinto." He looked at me through his gold-rimmed spectacles with an expression that was melancholy and comical and asked if I understood. I said I did. As I listened to him I was thinking that I'd intended to ask him about the war, and instead we were talking about the weather, the seasons, Shinto and how the Japanese love nature. There was something artificial in the conversation but the *kimochi*—the feeling—was good between us. I felt it was a good moment to begin asking questions. I asked what it was like in Japan just before the Second World War. Was there an atmosphere of idealism and pride? Harry thought for a moment.

"I was carried by the current and dragged along. I was still young, you know." He cleared his throat. "You learn later. That's what happened to me. I learned a lot later, after the country was defeated. I wasn't particularly conscious of the military. I didn't want to fight. I didn't want to kill anyone."

Had he ever considered that what was happening was wrong?

"I couldn't say it openly, because of my weakness. In those circumstances you have to follow—" I could see he was having difficulty finding the right word. He clicked his fingers softly, as if to call the word from the air. "You have to follow the—you know."

He told me he had been a liaison officer with the local population in the Philippines. "I tried to call people from their hiding places, to get them back to their villages. I was happy to help the people. I had to go to the countryside. There were people hiding out there, maybe for a year or so. This work went on for a while, maybe until Christmas 1941. Then we moved to Manila. I was a civilian, but I was doing liaison work there between the Japanese army and the people. It was a sort of public relations job." I interrupted to ask if he was in the intelligence service and he said yes, he was.

"MacArthur came back, the situation went the other way and the HQ had to move north. The Japanese army rounded up so-called guerrillas and the people. They started to kill guerrillas and villagers, and the case of the war crime took place." I asked what the charge was at his trial.

"I was part of, you know, the planning and the execution of the plot. Yes." He paused. "They rounded up Chinese and Filipinos and executed them. Not only in my town, but other places. There were many kinds of excuses given by the garrison commanders. Finally it happened in my town." I could imagine the same words, the same sentences repeated during his trial.

"The planning and execution of the plot," he paused, "the incineration of the town. In fact it was partly done by the Japanese garrison and partly by the American bombing." For a moment I forgot which war we were talking about. The words "American bombing" made me think of other more recent wars. I was only half listening to what Harry was saying. I looked at what I'd written: "Massacring . . ." The sentence was unfinished. I asked if there was anything he could have done to prevent the massacre.

He took a deep breath. "I did my best to ensure it couldn't take place. I couldn't do much, you see. I was at one meeting where a plan for the massacre was being discussed, and a senior officer was against the plans and I agreed that it shouldn't be done. That was when my opinion was expressed. I wasn't an officer or a soldier. I was just a civilian attached to the army."

"What happened?" I asked.

"My view was not very effective. The commander forced the garrison to carry out the action. Six hundred Chinese were killed in a coconut grove. And sixty Filipinos." Harry was silent. I felt I had to say something, so I asked how they had died.

"I don't think by shooting. Mostly by bayonet and by beheading with the Japanese sword—the *katana*." He frowned and shook his head. "But to kill six hundred people—no officer could use a sword on so many. I guess the soldiers used their bayonets." I studied his face. He was telling me about a coconut grove in the Philippines fifty years ago, and we were sitting in a Tokyo restaurant full of men in business suits and waitresses in smart orange and white uniforms. I thought of the blindfolds, if they had any, and the heat, and the sound of insects. I looked at the men in suits at the table next to us, who were eating Pacific prawns, and at Harry Sasaki, who was breaking a bread roll. He looked up from his plate.

"War can make people crazy," he said. "You can't tell what's going to happen. You can't imagine how it is when your comrades die. I saw several die. They didn't shout '*Banzai*' or 'Long live the Emperor!' They used to say '*Okaa-san, Okaa-san*—Mother, Mother.'

"I had a friend, a special friend," he sighed. "The Filipino guerrillas knew he was a good man but they had to kill him."

I asked why. Harry laughed.

"Because he was Japanese. Everyone hated the Japanese at that time. Nobody picked him up. Nobody tried to help him. He died, and his body was left to rot. I tried to find his grave. Four years ago I went back with his three sons to try to find his grave. There was nothing there. I asked some ex-guerrillas about what had happened to him. They showed me the place where he died, and told me how his head was this way and his legs were that way, but there was nothing. Dogs must have taken all the bones away." Harry shook his head. "The young people from that time are old now. What we've gone through. Now people are repeating the same thing. Nothing's been learned.

"I tried to fight against evil." Harry laughed an old man's laugh, dry, resigned to the past. "I tried to fight against evil and—" I waited for him to finish the sentence. He looked at me through his spectacles. "Sometimes you can't win over the evil," he said. "The evil took place. Despite my intentions, I was involved in evil and sentenced to thirty years' hard labour." The way he presented the crime and punishment, in one sentence, joined together by the word "and" was like an accusation, confession and statement of belief, all in one. I asked if he could have acted otherwise than he had. He considered for a moment and said, "Well, I don't know what I could have done."

A waitress arrived and placed our orders on the table. Harry drank some water. I waited until the waitress had finished arranging the dishes before asking Harry if he thought he had had a fair trial.

"My trial, it wasn't fair at all. But some kind of trial had to be conducted. It was necessary. Being objective was difficult at the trial, and it's difficult now. The prosecutor and the judge tried to investigate everything but they were human beings." I wasn't sure what he was saying.

"At the time of the trial no Filipinos could speak in favour of Japan." He paused and I thought he had finished. But then he continued. "As I told you, I was between the Japanese army and the people. I was like a middle-man. On the day of the incident, all the men, the Filipino men, were rounded up and assembled in the church to be taken away. I was there. It was my job to tell each man that he had to stay or could go. I was a liaison officer, so I'd got to know a lot of people, including a lady from a group of young Filipinas doing charity work. This lady used to contact me for rice and other provisions, and that's how she helped the poor people." Harry hesitated. "We knew each other. At the time of the incident, when the people were gathered in the church to be taken away, the lady came to me with her girlfriend and asked me to save her brother. That's what I did. I saved him.

"She was called as a witness at my trial. The prosecutor asked her if I was guilty of the crime. She said yes, that man should be executed. The prosecutor asked her why and she said, 'Because he is Japanese.' " Harry looked down at the table, as if he was looking over a distant landscape, and I wondered about the relationship between the young Japanese liaison officer and the young Filipino lady who did charity work for poor people. Harry cleared his throat.

"When I was in prison I wrote to her. I asked her why she said such things at the trial. I thought perhaps she was forced to by the prosecutor. But she never answered. It's difficult to be objective. It's the kind of contradiction that's hard to get out of." Suddenly he was an old man talking about things that happened a long time ago. I asked if he was tired but he said he felt fine.

We returned to the trial. "The judge read the facts, the story, the written facts, and made his decision and passed sentence on everyone involved. The court was influenced by the politicians, the witnesses were influenced by their fear of being tried as collaborators. It's normal. Everyone is a victim of circumstances. I was carried by the current. I guess it was the same with the lady. But what made her say 'Because he is Japanese?' "

○

The market's dead.

Yamaguchi's face is a weird putty colour and his eyes are half closed. He's listening to a miniature stereo system with speakers the size of cigarette packets arranged on either side of the Reuters screen. It's his way of showing his seniority: the higher up in the company, the less there is to do. The don't-care expression, the sulky lines of his mouth, the lower lip pushed out a bit—the eyes half closed as if he was about to fall asleep—remind me of the faces of bully boys at the back of the class in the school where I taught when I first came to Japan. It's a look of spoilt indifference: teenage cool, Japanese-style, imitated from Western films of rebellious youth; James Dean and Marlon Brando.

Yamaguchi's in his late forties. He was less than a year old when they dropped the bomb on Hiroshima. His parents suffered the horror of defeat and the humiliation of living under the rule of a foreign power but he was too young to know what was going on. During the Korean war, when white men and yellow men were killing each other, Japan was making money selling jeeps and trucks and uniforms and ball bearings. Possibly some of the ball bearings paid Yamaguchi's fees at Waseda university.

As a postgraduate in Europe, he listened to the Beatles and the Rolling Stones while white men and yellow men were killing more of each other in Vietnam and Japan was making more money. After the oil shock Japan became Japan the fragile superpower. All the time it was lending money to America in its poker game with the Soviet Union. Eventually the Soviet Union had to drop out of the poker game, leaving America the winner, owing Japan billions of dollars in US Treasury Bonds.

For most of Yamaguchi's life things have gone well for Japan. He isn't one of the *salarimen* who made Japan—that was his father's generation. But he uses the systems they made and spends the money they accumulated and he's proud to be Japanese.

"Japan is number one," he says, in his blue and yellow Hermès tie and his Prince-of-Wales checked suit from Savile Row, smoking Marlboro cigarettes, listening to "Qué sera sera"—whatever will be will be—on his pocket stereo system.

I like this music. My mother used to sing it to me. I remember her singing "the future's not ours to see" and feeling sad, perhaps because she was sad, or because the future was somewhere else, far away from where I was happy. I remember the remains of the day, the shadows of the leaves moving on the walls of my bedroom, and my mother singing this song. Now I know. This is the future that was invisible, and I'm sitting in front of a screen full of numbers on the seventeenth floor of an office block in Tokyo, watching Yamaguchi smoking a cigarette.

He's opened his eyes and noticed me looking at him.

"We don't know what's going to happen, do we?" he says and gives one of those switch-on switch-off smiles and turns up the volume as if the music had a message he wanted me to hear.

"The future's not ours to see," he repeats, "nothing's certain. We can't be sure of anything." And he gives another switch-on switch-off smile.

He's using silence Japanese style, like a threat without words to make me feel bad. But I don't, I just wonder why he wants to make me feel bad. Perhaps I can guess why, but I'm not saying, like Yamaguchi.

Is it difficult for him to understand me? Is it as difficult for me to understand him? Do our faces speak the same language? Do our silences have the same meaning? Like a lot of Japanese, he underestimates foreigners' sensitivity to the unspoken word. Sometimes he shouts his thoughts by what he doesn't say.

Occasionally when I catch sight of the shadowy reflection of my face in the computer screen looking out of the green shade through a shining window, like a visitor from another world, I feel I'm looking at myself through the eyes of someone else, like Yamaguchi.

There he is.

Here I am.

In the nebulous dimension on the other side of the screen,

my double moves when I move, watches me watching him, silent as a fish.

"Qué sera sera."

◯

Within a couple of weeks of arriving in Tokyo the weaknesses in the company's operations were clear. The same weaknesses are still present: communications and sales. I've discussed the problems several times with both Yamaguchi and Laroche. The frequent breakdowns in transmissions from London, during the conference call. Often the sound quality is so bad it is impossible to hear what is being said. Sometimes there's no contact with London or it's lost after only a few minutes. The Tokyo office isn't receiving any information reports from the European offices, while other companies are receiving reports on a daily basis. Company research is taking too long to reach Japan; some reports have arrived in Tokyo three months after they were written.

It seemed a good idea to find out why it was taking so long and try to do something. Only twenty per cent of the clients on the primary list had been contacted in the previous twelve months. No one was contacted on the secondary list. Yamaguchi's explanation was simple. The market conditions weren't right. Laroche seemed indifferent. "He's your boss," he said, "he knows the business. I'm just an engineer." I suggested the company could make contact with more clients and translate sales reports into Japanese for Japanese clients. I offered to organise a monthly report on the fifty major European companies in Japanese for clients with limited experience of European markets. Laroche said he'd think about it.

Almost nothing has changed. The conference call with London is still interrupted by technical difficulties. Liaison between the offices is intermittent and unreliable. Yamaguchi has finally arranged introductions with half a dozen clients, all from the secondary list, all no-hopers. There are still no sales reports in Japanese. Reports from Europe are still arriving three or four weeks late.

Head office thinks of Japan as a problem area. The same criticisms keep recurring. Japan is OK—the problem is the people. They speak Japanese. They're difficult to understand. They take a long time to make decisions and ask unnecessary questions. They're boring. They play by a different set of rules. They have a different attitude to the truth, they're suspiciously polite and they never say what they really think. They're all the same, like ants or robots, and they have no individuality. It would be easier to pretend they don't exist but they have the money and technology which command respect. Worst of all, they don't have a sense of humour.

The old men on the fifth floor try to ignore Japan, which only makes things worse. They assume the person in charge of the Tokyo office knows what's going on. But he doesn't speak the language—he is a foreign man surrounded by the sound of Japanese. He says what they want him to say. He knows what they want him to know. The whole operation is controlled by the Japanese. If the Japanese wanted this side of business to go well there wouldn't be so many problems. Someone in the office—or outside it—doesn't want the operation to work.

○

Tanya's next door reading *Vanity Fair* and I'm here in the bedroom, looking out of the window, thinking of Becky Sharp, and wondering what I'm doing in Japan.

Sometimes I feel like I'm doing time: the sentence is as long as I like. The old men on the fifth floor said they hoped I'd be here for a long time. "Pretty little things over there," one of them said, "you might find yourself marrying one." I thought of Sachiko when he said that. I imagined being here in Tokyo with her. "Yes." I said. "Who knows?" The old man smiled as if it was all decided. That was the agreement. They wanted me to be here for a long time, as long as I like; an open-ended assignment, an indefinite posting. Ideally I meet a Japanese girl, marry her and raise a family like Alex or William.

I know the old men's attitude to people who live in Japan. They think there's something strange about people who sit cross-legged on the floor, eating raw fish with chopsticks. They suspect someone who has lived out East. Some of them are jealous. They imagine a life of luxury and credit-card sex. The ones who come over for a month or two are the worst. They learn a dozen words of Japanese, read a couple of books about Japan, and use the Tokyo underground. They attend a few meetings, talk to some English-speaking Japanese, go to a few discos and visit a steam-and-cream massage parlour. They have a great time. They know Japan. They go back home and bore people at parties with their special understanding of Japan. But they don't know what it's like to live here. They can't imagine. It's something to do with time. It's like a prisoner and a prison visitor, looking through the same window, seeing different worlds.

I'm free to go but I feel I should stay. I want to look back on the time I was here and feel a sense of achievement: I introduced those clients, I set up that operation, I made that deal.

One or two people on the fifth floor know who I am, but as far as they are concerned I am a commodity. They invest money and they expect a return. It's difficult to feel a personal loyalty to such people—it's more like a business relationship. They pay me, I do what I can.

Tanya says I should leave the company. She wants us to go to the States, we buy a Thunderbird convertible in New Orleans and drive across America and I write a book about it. I grow my hair and wear red lizard-skin cowboy boots. She wears denim hotpants. We drive across America chewing gum, listening to Canned Heat, Mozart and the Beach Boys.

Tanya thinks it would be more fun than working in a bank in Tokyo. The book gets made into a film and we live happily ever after.

○

Sometimes the garden of the old house next door is so still, nothing moving, not a leaf, not a bird, not an insect. It's like a moment in a dream, or a film, the moment before something happens, but nothing happens. Everything is as it is, more or less as it always was: Japan a hundred years ago, except the trees are growing out of shape and the ornamental pool is dark and stagnant and the stones of the path are covered with pine needles.

The leaves of the willow tree are absolutely still. The old house is silent. The doors are closed and the windows shuttered. Nobody lives there. Nobody sees the dusty path, the overgrown pool and the stone lantern. Only someone spying from here can look over the hedge and see what it's like. It's become the sort of place where things move when there's no wind, even in sunlight. Although at the moment everything's still, it's as if something in it senses me watching, and it's waiting for me to look away. But I want to stay here for a bit. I like looking at the old house with its dilapidated garden. It's like seeing a *haiku* come to life: sunlight on weathered wood carved long ago by a forgotten craftsman; moss-covered steps, a rusty bicycle tangled with convolvulus.

It's a place where time passes in a different way, according to the seasons, measured by the sun and the moon and the stars, like Japan before the foreigners came with their machines.

○

Tanya's buying the tickets because she knows the underground better than I do. She just turned round and saw me using this and she frowned. She didn't want me to bring it. She says whenever I use it we have an argument: I change, I become someone else. She doesn't like it. I promised it wouldn't get in the way—I'd only be using it in between conversations, like now.

A twenty-foot cowboy in golden sepia light gallops across the screen on the front of a building. I want to buy one of those silver helium-filled balloons and let go of the string. So many people. The last time we were here was with Joe, by night and everything was made of different coloured lights. Now it's all grey and white concrete, plate glass and red and yellow plastic signs under a luminous grey sky.

Tanya's bought a couple of T-shirts with Japanese-English slogans. One says, "We sincerely believe the meaning of our life is new age style fashion. If we are to speak honestly our happiness is simple and blue sneakers. PS we wish you a good day. Established since 1990." The other says, "Milk Boy Sensation." While Tanya was trying one of the T-shirts a girl shop assistant came into the changing room. She didn't say anything. She just looked at Tanya's breasts, pointed at them and said, "big," touched her own and said, "small," then made a little bow, and said, "*Sumimasen*—excuse me," cupped her hands gently under Tanya's breasts and lifted them slightly. Then she made another little bow and left the cubicle.

○

We were in one of the lanes in Piss Alley. Tanya said it smelt like the elephant house. She was complaining about something, probably the recorder. I was feeling tired and irritable. In front of us the road divided. She went one way and I went the other. For a second or so I felt relief but then I missed her. I looked for her but I couldn't find her.

A man was walking towards me, he had grey hair over his collar and a thin grey beard. He looked like one of the men who sleep on cardboard inside the underground stations. As we passed each other he smiled as if we both lived in the same village. I carried on walking for a minute or so, but I was still thinking about him. Like the smell of incense or the sound of a bell, the thought of him remained with me. I could see him in my mind's eye, as clearly as if I was thinking of my brother.

It's happened before and every time it happens there's the realisation that it's happened before. Like the meeting with the Moroccan water seller.

I walked back the way I'd come. I wanted to find him. I saw him in one of those noodle shops made of wood and plastic. A man in a vest behind the counter was doing something in a cloud of steam. The old man was sitting at the counter with his back to the door. The other customers were a couple of construction workers, wearing yellow helmets, a man in a boiler suit and a crumpled-looking *salariman*. I sat next to the man in the boiler suit and ordered a bowl of noodles. There was an empty seat between me and the old man.

The man in the boiler suit was slurping his noodles like a dredging machine. The crumpled *salariman* was arranging the pages of a newspaper, aligning each page so that it fitted exactly against the corner of the page next to it. Beside him was a small pile of grimy newspapers, neatly folded. Just as I thought he'd finished folding the newspaper he frowned, opened the newspaper, and started arranging the pages again, making sure the top and bottom of each page were exactly in line with the pages on either side. He was wearing a suit and tie but the collar of his shirt was grey with dirt and in the lapel of his jacket, instead of a company button, there was a safety pin with a scrap of white thread hanging.

The old man was searching around inside a small canvas satchel on his lap. The straps of the satchel had been mended with string. He was wearing a dark blue coat, faded by the sun and rain to an almost colourless grey over the shoulders. He took a pocket notebook out of the satchel. He had pale brown eyes, the sort of colour that suggests a trace of Ainu blood. The man in the vest brought a bowl of noodles and a stand of throwaway chopsticks. The old man chose a pair of chopsticks, split them and examined the wood for splinters.

I don't know why I wanted to talk to him. He was different:

the way he looked at the space in front of him as if it were a mirror. I waited until my bowl of noodles arrived and asked him to pass the chopsticks.

"Certainly," he said. I didn't expect him to speak English and I thanked him in Japanese, but then I asked in English if he understood what I was saying. He said his English wasn't so bad. His voice was soft and clear. He explained how he'd worked as a driver for the Americans during the Occupation and listened to the Armed Forces radio to learn the language. Before the war, he was about to go to university but he was called up for military service.

It was hard to imagine him, fifty years ago, a young man in uniform going off to fight the Chinese in Manchuria. He didn't talk about the war. All he said was, "I came back." I asked where he lived.

"I am like a sparrow," he said. "I go from place to place." It might have been a phrase picked up on the Armed Forces radio. I wondered what happened to him in Manchuria. Perhaps he came back and found his family killed in the bombing. But he didn't seem like a crazy.

He asked what I was doing in Japan and I told him.

"Money is a sickness," he said, "people get it, then they die. Japan is sick." The other side of him the crumpled *salariman* was folding his newspaper. Sometimes what the old man said was like fortune-cookie wisdom but the look in his eyes had a strange authority. I think he liked me. He said he was sure I would do great things for Japan.

"*Ganbarimasu.*" I said, "I'll do my best."

We sipped at cups of hot green tea and talked about Basho who went from place to place like a pilgrim, writing poetry. He placed his hand on the travel-worn satchel beside him and said, "This is my book," and laughed.

He asked my name and I gave him my *meishi* name card. He didn't have one of his own, but he wanted to write his name for me. He took a pen from his satchel and wrote Isamu Tadano in capital letters on a paper napkin, then changed the way he held the pen so that it was vertical to the paper, like a bamboo brush, and wrote several *kanji* characters.

"My name," he said, "Isamu Tadano." He smiled and we bowed to each other. When he smiled, he reminded me of the picture of Basho in my copy of *The Narrow Road to the Deep North*. Then he paid his bill, picked up his satchel and was gone, leaving an empty space between me and the *salariman* folding his newspaper.

○

Tanya's not back yet.

The house is very still and the windows are open. I'm sitting cross-legged looking at the garden in the twilight, listening to the sound of Tokyo. I'll let the recorder run for a bit.

There.

Most of the time I don't hear it, but when I listen for it, like my heart beat, it's there. The thunderous murmur which is almost inaudible, because it's always there like the sea: the sound of power, the subliminal character of a great city.

Sometimes when I notice it, it disturbs me because it reminds me I am alone, not just by myself, but alone in the way one is alone among millions, a foreigner in Tokyo, and I start thinking about things like what I'm doing with my life and what if I died here.

The colours of the leaves have turned to shadows. The sky is a sort of sepia orange and Tanya's still not back. I'm not worried. I know she'll be back. Time by myself has helped me realise something I've been avoiding. While Tanya's here I'm distracted from Japan; she's not really interested in it. Tokyo is like Los Angeles and the Japanese are OK but she has no particular feelings about them.

"Japan is OK," she said. "But the Japanese are a bit samey." I think I know what she means. It's the blandness. But then I remember the old woman at the vegetable shop who folds the empty cardboard boxes flat and stacks them in a neat pile, who smiles every time I go past and the man at the dry cleaners with the sign on the door which says in English "We love leather" and the master and his wife in the *sushi* shop, and I think of Sachiko and I know it's not really true, because sometimes there's a feeling that isn't just good manners and polite smiles, a feeling that only happens with Japanese people and I miss it because I'm here with Tanya.

After living in a foreign country for a while someone else begins to develop inside—like another self inside oneself, speaking a different language, thinking different thoughts, almost a different person—an invisible presence behind the mask of one's own face.

Tanya doesn't know my Japanese self—when I'm Japanese she hardly notices, she just thinks I'm being difficult.

Somewhere along the line part of me has become Japanese. It's the only way I can explain it. Maybe it happened the first time I came to Japan, when I was living in Kashima or Kyoto. Maybe it happened with Sachiko. Ever since I was with her a part of me sees life, maybe not through Japanese eyes, but sometimes with a Japanese perspective, sometimes with a Japanese heart.

In London I felt as if part of my life was missing and I thought it was Sachiko. Now I know it wasn't only Sachiko, it was Japan.

○

The market's like a frozen mammoth: it might just be in suspended animation but everything says it's dead.

Yamaguchi looks as if he didn't sleep over the weekend. His eyelids are halfway over his eyes and he keeps licking his lips as if there's a funny taste in his mouth and he can't get rid of it.

Yesterday Tanya and I went to the country to see Conrad and Fumiko. I thought it would be good to get out of Tokyo; see some trees and mountains, breathe some clean air. We arrived in the early afternoon but Conrad was working in the dark room and Fumiko had gone to a parents' meeting at the school, so we went for a walk along the river to the village shrine. The air was still and warm. The path was overgrown with shrubs and bamboo grass and between the bushes strands of cobwebs floated like airy obstacles in our way.

On the other side of the river, heavy trucks full of stones from the local quarry thundered along, engines growling and air brakes hissing as they changed gears, taking the bends of the road. We stopped for a rest by a big rock with a pine tree growing out of it. It was like a tourist poster of rural Japan: the mountains half disappearing in mist, the pine trees, the great boulders at the water's edge. I tried to imagine what it was like when the only traffic through the village was ox carts and pack animals, a few riders maybe, but most of the passers-by would have been on foot; pedlars from Edo, selling combs and ribbons and mirrors; the occasional monk on a pilgrimage with a begging bowl in his hand and a basket over his head, to protect him from worldly distractions.

"What are we doing here?" said Tanya.

I thought she was asking why we were standing by the rock with the pine tree, looking at the river. A group of bikers were revving their machines on the other side of the river—a weekend wild bunch from Tokyo—junior *salarimen* in motorcycle leathers going for a burn-up in the country. I waited for the noise to die away.

"I don't know," I said. "Why are you here?" I wish I hadn't asked. The question sounded like an accusation. Tanya was silent. Then she turned towards me and said, "I'm here because you're here."

I was thinking of why I came to Japan the first time: to hear the sound of a temple bell and see the sparrows flying out of the nose of the Great Buddha at Kamakura and meet the people who invented the sound of one hand clapping. I thought of Kashima, learning Japanese and practising sword strokes in the old *dojo* hall with the heavy wooden doors pushed back and the rain falling into the dark green shadows of the forest. I thought of Kyoto, living with Caro in the little house in the overgrown garden next door to the monastery, waking up every morning to the clatter of wooden bells as the monks began their meditation.

I kissed her.

We walked along the path in silence until we came to the steps of the shrine. It's a place that's special to me. It's not the sort of shrine which has bus loads of tourists visiting it. It's just an ordinary village shrine. The stone *shishi* dogs on either side of the steps look as if they were made by a local stone mason— their expressions are as fierce as well-fed pugs. One is grinning as if it's just done something mischievous and the other has a squint. The concrete steps between them are uneven.

Tanya looked at the two flights of steps and asked if it was worth the climb. Halfway up we passed under the archway of a stone *torii*. Years ago I read a story about a gate between the past and the future. From one direction, the traveller entered the past; from the other direction, the future. Almost every time I pass through a *torii* I remember the story.

At the top of the steps we went over to a rough stone basin brimming with water. On the edge of the basin was a bamboo cup with a long wooden handle. I dipped it into the water and poured some over Tanya's hand then my own. The water was cool. I wiped my forehead and pushed my fingers through my hair.

It was quiet. The pine trees around the shrine muffled the sound of the road below. I walked to the shrine, closed my eyes and clapped my hands. Sometimes when I clap my hands I imagine the sound of hand clapping travelling through the air to the ear of the *kami-sama* who is present in an instant, listening to my thoughts, a benevolent presence hidden somewhere in the shrine or the surrounding trees. Sometimes I just clap my hands and listen to the silence.

I thought of people coming to the shrine for hundreds of years, who stood where I was standing: farmers giving thanks for the rice harvest; husbands and wives presenting their new-born children to the *kami-sama*; soldiers going away to war praying for a safe return; and lovers praying for each other. I stood for a while, maybe a minute or so, then I opened my eyes and turned round. Tanya was sitting on a step smoking a cigarette.

I was sure she was smoking a cigarette to annoy me but I didn't say anything. She asked what the matter was. I said I was fine. We walked back down the steps under the *torii* past the *shishi* dogs and followed the path along the river. I felt sad and angry as if I'd offered her a present and she'd ignored it or rejected it.

It was humid—*mushi-atsui*—the sort of weather which makes every movement an effort. My shirt was sticking to my back and my lips were salty with sweat. Tanya wanted a rest and we stopped where the path runs close to the river. Neither of us said anything for a while. The rumble of the lorries on the other side of the river was oppressive. We didn't talk for so long it became like a children's game, but still neither of us said anything. I made a joke but she didn't smile.

Every silence is different. If she were Japanese I would have interpreted her silence in a Japanese way. Perhaps I had my signals crossed. I asked what the matter was.

"You." She paused. "Japan."

I asked what she meant.

"You don't have to be here," she said. "You're free to go whenever you like."

It was like the breaking of a spell.

I hadn't thought about freedom for a long time. While living in Japan it's easy to forget. It's not part of the culture—there's no European tradition of liberty or freedom, only the Buddha's liberation from suffering. The world outside Japan is another universe, with a different language. I wasn't sure Tanya and I were speaking the same language. I said something about working for the company and getting to know Japan a bit better. I knew she wanted me to say something else, but I couldn't.

Being in love with a place can be like being in love with a person. The same kind of pain and happiness and the same loss of freedom in exchange for being where one wants to be. I felt as if Japan was like another woman and Tanya was jealous of her. We started walking again.

The thought of living alone in Tokyo doesn't make me feel good.

○

The sky is dark grey over Tokyo Bay and rain is scattering against the window, trembling in crazy diagonals and disintegrating in quicksilver mazes as another gust of wind and water is dashed against the glass.

Here behind the glass, under the long white lines of fluorescent lighting, among the screens and telephones and fax machines, conversation is subdued by the violence of the storm. It's the start of the *tsuyu*, rainy season, and this is the typhoon that swept out of the Pacific some time yesterday and hit Tokyo a couple of hours ago.

I'd forgotten the rainy season, like the Japanese who say, "In Japan we have four seasons—spring, summer, autumn and winter," and smile as if Japan is the only country in the world which has four seasons. If someone asks about the *tsuyu*, the rainy season, they suck their teeth and say the *tsuyu* is different.

My first *tsuyu* was in the country in Kashima. I remember the grey skies over the rice fields and the smell of the earth and the pine trees in the still, humid air. When it rained it was like the rain in the Bible—the flood gates of heaven opening, so much water falling out of the sky it was like the sea pouring through the clouds. "Rain" wasn't really the word for it, the *tsuyu*.

I remember practising swordsmanship in the *dojo* of Kashima

Jingu shrine during the rainy season. I used to pull back the great wooden doors and let the sound of the rain invade the stillness of the building and I thought of men hearing the sound of the rain before I was born, practising the *kata* strokes I was practising, using the same flick of the wrist to dislodge the invisible blood from the blade of the sword before sheathing it. After the rain, I watched the mist drifting through the bamboo grass framed by the door of the *dojo*, and when the sun came out it was like a gold-flecked folding screen of greens and yellows. Then the sun disappeared and the colours faded back into a shadowy confusion of dripping stems and leaves.

Memories of past lives.

I like the *tsuyu* because I lived in the country. In Tokyo the *tsuyu*'s a nuisance: it blocks the drains and in places the streets are ankle-deep in water, umbrellas in racks at the entrances to cafés disappear and it's impossible to get a taxi. In the country it's different: the rain pours into the fields and the forests like a relentless blessing.

Yamaguchi's just arrived back from lunch. He's slumped into his chair, blinking at the room and moving his mouth as if he's got something stuck between his teeth. It's the third time this week he's taken a long lunch and come back drunk. It's none of my business. But when he's had a late lunch the conference call with London always goes dead before they can ask us any questions. Laroche doesn't seem to mind. It's difficult to see what Yamaguchi's doing here. In six months he's introduced me to half a dozen clients. He's only been working on equities for a year. He was on the fixed interest side of the business. It's a different culture. Sometimes it's hard to make the transition.

His face tells the story: the pale, slightly sweaty skin, the evasive eyes, not quite focusing on anything in particular, the puffiness under his eyes and the discontented lines of his mouth. He's not a happy man. He's earning two or three times what the average *salariman* receives and still he's not happy.

His face reflects the principal emotions of the market: fear and greed. Most of the time everything's hidden by a mask of professional confidence and goodwill—but sometimes, like now, when he's drunk, or tired, the mask slips.

I'd like to feel sorry for him but I can't, because he chose his way long ago and now it shows in his eyes that are like the shadowy holes of a mask behind which there's only the echo of a man.

There are a number of people like Yamaguchi in this business. You can see it in their faces—when you look at them; it's in their eyes—a dirty nothingness that goes right down to the centre of who someone is: a dark space where the person used to be. Hollow men. Talking numbers all day, things like right and wrong get to seem irrelevant. There's no way to quantify a moral position, so why bother? People who talk about the bottom line don't waste their time with the finer points of the human soul; you are what you're worth—in yen, dollars, or roubles—and the rest is non-fungible.

○

Tanya's in the sky somewhere over the South China Sea and I'm here in Nakameguro, with a cold beer and a handful of dried octopus on the table, talking into this machine.

We went to the airport together. We'd said all the things that needed to be said. I knew why she was going, and she knew why I was staying.

Japan.

Japan. Why Japan? It's like a *koan*. I think of Zen monks meditating on the meaning of *koans* for months or years and suddenly understanding everything in a moment of *satori* awakening.

Japan is my *koan*.

It's not a rational thing. I wish it was. I'd go out and buy one of those books that explain Japan and I'd be cured. No problem.

But the most important part of Japan is never mentioned: it's a feeling—the *kimochi*. Sometimes it's good, sometimes it's bad: *Nihon no kimochi*—the Japan feeling.

On the way to the airport we talked about things we'd do when I came back. I began to have second thoughts about staying here. Like Tanya said, Japan's OK if you're Japanese, but it's different if you're a foreigner. Talking about other countries made me feel claustrophobic.

I looked out of the train window at the rice fields and the pylons and remembered the sensation of the country closing in on me, when I first came to Japan and took the same train north from Tokyo to Kashima. I tried describing it to Tanya, the journey with old Oba-sensei, with his shiny black hair and gold teeth, telling me about his time in China during the war: the massacre in Nanking and the troops firing their machine guns until the barrels were red hot and the officers using their swords until their hands and fingers were so raw and bloody they couldn't tie up their boot-laces. I told her about Oba-sensei congratulating me on my fortunate selection by the school and quoting Longfellow's line, "I shot an arrow in the air/it fell to earth I know not where," to explain how little he knew about me before I arrived.

I'm not sure I was making much sense to Tanya. I was afraid if I stopped talking I'd start crying. She was sitting there, smoking a cigarette, looking at me and through me, not saying anything and I was talking about whatever came into my head; how Japan is like a quicksand—the more one tries to get out of it, the more it sucks one in—or a maze without a centre—a sphinx without a riddle—or like Peer Gynt's onion, peel away the layers one after another and in the end all there is left is mush and tears.

Finally she interrupted me. "Why bother?" she said. "Japan can look after itself, it doesn't need you. The only mystery about Japan is in your imagination."

As we arrived at the airport, I had a hollow feeling in the pit of my stomach. I thought I was going to be sick but the feeling passed and then I felt numb. By the time Tanya checked in we were both on automatic: we were talking but I can't remember what we said. Then the flight was called, we went towards the barrier and kissed and I was back in Japan.

It was an odd feeling, like swimming in deep water after holding on to the side of a boat: a sensation of being above an invisible abyss.

Now I'm back here in Nakameguro, thinking about that invisible abyss. It's here. I can feel it. It's not just Japan, it's something inside Japan: one can't see it, but one can feel it, like an absence—a deep absence, at the heart of Japan—or maybe it's in me.

Places aren't the same without people. Now Tanya's gone, Japan's a different country, the way I feel about it has changed.

○

The market is active. Yamamoto has just been round the dealing room offering people *manju* cakes from the hot spring where she went for the weekend. I don't like *manju* cakes, but I took one because it would have been rude to refuse. Now I'm sipping a cup of green tea to wash away the taste, trying to justify my existence.

Laroche is walking about the dealing room winking and smiling at people and they're nodding and smiling at him and everyone's happy, playing the game of let's-pretend-we-all-feel-good-together.

But I don't feel good.

If time is money how much is a year of my life worth?

How much would someone of sixty pay for a year of free time at thirty?

If the doom merchants are right and the planet's dying, watching Laroche grinning at the secretaries and listening to Yamaguchi tell people to buy shares in European insurance companies is a phenomenal waste of time. There are other things to do with life.

Here we are with our MBAs and our law degrees sitting at desks looking at screens, talking money and living by numbers: people changing money, money changing people.

Gentlemen prefer bonds.

○

It's ten o'clock in the evening and I'm downstairs at Nakameguro looking out of the window at the shadows of the trees against the sepia orange glow of the night sky over Tokyo.

Some places they measure time from the birth of Jesus or the escape of the Prophet Muhammed from Medina to Mecca; here they count from the start of the Emperor's reign. The death of the previous Emperor is year zero. Japan changes its stationery. Different calendars and bank notes are printed and it's the beginning of a new era. Time measured by Emperors isn't time leading to a day of judgement or resurrection. It's time that goes on, life after life, passing through nature to nirvana. *Namu-miyō-hō-ren-ge-kyō.*

Today I had a drink after work with Fujikawa, the chief bond dealer. He's in his mid-forties, a graduate of Tokyo university with a wife and family in Chiba prefecture. He doesn't speak much English. He was recruited from Mitsubishi because he knows all the right people in the business.

We went to a bar on basement level three, with decor like a Munich beer cellar. He ordered a couple of big steins of lager and asked how I liked Japan. We spoke in Japanese. I said what a Japanese would say, *"tsuki desu*—I like it." Then he asked a whole string of questions: Do the Japanese work too hard? Are they really economic animals? Is Japan number one in the world? He seemed more interested in showing how international he was, asking such questions, than knowing my answers. I said in Japan there are three religions: Shinto, Buddhism and work. He laughed. *"Kinben-bitoku,"* he said. "Work is virtue." He was drinking German beer, wearing a Hermès tie, talking to a foreigner, but he was Japanese and proud of it. He told me with a grin he'd never been abroad, only Okinawa.

What about Japanese girls? His mouth was smiling but he was watching me carefully—a trick question, maybe. He could have been thinking about inviting me to a hostess bar or a massage parlour; or he could have been one of those people who dislike the idea of Japanese women with foreigners. I said Japanese women are pretty but so far I hadn't met the right one. He relaxed a bit more when I said that. It was like answering a password correctly. I thought of conversations with Japanese people when I'd given the wrong answer or said something I shouldn't have said and there was an invisible barrier like a force field separating us. But it was OK with Fujikawa.

"*Ningen-kankei*," he said. "Human relations. *Mina ningen*," he smiled. "Everyone's human." The way he spoke suggested some people were intelligent apes, but he was prepared to communicate with them as if they were human. He complimented me on my Japanese. There was a trace of surprise in his voice which reminded me of people in the country, when I said something in Japanese, who looked at me as if I had a parrot on my shoulder. Fujikawa ordered two more steins of lager.

"We Japanese are shy," he said. "We're difficult to understand, like our language." I nodded. If I'd disagreed and said Japanese was easy, it would have hurt his feelings. Fujikawa believes Japan is unique and when it comes to global society foreigners are second-class citizens. The country has the oldest monarchy in the world and the most advanced technology and it's the richest. The strength of a people is in its myths and traditions, the country with the most advanced technology rules the world, and the one who has the money gives the orders. It was like listening to a tape of Ishihara's book, *The Japan That Can Say No*. I agreed with almost everything he said. He was talking to me more as a Japanese than a foreigner. Maybe it was the beer. He began telling me how the Japanese had a special quality, a kind of innocence, like Pacific Islanders before the missionaries came, a simple gentleness of heart, an unpolluted dignity of spirit.

"*Yamato-damashi*," he said. "That is the true Japanese spirit. *Yamato-damashi*."

As the beer in his glass went lower, his voice went higher and his face got redder. He wasn't really talking to me any more. He was lecturing the face in front of him, like his father or his *sensei* had once lectured him. It wasn't a conversation, it was a lesson. I was younger than he and he was buying the drinks so I listened in silence while he explained how Japan was different from anywhere else in the world. He mentioned all the usual things: *Koto-dama, sabi, wabi, shibui*, almost every element of Japan's self-image, the inscrutable mask which amuses the Japanese and confuses foreigners. At the end of it all he said it is difficult for foreigners to understand Japan because the Japanese don't really understand themselves. Then he looked at the pile of empty pea-skins on the counter and sighed. He was entering a twilight phase of drunkenness which happens to a *salariman* who's had a few drinks, who's thinking about getting the train home and wishing he wasn't married.

Fujikawa shook his head. He was looking at the pea-skins and I was waiting for him to say something. But he didn't. Perhaps he was in a valley somewhere in his past. Perhaps the pea-skins reminded him of something in his childhood. He sighed again.

"US Treasury Bonds," he said in English. "US Treasury Bonds." He repeated the words in a voice which sounded as if he was imitating someone else's way of speaking, maybe Laroche's or Clather's. He could have been contemplating some esoteric poetry in the movement of the long bond yield. I nodded my head gently, to show I was listening. The expression on his face was like a *samurai* in a film; strong, stoic, *gaman-tsuyoi*.

"*Nippon-jin desu*, I am Japanese," he said. "I buy and sell United States Treasury Bonds." There was another long pause, another long sigh and finally he added, "That is my life."

For several seconds we sat there with the meaning of what had just been spoken silently unfolding between us. Then Fujikawa looked up from the pea-skins and said he had to catch a train.

All the *nihonjin-ron* talk about Japan made me feel I should behave like a Japanese and I went with him to the subway station. At the entrance two middle-aged *salarimen* were supporting another, older man with an orange-pink face. He looked like a section chief or a small company boss. He was mumbling how he'd drunk so much he wasn't sure he could find his way home and they were telling him not to worry, they'd look after him. He had his arms around their shoulders and they were more or less holding him upright, walking him along, like two loyal retainers supporting their wounded leader from the battle field. As they got to the ticket gate, the older man suddenly straightened, let go of his companions' shoulders, produced his ticket and walked through like everyone else. On the other side he stood waiting for them, still as a tree about to fall over, I thought, but once his two helpers were through the ticket gate he lifted his arms like a clumsy bird, the two men bowed their heads, took his weight on their shoulders again and they all staggered onto the platform.

Fujikawa got his train. I stood on the platform, watching him as the doors closed and we bowed to each other as the train pulled out of the station.

Travelling back to Nakameguro I thought about the meeting and wondered why he asked me for a drink after work and what he really meant when he said that here in Japan there's only one way of doing things, not the right way or the wrong way, only the Japanese way.

○

It's two o'clock in the morning.

I've read a hundred pages of the *Morte D'Arthur* and I'd like to go to sleep but I can't, something won't let me, like there's something I haven't done or something I don't understand keeping me awake.

Maybe this is how people feel when they confess to things they haven't done.

Maybe it was the fried oysters.

I'd like to telephone Tanya but I don't want to talk to her *ansaphone*.

Perhaps it's just my imagination. While we were together I didn't think so much about coincidences. Now I have more time to think about them.

Sometimes I feel I'm here only as long as someone lets me be here, and they could just press a button and I'd be gone. Sometimes, it seems as if it's all in my imagination, but then I remember things which have happened. I try not to think about them. I try not to think about why, because there's no point asking why in this country. It doesn't get anywhere. It's like fishing without a hook. Daruma said: "I looked for it, and I couldn't find it" and he should know. But I can't help it.

Why don't the people here ask why?

○

It's Saturday afternoon and the sky is grey. The air is still and warm and heavy. I just walked to the supermarket and back and my shirt is soaked with sweat.

When it's like this people close their windows and turn on the air conditioning but I prefer to have the windows and doors open and occasionally there's a light wind, like someone breathing, that seems to come from nowhere. It's the weather for using a fan, but the only fan I have is a plastic one from Cathay Pacific and it's in the bedroom.

There's *sumo* on television.

It's a mystery why so many people want to see big fat men in silk jock straps trying to make each other fall over.

I remember the *sumo* stable in an underground car park in Osaka—the floor was covered with sand. The men, made gentle and good natured by their size, were sitting around eating bowls of *chanko-nabe*. One of the younger ones said it was his duty, his *gimu*, to eat as much as he could. It seemed like a metaphor for Japan's *amae*: every Japanese feels it's a duty to consume Japanese goods, and now Japan has a *sumo* economy.

I like the way they grab the salt and throw it into the air: getting rid of the sweat in the palm of their hands. I like the wrestlers who lick their fingers afterwards. Just before the fight they want to taste the salt. It's a good sign, it shows hunger for life, like the Zen parable of a man holding on to a tree root over the edge of a cliff: below him rocks, above him a tiger, and a black and white mouse nibbling at the root: the man notices a strawberry beside him and picks it.

When there's a close-up of a wrestler it's possible to see the strength of the man's *ki* spirit in his face. Sometimes in the final seconds before a bout his concentration slips and he loses the focus of his *ki*, he's not ready. He has to get up and walk around a bit, find his equilibrium and centre his *ki*. Maybe throw some more salt in the air. Then there's the timing. They're waiting, just about to begin the fight, trying to choose a moment when the other's *ki* is weaker.

*Tachiai!*

It's all over. The smaller one stepped aside, the bigger one couldn't stop himself and fell, but he managed to pull his opponent down with him.

It must be hot in Osaka. People in the audience are fanning themselves with their programmes. Seeing them sitting in rows, with their fans and their programmes flickering like insect wings, makes me feel uncomfortable.

○

As I was getting the fan from the bedroom I looked out of the window. The *shoji* in old man Uehara's house was pulled back. The old man was kneeling in front of the *butsudan* cabinet containing the ancestor tablets and photographs of the dead.

He was wearing a light grey *kimono* and the smoke from the incense was drifting round him. The electric light was on. With no one else in the house the shadows in the empty rooms must be oppressive for the old man.

He leaned forward to tap a round bronze bell and I heard the sound, faintly, softened by the humid air. Then he picked up a rosary from the *butsudan*, looped it over his left hand, put the palms of his hands together and began to pray.

Every now and again he took his right hand away from his left hand which remained still, holding the rosary, then brought his right hand back again, slowly, to tell the beads of the rosary, another one of the 108 beads: the 108 mortal sins in the Buddhist Canon. Then I understood. There it was; the prayer, the rosary, the ritualised gesture of the right hand leaving the left hand and silently returning at another prayer's completion: the sound of one hand clapping—in my neighbour's house in Nakameguro.

○

It's after midnight, almost one o'clock on Sunday morning and I've just been to see Joe. We had dinner by candlelight. The parrot was on top of its cage and the dogs were chewing the cat under the table and the light from the candles was flickering in the shadows of the potted plants and Joe was drinking gin on ice. He wanted to get drunk. He said sometimes it was good to get drunk and that's what he was going to do, he was going to get drunk. We smoked Kretek cigarettes and he talked about growing up in Indonesia, with the young orang-utan as his playmate.

"I miss that creature, Perry," he said. "It was like a brother. We understood each other. Maybe it sounds crazy, but we loved each other. I felt terrible when we had to leave Indonesia. They had to put him in a zoo." He said the experience changed his life, it taught him how different species could communicate love on many different levels, maybe an infinite number of levels, not just ape with man and man with dolphin but maybe man with some other kind of creatures altogether, like alien life forms or intelligences from other parts of the universe.

"I don't believe the crap on television about extraterrestrials," he said, "but some people born on this earth have different ideas which didn't originate on this planet." I asked him what he meant.

"Language," he said. "People think it's the only way to communicate. But language is a barrier to communication. This planet's like a tower of Babel." He wrinkled his eyes and shook his head as if he was watching a documentary film of some atrocity.

"Humans as I see them are the most . . ." he sighed. "I see human beings in a way no human beings would ask me to see them. But when I talk about them like that, they get upset. Look what's happening to the planet. I tell you, this planet's a tower of Babel. Just the sentence 'I want to go home' has a hundred different meanings.

"These pictures going round," he murmured, "I just have to tell them to shut up and they will."

There weren't any pictures on the wall and his eyes were closed. He was breathing heavily. I took the empty glass from his hand and put it on the table.

○

It's raining and the sky is grey but there's a bright island of sunlight, shining on the sea, over towards the horizon.

The market's like a blind man in a lift, it doesn't know where it's going.

Yamaguchi is filing his nails while he waits for someone in Mitsubishi to call him back with an order, maybe.

Last night I saw Takahashi. It was good to see him again.

In a way he is my *sensei*: he taught me about the market when I came out to Japan; he explained the vocabulary and showed me how to read a company balance sheet in Japanese. He taught me to buy on rumour and sell on fact and never be afraid to take a profit. He taught me that optimists make more money than pessimists—if there weren't any optimists there wouldn't be a market—and he gave me a way of looking at the market. Not just the technicalities but a philosophy. He taught me more than I know.

We went to a little place on the Ginza, somewhere on the fifth floor; expensive, low lighting, polished stone and smooth wood. The girls had beautiful smiles and perfect manners and they weren't trying to fill our drinks every ten minutes. It was the sort of place where nobody pays the bill because it's sent automatically to the company.

Takahashi sat there, an ugly middle-aged man chain-smoking Camel cigarettes, exhaling the smoke from the sides of his mouth with a pained expression, looking like one of the grotesque hermits in a picture of the Buddha passing into Nirvana. He often looks in some kind of distress. It's his mask. I've seen him looking as if his dog had just been run over while he watched the price of his stock go up ten per cent in a morning. He's shy; he hides in the lines and shadows of his eyes. Even when he smiles, I can't see who he is completely. But I trust him, because he was a good *sensei* and I owe him a lot. My *on*, my debt, my moral obligation to him, is what he taught me, and as my teacher he has a responsibility for me. Sometimes he telephones me to see how I am, tells me what shares I should be buying, and we talk about the market. Maybe he also wants to find out what's going on between here and Europe, but why not? That's how it works. It's never difficult with Takahashi. He doesn't bruise people to get information, and he's good at his work because people feel comfortable with him. Last night he told me his theory of investment analysis.

"Even now I am not a rich man," he said. "I must work. Perhaps I will never be rich. Every year it costs more money to be rich." We were drinking a bottle of brandy that cost 500 dollars minimum, but we could have been in a *nomiya* drinking place, under the railway arches as far as Takahashi was concerned. He's like a lot of Japanese of his generation who grew up in the poverty after the war. He still thinks poor although he's probably a dollar millionaire.

He told me how to make money. The most important thing is to know the market and to know the market one must understand human nature: knowing what's going to happen isn't as important as knowing what other people think is going to happen.

"The market is a mirror," he said. "It reflects the emotions of fear and greed. According to Napoleon people are ruled by two emotions: fear and greed, they are afraid to lose what they already have, and they're greedy for more. By itself fear, fear is meaningless. So is greed. But with money there's a market." He lit another cigarette.

"Thinking of everything in terms of money is tiring. It is easy to forget what it is like to be human, therefore I read books: Virginia Woolf, Sartre, Dostoevsky—people who try to explain human existence. They help me to endure the unendurable, and teach me to understand human nature." He looked at me through a cloud of cigarette smoke. "So when I read *The Gambler* I help myself." He smiled. "And I become a better investment analyst."

I told him how many books I read in the last year and he pretended to be shocked at my laziness.

"Perhaps you are very busy?" I wasn't sure how much he knew, but I guess he had a pretty good idea. I played for time, Japanese style and sucked the air in through my teeth. Takahashi nodded and said it was the same everywhere.

"We must learn to forget," he said. "It isn't possible to know everything, not yet anyway. We must forget things. Today's information is more important than yesterday's. Tomorrow's information is more important than today's. Nowadays, nobody can remember all the information: the mind cannot hold it all. We must forget to remember."

Sometimes the way Takahashi says things he seems to be speaking another language, between Japanese and English. I think I understand what he's saying but then I'm not sure. Perhaps he wants to say something else. I have second thoughts. I listen to what he says and it seems he's talking about another thing altogether. When we first met it was difficult, I wanted to understand exactly what he meant, I tried really hard, but it was like catching smoke rings. Once I asked him directly and he said something about Western minds moving in straight lines and Japanese minds moving in circles or spirals. Another time I said I didn't understand what he was talking about and he said it didn't matter, but it was important to be patient: sometimes the tea isn't visible till it reaches a certain level in the cup.

I don't know if he enjoys playing at being my *sensei*, or if he really means it. But I enjoy our meetings. I described the situation here in the office and he told me not to worry. If I need any help I only have to call him. He said I should buy shares in Mitsubishi.

Yamaguchi is filing his nails. Like Takahashi he's lived abroad, he's seen Japan from the outside and he knows what it's like to be a foreigner. They both had problems coming back. They'd picked up foreigners' habits. Other Japanese people were suspicious of them: they were selfish, rude, too individual, they'd become *gaijin-kusai*—they smelt like foreigners and it wasn't just the meat they'd eaten while they were away. The biggest problem was the loss of their pure Japanese spirit. Whatever they were doing abroad, the general feeling was that something had rubbed off on them. They couldn't be trusted to do what most Japanese would do—they might do something foreign. The consensus was that by living away from Japan they'd become unpredictable, more difficult to get along with, unreliable.

Takahashi and Yamaguchi. Two men, more or less the same experiences, but very different people: Takahashi explores the strange world of Dostoevsky, Yamaguchi drinks himself into a caricature of a typical *salariman*.

○

The sea is grey, the sky is silver over Tokyo Bay.

I've called my clients with comments on the latest set of company figures. Saito is thinking of restructuring his portfolio. I have to suggest a model portfolio. He wants his holdings to reflect the market—sector by sector—but only the best stocks. No rubbish. He rolls his "R"s like an Edinburgh fund manager, although he's never been outside Japan. He doesn't understand English, but he likes to speak it, so every day I talk to him in Japanese and he asks me questions in English. We have a relationship. He even laughs at some of my jokes—sometimes when I'm not joking. He says he wants to learn the English sense of humour.

"As you may know," he said, "we Japanese have no sense of humour."

Yesterday evening the office celebrated another year of business with a party in a Chinese restaurant. Before it started people who joined the office in the year were called forward by Laroche. Laroche described me as a temporary representative from the London office. He spoke in English. I thanked him in Japanese and said I looked forward to a long and happy relationship with everyone in the office.

Around eight o'clock people started leaving for home and the rest of us went to a disco. The women outnumbered the men, three to one. There were problems getting in. The man at the door didn't realise that Laroche, Casey and I were in the same group and tried to stop us entering. A while back some orange growers from California on a goodwill visit to Japan had visited the club and the manager was still nervous about foreigners.

The place was smart but not exclusive. I sat at a table with a couple of secretaries from the accounts department. They were nice young women in their early twenties with pretty smiles and bad complexions covered in foundation cream and powder. One of them had been to England.

"Bournemouth is beautiful," she said. She described her three days in London. She visited the statue of Peter Pan in Kensington Gardens, fed the squirrels and the ducks and ate an ice-cream which made her sick. She liked England. The other had an Australian pen-friend called Costas. She did not understand all his letters. Often she had to look words up in a dictionary and sometimes they had strange meanings.

I danced with both of them. They danced in time with the music and so did I, but we might as well have been on different dance floors. Sometimes, towards the end of songs, small groups came together on the dance floor and danced in unison, co-ordinating their movements like professional dancers.

One group formed around Laroche. It began with half a dozen secretaries dancing round him, waving their arms in rhythm and in a couple of minutes almost everyone from the office who was on the dance floor had gathered round him, swaying to and fro and Laroche was in the middle wriggling his hips, grinning like a TV presenter, with the sweat dripping out of his hair.

○

It's eleven o'clock on Sunday morning.

The sun's shining, the crows are making a noise in the trees overlooking the cemetery and there's a smell of *senko* incense in the air.

Yesterday afternoon I saw Tony. He was with a young woman called Noriko. He introduced her as his assistant. He's going to teach her how to run the business in Tokyo while he's out of the country. We went to Kamakura for the day. On the way Tony explained why he needed a new assistant.

His previous assistant was with him for a year. He took her

for trips to Hong Kong, Hawaii and a couple of visits to Europe, showed her how the business worked and introduced her to clients. A month ago, she complained he wasn't paying her enough and she was leaving. He offered more money but she wasn't satisfied.

"Japanese girls these days," Tony shook his head. "That's all they think about. Money." He asked Noriko in Japanese if the most important thing for Japanese girls was money and Noriko giggled and said yes.

A couple of weeks ago the tax office called. They had information that Tony falsified his tax returns: profits on sales had been understated. Tony checked the sales receipts and found discrepancies. It took a while to piece together what had happened. At first he couldn't believe it.

"I trusted her and she fixed me up. She was planning it all along." Tony grimaced as if he'd just found a curly hair in a piece of *sushi*. He'd bargained with Uzbeks in the bazaars of Kabul and Mazar-i-Sharif and got a fair price, he'd done deals with Hong Kong Chinese and Koreans and made a profit, he'd started a company in Japan and he was still in business after ten years.

"I thought I could judge character," he said. "I never guessed. From the beginning she was filling in the wrong amounts. She made a pinprick in the paper beside the numbers she changed. She was cool. Very cool." There was something like admiration in the way he talked about her.

"We even spent a weekend together at an *onsen* hot spring." He grinned and then looked thoughtful. "Incredible actress— all the time she was spying on me. That's what they're like here, isn't it? It's all an act. They wear masks and watch each other. They've been doing it for hundreds of years, dobbing each other in."

I asked him what dobbing was. He was surprised I didn't know.

"A dobber's a grass, an informer, someone who goes to the police and says you've been a bad boy. Japan's a dobber society.

It's a citizen's duty—it goes back to the Tokugawa shogunate. If you punish a whole village for a crime committed by one individual you get everyone watching everyone. They conform to the norm and no one gets out of line—the group makes sure of that. It's the group's way of protecting itself. That's how you get the Japanese saying: 'The nail that sticks out is beaten flat.' " I understood why he felt bad about things—but he was talking as if Japan was some kind of police state.

"Believe me, Perry," he said, "living in Japan is a mind-over-matter experience—they don't mind and you don't matter. If you cross the line, it's different. In the interests of *wa*, for the sake of harmony, you may be persuaded to change your position. Or you may find yourself in a no-go situation." I asked where he crossed the line but he wasn't sure. Perhaps someone was interested in the business. They'd seen what he was doing and they wanted some of it for themselves. Probably they promised backing to the girl. Now they had a list of his clients and he had to find several hundred million yen.

"The worst thing is the loss of confidence," he shook his head. "I thought I knew these people. Now I don't even trust myself."

By the time we got to Kamakura, Tony was in a better mood. We went to the Great Buddha, took photographs of each other standing in front of it and went inside. Noriko had claustrophobia so we came out again.

The sun was shining and there were birds flying around the Buddha. They reminded me of the *haiku* about the swallows flying out of the nose of the Great Buddha of Kamakura. The *haiku* was one of the reasons I came to Japan but it was hard to see how a swallow could have flown out of the bronze nostril, unless it built a nest there. Perhaps the *haiku* writer only imagined it; a poetic Zen joke at the Buddha's expense. I looked at the Buddha's face and thought of Basho gazing at the deep-lidded eyes, seeing the same line of hills and the sky over the Buddha's shoulder.

Noriko wanted to have lunch in a restaurant she'd read about in a magazine. Tony teased her, saying we could have a burger in McDonald's when we got back to Tokyo but we ended up where Noriko wanted to go. Tony groaned when he saw the bill and Noriko laughed.

The train back to Tokyo was crowded. Tony and Noriko found seats, but I stood almost all the way, next to a Buddhist priest in his robes. He was in his mid-sixties. His face was red and his breath was sweet with *sake*. A couple of times he almost lost his balance and steadied himself by holding on to my arm. He apologised in English. The second time he asked if I was American. I told him where I came from and his face went into a big grin, as if I was pointing a camera at him. The grin stayed in place for a few seconds but then it turned into a weird expression, between a smile and a snarl, as if the *sake* he'd drunk had affected the control of the muscles in his face.

He said he liked foreigners. He was sober enough to talk in English sentences that made sense, but he was only in partial control of his face, and when he said the word "foreigner" a tiny muscle flickered in his upper lip. He gave me his *meishi*.

He was head of an organisation which arranged contacts between foreigners and various Zen temples. He shows visitors round and interprets to them. He told me how much he enjoyed his work.

"Many foreigners are interested in Japanese Buddhism. I am very pleased to help them." He smiled but his eyes were angry.

He kept saying how happy he was to talk to foreigners but his face said something else. It was embarrassing to hear him describing how, if the whole world was Buddhist, there wouldn't be any wars, while he glared at me through the lopsided smile on his face. Perhaps he'd met too many pilgrims in search of enlightenment—people thinking Zen could be the answer to the question of the meaning of life. I could almost sympathise with him, but then he started telling me how it's difficult for foreigners to understand Japanese Buddhism because foreigners all think logically, and they can't make their minds empty and they have problems kneeling in the *seiza* position of meditation.

"If you do not do things the way we Japanese do things, you cannot understand the Japanese mind." He smiled almost all the time but the only point the smile began to look natural was when he was describing how difficult it was for anyone who wasn't Japanese to practice Zen. Obviously it made him feel good and I wondered why. It made me feel irritable. I asked if the Buddha mind is the same in everyone. The question stretched the grin across his face again.

"Of course, the Buddha mind is the same in everyone," he smiled, "but almost nobody knows their Buddha nature." He was pleased so many foreigners came to Japan to study Buddhism. He hoped they would discover their Buddha nature in Japan.

It wasn't just the ghostly sneer trembling on the edges of his smile that repelled me. It was also the anger in his eyes: something I suspected was there in other Japanese faces I'd seen from time to time: a hostility towards my presence as a foreigner, resenting the invasion of territory, wherever it was; a restaurant, a shrine, a bus stop or a railway carriage.

By the time the train got into Tokyo the muscles in my cheeks were stiff from smiling back at him. I finished bowing goodbye to him as the others appeared. Tony asked who he was.

"They're all scroungers," he said, "think the world owes them a living." He told me about the head of the Buddhist monastery in Kyoto who ran a chain of massage parlours and who was charged with tax evasion. He hadn't paid the necessary percentage to the right people so they informed the tax authorities.

While Tony was telling me the story of the priest with the massage parlours I thought of the year I lived in Kyoto when Buddhism was an important part of my life. I practised meditation in activity, like Hakuin recommended. I was looking for *satori*. I wanted to hear the sound of one hand clapping and see the light. I didn't know about Zen monks with real estate holdings paying cash sweeteners to *yakuza* gangster-related construction companies. Buddhism was the religion of the two old nuns I met in Kashima, who lived in an ancient farm house on the edge of a rice field, with half a dozen pairs of dark blue serge knickers fluttering on the washing line, laughing at my first clumsy attempt to say *Na-mu-miyō-hō-ren-ge-kyō*.

Before Zen, chopping wood and drawing water. After Zen, chopping wood and drawing water.

The sun is shining, the crows are silent, and I'm hungry.

○

The sky is a swimming-pool blue. The sea is a swarm of golden bees between the silhouettes of buildings.

The market's like a *pachinko* ball: it needs money to get it moving and it could go anywhere.

Sometimes this business reminds me of Lao Tzu's definition of the *Tao*—the way of all things: the one who says, does not know—the one who knows, does not say. Like insider trading.

People in personnel know where the bodies are buried, metaphorically speaking, which explains why they often get to the top. I'm not in personnel, I don't know where the bodies are and I don't want to dig around in anyone's backyard, any more than I want someone to open my desk and read my papers.

The enemy of my enemy is my friend.

But if nobody is my enemy, who are my good friends? The people who keep an eye on me, who want to know what I am doing and check to see how I am.

It's a confession of friendship to say the relationship's mutual.

Maybe Larry Whale is right: Japan is a sphinx without a riddle and the only mystery is why anyone thought there was a riddle. As it says in the last verse of the Sandokai: "I say respectfully to those who wish to be enlightened: do not waste your time in vain."

If Japan has a mystery it is like this.

○

It's five o'clock on Sunday evening.

This morning I was standing on the top of Mount Fuji.

A couple of days ago, Forbes called me. He'd got a party together to climb Mount Fuji and did I want to come along? Everything was organised, a bus, food, shelter, no problem. The meeting place was in a car park near Roppongi.

The bus was full of foreigners—most of them from the Tokyo cocktail party crowd. There weren't many Japanese faces but I saw a pretty young woman with short hair and red lips looking out of the window and the seat next to her was free so I sat beside her. It was Fujiko. The last time I saw her was at Forbes' when her hair was long, over her shoulders. I said I liked the way she looked and she smiled.

Her smile was like the answer to a question I'd been asking for a long time.

The traffic out of Tokyo was very heavy and it was dark long before we reached the mountain. Forbes had booked our group in at a hostel, halfway up the mountain where the road ends. The place was organised for climbers: mattresses on the floor and no sheets or pillows, only blankets. Everybody lay down to sleep in the clothes they were wearing except a man from Barings who changed into pyjamas. Fujiko found a couple of mattresses next to each other. The room was full of people and there was less than an arm's length between us. She lay on her right side, facing me, with the blanket tucked around her shoulders and a slightly wide-eyed expression on her face like some Japanese women have when they know someone's looking at them. I thought about us in bed together. She looked into my eyes and I saw a gentleness.

Forbes announced an early start in the morning and said if everyone was ready he would put the lights out. Fujiko whispered goodnight to me and I answered *o-yasumi-nasai*. She closed her eyes. Her mouth became a smile and she whispered *o-yasumi-nasai*. Then it was dark.

In the morning we got up later than most of the others. Several of the group had already started up the mountain. It was a fine day: the sun was shining over the landscape below and the side of the mountain stretched up into the sky above. The sight made me want to sit down with a cup of coffee and a newspaper.

It was OK for the first couple of hours but gradually the path became steeper and the sun seemed hotter and people's conversations slowed down and slipped into longer and longer silences. As we climbed higher we began to meet other people on their way down from the summit who smiled encouragement and greeted us. "*Ganbatte*, do your best, keep at it, do your best, *ganbatte kudasai*," and we answered, with as much breath as we had, "*Hai! Ganbarimasu*—we will do our best!"

The image of the Coca-Cola machine in the lane here in Nakameguro kept appearing in my mind's eye. I could see the condensation on the red and white tin, feel the weight and the chill of it in my hands, hear the sound as the seal was broken. But I couldn't get the taste. I was climbing Mount Fuji and all I could think about was Coca-Cola. I felt I should have been thinking about something Japanese, like Issa's *haiku*—"Oh snail, climb Mount Fuji, but slowly, slowly"—or Buson's— "Fuji, a single summit, there above the green leaves, that's how it is!" But there weren't any green leaves and I couldn't see the shape of the mountain, only rocks and boulders and pebbles and a dusty path winding upwards.

At last we got to a stone-built tea house with wooden tressles outside and people in sun-hats and hiking boots sitting drinking tea and soft drinks. I bought a Coca-Cola but it wasn't cold so I had a cup of hot green tea. We climbed for another couple of hours and stopped for lunch while a procession of people went past; small groups dressed in hiking gear and track suits, students carrying rucksacks, and *yama-bushi* pilgrims in white robes of purity with staves. Some of the pilgrims laboured under large packs and their almost invisible progress up the mountain was like the snail in Issa's *haiku*. The sun was high overhead but the air was cool and the wind was blowing.

In the late afternoon we came to another stone-built shelter where Forbes and others in the party were drinking champagne and *sake*.

We sat and gazed at the landscape below changing as the sun moved across the sky and the light turned from yellow to gold. It was like a vision of a country in an ancient legend; a land where there might still be dragons, knights and beautiful princesses—even if the dragons were only made of paper, ink and water, decorating the sliding doors of temples and restaurants, and the knights were *salarimen* and the beautiful princesses had become bored housewives or *mama-sans*. Looking out from the sacred mountain over Japan in the glow of the setting sun I thought I could see how the Japanese believe in the myth of Japan, that is their strength, and the way the myth becomes a reality.

Beside me a *yama-bushi* pilgrim, a man in his early sixties with a weather-beaten face and gold teeth, was murmuring a prayer to himself. The land below was already in shadow. As the last of the sun's disc slipped beneath the horizon the man unhooked a conch shell from his shoulder and blew it. The sound rang out like the roaring of the sea made into music. I thought of the sound of the conch shells of war in the *Bhagavad-Gita* that signalled the great battle between good and evil as the cool evening air rolled over us in an invisible wave and the sky began to darken.

We went back inside to join the others. Lamps were lit. There was a party atmosphere. People sat where they could find a space or stood, shoulder to shoulder, singing songs and talking. We ate noodles and drank *sake* and the man with the conch tried to explain why Fuji was a holy mountain. It was beautiful, but that wasn't the reason it was holy. The mountain's present shape only dated back a few hundred years to the last time there was a volcanic eruption and Fuji blew its top. Before, it was sacred to the Ainu, the aboriginal inhabitants of Japan, who gave the mountain its name. As the highest mountain in the country it was the part of Japan closest to heaven.

The gold gleamed when the pilgrim smiled and his eyes were bright in the lamp light. He was a good man and he wanted me to understand his beliefs. He was a country man: the sort of person I used to meet when I went for bicycle rides in the countryside around Kashima. Yamaguchi and Takahashi, with their dealing screens and fax machines, were in another world from his. He was a farmer and every year he and other members of his village made a pilgrimage. It was a village tradition and they enjoyed the outing. It was a good way to see Japan, pray for the spirits of one's ancestors, and acquire merit for the future life.

I liked the sound of his conch and he asked me to come outside. The sky was dark and the air was cold. Below us lights were moving in the shadow of the mountain. He took a cigarette lighter from his pocket and lit a lantern on a stick which he placed on a low wall in front of us. Then he raised the conch and blew an echoing note. The sound of the conch cleared my head, I remembered the same mysterious roaring from another time in the Himalayas with Caro and the Sadhu holy man who blew the conch to sanctify the place where we were and protect us from evil.

The man blew the conch again and stared into the darkness. After the third or fourth time, he gave a cry of excitement and picked up the lantern and swung it from side to side. He gave another long quavering blast on the conch and pointed down into the dark, towards one of the threads of wavering lights and I saw it—a single light, not moving like the others, but going from side to side, answering the movements of the lantern in his hands and faintly, against the wind, there was the sound of another conch echoing.

The journey to the top took several more hours and the night was already beginning to fade from the sky as we reached the summit. Fujiko and I congratulated each other. There were a lot of people. Some had slept in tents, others had stayed the night in shelters. Everyone was waiting to see the first rays of the rising sun from the top of Mount Fuji. As it became lighter the numbers grew, climbing onto boulders and huddling together on outcrops of rock to get a better view. We stood next to a man with a white stick who was holding on to the arm of the man beside him.

The wind was cold. Clouds drifted below us and looking down through the floating grey strands it was possible to glimpse the darkness of the land still in shadow, like a lost Atlantis, under a misty sea. It was like being an extra in a religious epic, with hundreds of people standing on rocks looking towards the East, waiting for the Apocalypse. The man with the white stick asked his friend if the sun had risen. The friend glanced at his watch and said the sun would rise in another minute or so, Tokyo time. The blind man nodded.

Fujiko looked at me and we smiled at each other. Behind us an electronic bleeper started up. The blind man asked his friend if the sun had risen yet, the man checked his watch. The sky on the horizon was definitely lighter. Another bleeper started up. The blind man half turned to his companion who told him not yet. It was cloudy, it was difficult to see. But the sky was glowing brighter. There was a click of a camera, then another click. The blind man raised his head like someone listening to music and then the light came into his face in a smile as his friend told him the sun had risen and all around there was a clicking and whirring of automatic camera lenses like a colony of insects come to life.

Some said *Banzai!* Others stood with their hands together in prayer. An old man with a towel tied round his bald head offered us *sake* which he'd cooled in some snow and we toasted *kampai* to each other from paper cups. I looked at Fujiko and thought perhaps this is as close as anyone gets to being Japanese, like a *haiku*, on top of Fuji, in the light of the rising sun, the taste of *sake*.

Thinking about it now, it seems like the end of a journey that began a long time ago.

We stayed at the summit for a while, but as the sun climbed the mystery of the place evaporated and it became like a vast picnic site, with people on benches eating from *bento* snack boxes, and groups of students shouting and singing songs together. We paid our respects at the small shrine and started back.

As we made our way down, the clouds disappeared and the landscape stretched out like a sunlit map below us, and we greeted the people toiling up the mountain with the greeting we heard so often the day before: "*Ganbatte!* Keep it up! Do your best! *Ganbatte! Kudasai!*"

○

During the morning meeting I was looking out of the window and I saw a heron flapping past flying over towards the Imperial Palace. When I got back I found a piece of paper on my desk, it was a fax message from England, in big, hand-written capital letters. "Stop wasting time in the bank. Get a proper job. Start writing. Love Bill." I folded the paper and put it in my pocket.

Yamaguchi looked up from his screen and asked if I'd seen the fax message on my desk. I suppose it was his way of saying he'd read it. He asked if the message was from the London office. I said no, it was from a friend, and he nodded, as if he'd known all along, but he was just checking to make sure.

Through the windows of my screens I watch the market changing, like the sea as the weather changes, dark and shadowy, clear and bright, a mirror of man's nature, paradoxical, sometimes predictable, suddenly irrational, moved by visible and invisible influences.

All one can do is try to steer a sensible course between ru-

mour and fact, the real and the imaginary, or else let the cross-
currents of hope and fear bring everything in a random way,
to where the *gurus* and the experts say it's meant to be.

○

Living in another country, one finds another reality taking
shape in one's mind, like a book.

○

Last night was the Philippines' Independence Day Party. Maria
called me from the Embassy and we had a drink together at a
little place near Satin Doll. She was wearing something made
of blue silk that changed colour like a butterfly's wing when
she moved. Electric blue and indigo. I said she looked marvel-
lous and she smiled.

"Men in evening suits," she said, "so smart, so polite." Her
hair was immaculate, her eyeshadow and her lipstick were in
harmony, and the pearls at her neck caught the colour of her
dress. I asked what kind of party it was going to be. She was
vague; it was all organised by the Tokyo Philippine Wives.

I wasn't clear why I was there. I felt like Maria's escort, which
I was, but the way some of the Embassy staff looked at me I
wondered what she had told them.

Everyone had a certain Philippine style: the men were in
tuxedos and their wives were in silk and satin dresses trimmed
with gold braid, with fans, like a chorus of flamenco dancers
from *Carmen*. There was a band of musicians playing on a stage
and a net full of balloons hanging from the ceiling and a lot of
candlelit tables round the sides of the room. Halfway through
dinner the stage was spotlit for a fashion show with Philippine
models wearing the latest designs from Manila: tropical, Span-
ish, American and Oriental with a lot of bright colours and
feathers.

After dinner I danced a couple of numbers with Maria but she had to talk to people and I danced with one of the models. She was tall, with blonde hair and slanting blue eyes. I guessed her father was in the US military stationed in the Philippines. She was nineteen and it was her first time outside the Philippines. We tried to dance a quick step. I showed her how to put her left hand on my shoulder and her right hand on my left hand. Her fingers were cold and moist. I asked if she was feeling all right, I thought she might have malaria. She said she was fine.

I sat at the table for the next few numbers and talked with a couple from Cleveland, Ohio. He worked for one of the big American car companies and called his wife "Honey." Her hair was apricot blonde. I tried to imagine her as a cheer-leader but it was too long ago: she'd become a wife who listened and smiled while her husband did the talking.

"I keep telling the people back home they better get their shit together or the Japs are going to walk all over us. Do they care?" He shook his head. "They don't even listen. They don't want to know what's going on here. Japan's a problem but it's too much hassle thinking about it. They hope it's going to disappear. They don't even bother to convert the cars from left-hand drive to right-hand drive for the Japanese market." I said it must be hard work selling American cars in Japan. "Like blood out of a stone," he said, "only harder. But it pays the rent."

Maria came back to the table with a woman on her arm. The woman's name was Elena: she had strong features and a good sense of humour that went with her face. She was in her thirties and unmarried.

"I always do what I want to do," she said. "I please myself. Maria understands. She's like me." She described how Japanese men changed their attitude towards her when they learned she was from the Philippines. Assuming she's from America, they're polite, but after discovering she's from the

Philippines, they presume she must be a prostitute and their language is laced with sexual innuendo.

"I don't like sex with little boys," she said. Her statement hung in the air like a question. I said I knew what she meant. I felt uneasy. I had the feeling she was making a pass at me. Something about her was artificial, as if she was playing herself and everything she said was remembered from a film script. Perhaps she'd been too long in Japan.

"I want a child," she said like someone talking about a make of car. She didn't particularly want to get married, but her hormones had told her to have a child. Would I consider being the father? I thanked her and said I'd like to think about it for a while, to get used to the idea. She said I could call any time. I felt sad and I wanted to laugh.

Across the table from us a Canadian was having an argument with his Japanese wife. He was drunk and rude and she was sober and angry but perfectly in control of herself. Her politeness was like ice, so cold it hurt. He wanted to force some response from her; but the more he tried, the less she said which only made him lose his temper further. Suddenly she stood up and smiled and said how much she had enjoyed our company. Then she smiled again and bowed. She was gone before her husband realised what was happening. He got to his feet and walked unsteadily after her.

"She's got balls," said Maria. "More than him anyway. An independent Japanese woman meets a foreign man. She thinks she's found a way out of Japan. He thinks he's found the perfect woman who always says yes. Then they discover they've both made a mistake." I remembered Conrad's description of the loneliness in his marriage with Fumiko, how there was always a part of him, separate and untouched by her, however long they spent together, which he said was a bitter-sweet freedom, like marrying someone with no religion.

Maria suggested we all go on to a Mexican bar.

It was up some stairs on the second floor in a building near Ebisu. The music was loud and the room was small and full of people drinking beers from the bottle. There was a good, raw energy. Maria met a friend celebrating his birthday who asked us to join him. Someone ordered a bottle of champagne. Then another. Maria and Elena left at midnight with a man from Mitsubishi. I was talking with a young Japanese woman. Her name was Miriam. She'd just come back from India and Pakistan with her boyfriend. She told me about a meeting with a holy man and asked if I had any experience of telepathy. I said perhaps I had but it was difficult to tell the difference between certain kinds of telepathy and coincidence.

"I knew I was going to meet you," she said. "I recognised you when you came." The music was loud and we were speaking Japanese. I didn't remember her from anywhere. I thought perhaps I misheard. I asked her to repeat what she'd said.

"I know you," she smiled. It was a simple, open smile and she seemed normal which made what she was saying seem even stranger. People were dancing and I asked her to dance. I liked her, but I was sure we hadn't met before. Her name was unusual. I wondered if she was American, perhaps a *nisei*. When we sat down I asked her where she came from.

"The same place as you," she said. It reminded me of conversations in India and other parts of Asia. She gestured to the man beside her. "Like my boyfriend. We all come from the same place." The man smiled and nodded. He had curly hair and a little beard. He looked like someone from the South of Japan, maybe Okinawa, but the bright brown eyes and the white teeth wouldn't have been unusual in America, Paris or Tehran.

"You must love him," she said in English. Through the champagne, the effect of what she said was like a strong black coffee. I said I didn't feel like going to bed with him but I loved the way she danced. I amused her. Perhaps I was drunker than I realised and I misunderstood what she was saying. Then she asked if I was a spy.

My defences were down. I was unprepared. It was like a trigger. I told her how I felt. I spoke in Japanese although what

I said was un-Japanese. I said her question was wounding, it wasn't the first time I'd been asked the question and every time it hurt me, and damaged my image of Japan. I told her how I came to Japan, wanting to understand the sound of one hand clapping of Hakuin, the *haiku* of Basho and the ink paintings of Sesshu and Sengai. I described my time as a foreigner in a small town in the country, learning Japanese and practising *kendo*: the strangeness and the isolation, teaching in Kyoto and working in a bank in Tokyo. I talked for a while, and at the end I said yes, I was a spy, like everyone who wants to understand another country. She apologised and I said it was OK but it was time for me to go home.

The three of us left the bar together. It was getting light, but there was still a full moon blowing in the sky. We leaned on a wall overlooking a deserted railway line and talked for a while about the moon and the clouds passing across its face like shadows and then we said goodbye. I'd like to meet again, but I can't find the piece of paper with her telephone number.

All I can remember is her name.

Miriam.

○

During the morning meeting Nakamura talked about the US Treasury Bond auctions. I was looking out of the window towards the mountains in the distance. The sun was shining and I could feel the heat on my shoulder and I thought about time and the shadow of my head in the light: how a man's life is the shadow of his actions in the light of eternity.

Nakamura discussed the effect of the President's popularity on the value of the dollar. Yamaguchi stared at his fingers as if he wasn't absolutely sure if they were his or someone else's and Laroche gazed at the ceiling. Nakamura's voice was a near-perfect monotone. Nobody moved. It was the sort of stillness which sometimes settles on gatherings of people who are only half listening. Over the horizon, the mountains were almost invisible against the sky. I imagined what it was like there, in the mountains: the light through the leaves, perhaps the sound of a stream. Nakamura finished his talk, Laroche announced a junket in Hong Kong for everyone on the sales side of the business and the meeting was over.

I hurried back to my desk because I wanted to write down the idea which I had during the meeting but Yamaguchi asked me to bring him a coffee and by the time I sat down to write the idea it had changed.

Time to call clients.

Later.

It's happening. It's finally happening. Saito is close to the first transaction in the restructuring of his portfolio. It's taken eight months talking to him every day to get to this point. He said he would place an order at the end of business today. If the German market eases a little and Saito's order goes through it will be my first deal.

Everyone said winning new business was difficult, but I didn't think that it would be like this.

*Ishi-no-ue-ni-sannen.*

○

It's lunch time.

The market's quiet and the dealing room is almost empty, only one or two people monitoring each section. Some of the secretaries are sitting in a small circle eating from *bento* lunch boxes.

Tokyo Bay is a mosaic of gold stars towards the sun, and the sky is so bright it has no colour, just a white light everywhere to the horizon. I like being by the window: it's good to look up from a green screen and there's the sea and the sky: it gives a perspective, a sense of freedom.

The marching songs of the old Imperial army echo up from a loudspeaker van in the street below.

A dragonfly flits by the window.

On Sunday I saw Fujiko. We met in Shibuya. It's a pity people here still don't often kiss in public. But the way she smiled and blushed, it seemed like the kiss I almost gave her somehow reached her anyway.

We had lunch in an Italian restaurant. The waiter was a Japanese man in his twenties with a spoilt, pretty-boy face who served us with a carefully calculated display of *ingin-burei*—dumb isolence Japanese style. Perhaps he was jealous. Perhaps he didn't like foreigners. I tried to ignore him but it made me conscious of how Fujiko and I appear through Japanese eyes: a Japanese woman and a foreigner. With Sachiko in London, there wasn't a problem: we were just a couple. With Fujiko in Tokyo it's different: she's Japanese and I'm a foreigner and even if it's not how we see ourselves a lot of people here can't help reminding us.

I asked Fujiko what it was like living with her American artist friend in Kamakura. She said she got used to it. Sometimes people said things, but mostly the criticism was implied, by a tone of voice, or a smile. It was a reason for living abroad; perhaps France, perhaps America.

She asked if there was the same kind of prejudice towards foreigners in England as in Japan. She wasn't sure if the meaning of "prejudice" was the same as "racism."

I said some people still think prejudice towards foreigners is a problem of racism. But the real problem is culturism: assuming one culture is superior or inferior to another, discriminating on the basis of culture, being prejudiced against other cultures.

I wanted to say racism is skin-deep, like acne; culturism is in the blood, like a virus, and there's no instant cure.

The waiter appeared and presented the wrong bottle of wine with an unconvincing politeness. He apologised in such an insincere way that Fujiko and I laughed, which probably delayed our fettucini another quarter of an hour. It didn't matter. We understood each other. The situation was us and them, and we were right and the waiter and all the other people like the waiter, with their hard eyes, cold manners and silences, were wrong. We were happy because we were right and they were miserable because they were wrong, which made it all the more fun.

Fujiko talked about the film producer in his mid-fifties who wants to have an affair with her. He says he has a *rorikon* feeling for her. If she agrees to come for a weekend to Hawaii he'll arrange for her to be his research assistant in a fictional documentary he's making about a teenage TV star who committed suicide. The way she described him, the man is a caricature of a rich, middle-aged Japanese, who can afford to do almost anything he wants. He has no morality, no beliefs or philosophy of any kind—only the will to make more and more money to satisfy his increasingly strange desires.

I'd forgotten what it's like to be with a Japanese girl. I'd forgotten the lightness and the humour, the pleasing tension and the elegance of control, the curious discipline of saying one thing and meaning another, and the art of knowing when yes means no, and no means yes, perhaps.

I told Fujiko I was out of practice and she said she understood. We were speaking another kind of Japanese: not the language I used in discussions with *salarimen* in banks and insurance companies with all the formalities, automatic greetings and expressions of regret or gratitude.

With Fujiko I was talking in a way I hadn't talked for a long time, not since I was with Sachiko.

I kept thinking about Sachiko. The colour of her hair, the sound of her voice, the light in her eyes, and her way of pausing in the middle of speaking, just long enough for another meaning to emerge from the previous sentence, then continuing, as if she suddenly remembered what she was going to say. And her sense of humour, and her strength of character. A lot of things about her reminded me of Sachiko.

She told me about her time with the American, an artist called Milton, and I told her about my time with Sachiko. One can tell a lot from how people talk about previous lovers. Some treat them as case studies and the conversation becomes an anatomy lesson, others lock everything away, like skeletons in cupboards or else they display selected parts, unnaturally preserved for public view. A lot of people prefer to forget everything. Only a few are prepared to remember. I liked how Fujiko talked about Milton.

She described the colour of his eyes.

Before she came to Tokyo she lived in the country. There weren't any foreigners, only the occasional missionary and they were always strange old men with dirty grey beards who talked about the crucifixion and love. She'd seen faces of people with blue eyes in magazines and films but it was only after coming to Tokyo that she met someone whose eyes were blue. Then she discovered there were different colours of blue; blue-yellow, blue-green, blue-grey, and the colours seemed to change the closer one was to someone. With Milton she used to look into his eyes and sometimes she saw the sea and sometimes she saw the sky. After making love his eyes seemed to change colour. She asked if there was any physical explanation. I said I didn't know but maybe it had something to do with blood going to the head.

After lunch we went for a walk towards Meiji Jingu. It was warm and the streets were crowded with people in smart summer clothes looking at each other's style. Under the trees and along the side of the road, there were foreigners with little stalls selling cheap novelties and jewellery, on the other side of the pavement from shops selling clothes by Chanel and Yves Saint Laurent and new antique galleries selling old Victorian school desks for a thousand dollars each. Near Harajuku the streets were crowded with day-trippers up from the country and tourists and foreigners on their way to see the street bands playing.

By the time we came to the entrance to the Meiji Jingu shrine the sky had clouded over. The white stones of the avenue between the pine trees and the grey sky were like a back drop to a dream sequence in a film: tiny figures moving along a road of white stones enclosed on either side by the tall dark walls of the forest.

Passing under the great *torii* spirit bridge, I thought of the last time I was there, ten years ago, with Philip and Kinuyo on New Year's Day, in a procession of several hundred thousand people, wrapped against the cold, moving slowly towards the shrine. The procession had a strange feeling; it wasn't just the odd sensation of being among a vast number of people moving in the same direction. There was also an undercurrent of something like hysteria. Everyone was perfectly ordered, everyone was in control, but there was also a sense that for no particular reason, it could all change suddenly and anything might happen. As the procession got closer to the shrine, the noise ahead of us became like the sound of the rain on the roof of the *dojo* hall in Kashima, but sharper and more metallic and people everywhere were throwing coins and notes wrapped around coins towards the great collecting boxes of the shrine.

I told Fujiko my memory and she said it was also the first time she'd been to Meiji Jingu for years. The mood between us was strange and we were silent as we approached the shrine.

We prayed together and as we were leaving, we passed a couple in traditional wedding clothes having their photograph taken. He was wearing spectacles and smiling, she was expressionless under a mask of white powder and an elaborate black wig and headdress. They were standing very still, watched by a group of aged family and friends, while the photographer arranged the folds of the bride's *kimono*. Fujiko didn't even glance in their direction, and we walked by the little gathering without saying anything.

Fujiko came back to Nakameguro and stayed till the early evening. I went with her to the station. We were closer than before but we didn't talk much. I think we were both thinking about what had happened. I said I hoped to see her again soon. Perhaps we could go somewhere out of Tokyo, somewhere in the mountains. She smiled as we said goodbye and then, almost as an after-thought, she kissed me.

"*Matte-imasu*," she said. "I'll be waiting."

○

It's eight o'clock in the evening and I'm waiting for the train to Nakameguro.

This is the time, after work, when everyone's going out with friends to a bar, or back to their wives and families, when I remember I'm a *gaijin* and it hurts like poverty or injustice. It's the pain of being other. I'm used to being one of a racial minority. Usually I can ignore it. But sometimes it hits hard like I imagine it hits waking up in prison. A sharp blow—an invisible wound, like the point of a stiletto through the armpit into the heart. Nothing shows, nobody knows what the matter is, but if nothing's done it's fatal. Internal bleeding. Like it was for Johnny Tallis. He was hurt and nobody looked after him. The reason nobody looked after him is simple and ugly. He was a *gaijin*.

Tony described a similar thing he saw last week at Roppongi crossing. A car swerved to a halt alongside the pavement. It had diplomatic number plates. Two men, not Japanese, maybe Middle Eastern, grabbed a foreigner walking along the street. They dragged him towards the car beating him about the face. There was a policeman directing the traffic at the crossing and Tony ran back to get him, but the policeman had already seen what was happening. Tony pointed at the struggling men but the policeman did nothing. Tony ran towards them as the car door slammed and the car pulled away into the traffic. Tony summed it up neatly. "One law for the Japanese, another for foreigners." He said it was a typical example of the Japanese problem; what he calls the Japanese "fuck-you attitude." His answer to the problem is simple.

"If the Japanese attitude is 'fuck you,'" he said, "fuck them."

Looking at the faces of the people around me, it's not so simple.

If I was lying on my back with blood coming out of the mouth, they wouldn't stand on my face. But they wouldn't help me either. *Ligada! Kitanai-mon!* They'd walk by on the other side like they did with Johnny Tallis.

It's taken me this long to realise.

Ever since Johnny died I've been blaming the Japanese for his death. Death by suicide. Death by misadventure or death by negligence. Sometimes doing nothing does more harm than doing something. In a way they killed him. The Japanese killed Johnny Tallis by doing nothing. Of course it was an accident, a regrettable misunderstanding, a most unfortunate mistake. But they killed him. The death has been between me and these people. All this time the shadow's been there. I didn't know it was there. I wasn't even aware of it. Or perhaps I was aware of it, but I didn't know what it was. All this time I've been trying to make sense of a shadow. Johnny's death cast a shadow and because there was a shadow I was looking for a reason why there was a shadow and I blamed Japan. The shadow of suspicion. Perhaps it was my fault. Perhaps it was only in my imagination and there was nothing there, only the shadow of Johnny's death and now even the shadow's gone.

But I'm still a foreigner.

○

The market's like a dinosaur's tail, it's not sure where it's going.

Yamaguchi's talking to someone in Mitsubishi about the prospect for economic growth in Europe at the beginning of the next year.

I just called Saito-san. He's still interested in the companies we talked about last week but he's waiting for the market to go a bit lower before committing himself.

This morning I talked with Kit Casey in accounts about expenses. He said my expenses should be higher; people might think I wasn't looking after clients, going to clubs and bars, and keeping the customers satisfied. He said I shouldn't worry about spending too much. He knows of some people, not necessarily in this company, making a lot of money on expenses. It wasn't any of his business, he has to work with the numbers people give him and he doesn't want to call anyone a liar, but he knows someone who made fifteen thousand dollars last year and that was just on travel expenses. "You'd be surprised who," he said. "Perhaps you know anyway." I asked who he was talking about but he wouldn't tell me. He thought perhaps he'd said too much already.

If it was a person in the company I can make a guess. But someone who massages their expenses might also be someone who looks in other people's desks and reads their papers.

○

It's after midnight.

The windows are open but the candle's flame is steady. After the lights and the noise and the people it's good to be alone by candlelight.

This evening I went to a party at Forbes' house. There were a lot of people there; about equal numbers of Japanese and foreigners. There were some familiar faces: not too many bankers, a few lawyers, one or two people in advertising and several journalists. I spent most of the party with an old lady called Dora, an Englishwoman who'd come to Japan in the 1930s. At university she read the books of Lafcadio Hearn and decided to visit Japan. She went by ship. When she arrived in Japan she knew it was where she wanted to spend the rest of her life.

"Sailing towards Tokyo, I saw Mount Fuji," she said. "It was like coming home." She married a Japanese diplomat and became a Japanese citizen in 1935. When the war broke out her husband was in South America and she was in Japan. She lived in Tokyo right through the Second World War. I asked what it was like.

"No problem at all," she said. "No problem at all. As a Japanese citizen I wasn't interned like some foreigners. And my neighbours were very good to me—much more helpful than English people." She was in her late seventies, but there was passion in her voice and anger in her grey eyes. "As for the Americans, they were barbarians." Towards the end of the war, when the Americans were dropping bombs around the clock she went to buy some meat from a local shop. Food was rationed. She had her ration card but there was nothing to buy.

"Even when the city was burning and hundreds of people were dying, they were so kind to me." Her eyes were glistening, with old age perhaps, or the pity of the past remembered. " 'Please, please, forgive us,' they said, 'we have nothing to sell you.' " She wanted to make sure I understood what she was saying.

"They asked me to forgive them because they had no food, while the Americans and the British were killing their brothers, and sisters. That's why I love this country," she said. "That's why I love Japan."

I made the mistake of mentioning the Bataan Death March. As far as she was concerned it was all American propaganda, like the stories about the Burma Railway. Her explanation was simple.

"The jungle isn't a healthy place," she said, "the white man isn't used to it; even the Japanese soldiers were ill. But the Americans and British blame the Japanese for diseases like dysentery and malaria. It's ridiculous—like stories of Japanese soldiers torturing their prisoners are exaggerated rumours. As for the War Crimes Trials, even at the time, everyone knew it was unfair. Justice is always on the side of the victors.

"The Japanese liberated East Asia from the rule of the white man and turned the countries from colonies to independent states. The dropping of the atomic bomb on Hiroshima was a crime against humanity and so was the bomb dropped on Nagasaki, a cynical experiment by America, testing its weapons on a civilian population." Her thoughts moved according to the passions of fifty years ago and while she talked about the special and unique qualities of the Japanese people I thought of the Japanese soldiers who maintained their military discipline and code of honour, who refused to surrender at the end of the war, and remained in hiding in remote islands in the Pacific. Dora, like those men, preserved a mystical belief in the superhuman nature of the Emperor and the density of Japan. Listening to her I was hearing the authentic voice of Japan in the 1930s, uncannily preserved in the body of an elderly Englishwoman.

Her thinking was Japanese, but the way she spoke her mind was English. Most Japanese of her age would probably have avoided talking about the war, at least with a foreigner, but Dora talked with the energy and conviction of someone defending the cause of truth and justice.

Her case was simple. In 1919, at the Treaty of Versailles, Japan as one of the signatories proposed a clause guaranteeing racial equality. The proposal was rejected by the other, Western countries. By this action, the Japanese people knew America and Europe really believed the white races were superior. The Japanese understood they would not be accepted as equal citizens of the world by white people. "From that moment," she said, "perhaps war was inevitable."

I asked if she missed England. The question seemed to surprise her. It was difficult for her to think of a reason for returning. Her life was in Japan. Her family and friends were here. She went back once, in the sixties, for her father's funeral. London was more or less as she remembered it, but the people were ruder.

"They seemed to have lost their self-respect," she said. "I saw no point in going back to live in such a country."

She preferred to talk about Japan and the strangeness of foreigners who live here, who do not speak the language but claim to understand the country. Like most old people in a country where something of the Confucian reverence for old age survives, she didn't expect to be interrupted. As she talked and I nodded, I thought of Dora before she came to Japan: reading literature at London University in the early 1930s, wearing one of those funny hats they used to wear, smiling for a photograph beside an old-fashioned car.

What made her abandon that past, her other life, so completely? Love certainly. But perhaps there was some other reason. Japanese diplomats rarely marry foreigners. In the 1930s someone in Dora's position could have caused suspicion. She might have felt the need to show loyalty to Japan. Perhaps at first she had to think herself into the part but gradually it could have become second nature and the role she chose to play became her personality. Or perhaps it's all a double bluff and somewhere behind her curious anti-Western, pro-Japanese façade, she's still an Englishwoman.

○

The windows of the train are open and the rice fields are golden. Fujiko's reading a book and I'm looking out of the window at the mountains on the horizon, glowing in the afternoon light.

The people in the carriage look different from people in Tokyo; their faces are copper-coloured, country faces, shaped by labour in the fields and lined by strong sunlight. A thousand years ago Sei Shonagon was amused and horrified by the appearance of country people and a hundred years ago in Tokyo it used to be an afternoon's amusement to go to the railway stations to watch the people arriving from the country. It was fun to stare at their strange faces, clumsy manners and hear their quaint speech.

Even now, looking at some of the other passengers, it's difficult to believe they're the same race as the people I see on the underground in Tokyo. But without knowing anything about him I trust the face of the man opposite me with his grizzled chin and his sticking-out teeth more than the smooth, well-fed features and the automatic smile of a *salariman* like Yamaguchi or Takahashi. I'm prejudiced. When I first came to Japan, I lived in the country and I still prefer it.

A long blast from the train as it begins the climb up into the hills. Fujiko looks up from her book and we smile at each other. A warm wind blows through the carriage windows carrying a fragrance of dry earth and wood smoke. The man beside me takes a photograph of his two friends sitting opposite, sleeping with their heads pillowed against each other. A dragonfly appears from somewhere, the man notices me looking at it and asks if there are dragonflies in the land where I come from. I say yes, there are, and he nods his head as if I've told him something rare and wonderful. "Ah," he says, "I guessed so. Maybe, it's the same everywhere?"

"Yes," I say. "I suppose it's the same everywhere." He smiles and his teeth are gold.

◯

The sky is dark grey.

The rain is trickling through the branches of the wistaria.

Fujiko is out of the room changing into a *yukata*. When she comes back we're going outside to bathe in the hot spring *rotenburo*. It's good to be with her.

Looking at her just now I saw so many people in her face and I wanted to tell her but if I'd said something the words would have changed the meaning of the silence between us. So we sat here, without saying anything, with the *shoji* windows pushed back, and the rain falling.

◯

The *rotenburo* is a rock pool under a maple tree surrounded on three sides by a bamboo screen. There was no one else. We took off our clothes and stepped into the water. At first it was almost too hot. We lay there, looking up through the steam into the branches of the tree, listening to the sound of the rain on the leaves. With her in the warm water, in the twilight, with the shadow of a tree above us, was like a strange and mysterious dream.

Then there were voices and three young men appeared: they took off their clothes and slid into the water near us. We all lay there, for a while longer, almost invisible to each other in the gathering dusk until Fujiko whispered that she was going to go back and as she got out of the water her body was like a white shadow in the darkness.

○

It's seven o'clock in the evening and Fujiko's asleep.

This afternoon we went to the temple in the village, called the Temple of Present Happiness, and met a priest who told us with a twinkle in his eye of another related temple in Nagano called the Temple of Future Happiness. He suggested we should pray in both temples.

There were rows of stone *Jizo-sammas* with little hats of damp, faded red cotton and a large *Jizo-samma* draped with strings of multi-coloured paper cranes. I thought about the women praying for the health of their children or the souls of aborted foetuses, and that reminded me of a statistic I read somewhere, about Japanese women, during the course of their lives, having an average of 3.5 abortions. It wasn't what I wanted to think about but the statistic wouldn't go away. I looked at Fujiko and wondered if she had already had an abortion, or if she was going to have one.

She was reading an inscription on a stone. She called me over. According to the inscription Basho visited the temple. Nearby there was a fountain of bubbling water pouring into a stone basin, with a long-handled bamboo cup resting on the rim. I dipped the cup into the water and poured it over my hand. The water was warm. I rinsed both my hands and raised another cupful to my lips; it had an odd taste, like warm mineral water with a hint of sulphur. I thought of Basho tasting the curious, almost metallic taste. It was like receiving something I'd been wanting for a long time. I knew, or thought I knew, a moment of Basho's life exactly, as if it were my own: the moment he tasted the water from the fountain.

When I first came to Japan and followed in his footsteps on the Narrow Road to the Deep North, it was a pilgrimage of the imagination. I hoped to find something on the way that might bring me closer to him. I went to Matsushima Bay and looked at the islands like dark clouds floating in a diamond sky and listened to the sound of the wind in the pine trees and the waves on the sea shore just like Basho's *haiku: Matsushima— Matsushima, ah Matsushima! Matsushima!* In Yamagata I heard the sound of the cicadas like a stone drill, piercing the rocks, and I saw the Milky Way like a silver mist over the shadow of Sado Island. I heard what Basho heard and saw what he had seen but somehow the immediacy I wanted was missing— there was always a distance between us.

Suddenly, without even thinking about it, I find what I was looking for, in the taste of water.

○

It's early morning and Fujiko's asleep, and I'm sitting cross-legged at the table by the window, as the sky grows paler.

She's lying on her side and her hair half covers her face. Her mouth is slightly open, as if a spell had caught her in the act of saying something. Her shoulder is bare.

It's the old question: if one doesn't know oneself, how can one know another?

I see her there and listen to her breathing and once again I'm drawn out of myself into the mystery of someone else. And this time, as always, it's different. Not love perhaps, but something close to love. We would both prefer it to be love but we know it isn't, which is a kind of freedom. Once or twice I've sensed her talking to me as if I were someone else, thinking of me as Milton, and sometimes when I'm with her, I find myself thinking of Sachiko. These things I suppose are inevitable: the echoes of other people, the ghosts of previous lovers.

Being with her has reminded me of a Japan I'd forgotten. Talking with people in banks on telephones and discussing money and politics in restaurants and bars is one Japan; listening to the sound of the water trickling into the pool and watching the shapes and colours of the mountains emerge in the early morning light is another.

The men in suits and Hermès ties have changed the way I feel about Japan; they have come between me and the country I used to know. Or perhaps they've showed me a Japan which was always here, like the pine trees and the sound of the crickets.

When I first came here I was looking for something, like a code, or a secret language which, once I discovered it, would enable me to understand Japan. I wanted to find its true meaning, gain enlightenment and enter *satori*. It's taken some time to realise there's no code and no *koan* and looking for the real Japan was like trying to catch the moon's reflection in a teapot, since it only existed in my imagination.

I met Sachiko and Japan became a person instead of a place full of people: I wasn't a foreigner. While we were together I was part of Japan.

But like every traveller who goes away, when I came back I found the place where I was had changed. Japan was different and I was a foreigner again.

It's getting lighter. I understand why the shuffling of Mah-Jongg pieces is called the chattering of sparrows. Fujiko sighs and turns over.

○

Fujiko's kneeling in front of a mirror and I'm watching her putting on lipstick, thinking about the ritual of a woman looking at herself in a mirror. She pauses every so often to touch a bit more lipstick to her lips but she doesn't take her gaze away from her reflection, except when I ask a question. She just leans forward slightly so that she can see me in the mirror.

I'm going to try and make her smile.

"The mirror reflects the heart," I say.

"Maybe," says Fujiko. Her expression doesn't change. I wait another few seconds and as she puts the vermilion pencil to her lips, I ask how I can make her smile and she looks at me, takes the pencil away and smiles.

○

It's mid-morning and I'm with Fujiko and we're walking along a little country road, past an old man in a baseball cap hoeing onions. On the other side of the valley the peaks of the mountains are half hidden in slowly moving clouds. Somewhere, probably over in the next valley, there's a sound which could be thunder, or it could be a plane in the distance. A path leads off the road, into the woods, and it looks as if it might lead somewhere interesting so we follow it. The *semi* are incessant. The path leads to a bamboo grove and a row of half a dozen gravestones.

The largest of the stones is almost the size of a man: a tall weather-worn boulder which could have come from the river in the valley below. It has no inscription, but the stones near it have dates going back two hundred years. For a few seconds I stand listening to the chorus of the *semi* and the distant murmur of the river through the trees. It's a beautiful place and I feel a curious kind of envy for those who are remembered here, and for their descendants, making their offerings of incense and *sake* with the breeze blowing through the bamboos and the light in the shadows shifting and flickering like sunlight under water.

The frosts have carved away the names. Looking at the stones, the weathered surfaces, I am on the brink of remembering something, as if I know this place from a long time ago. Perhaps I recognise it from a dream, or a picture, or a poem—

somewhere like Andrew Marvell's garden: a place to contemplate "a green thought in a green shade."

Fujiko's wearing open-toed sandals and the grass is still wet with last night's rain. "Let's go back," she says, "there are too many insects. There are always mosquitoes in graveyards."

Back on the road again we pass between fields of *soba* and come to a village where the houses are traditional wooden buildings. One of the houses has been turned into a museum. Two old *obaachans* welcome us inside. It's dark and it takes a while to get used to the shadow. There are three dusty cases of exhibits: fossils found in the local quarry; Jamon arrowheads made of obsidian, shaped like willow leaves; pieces of pottery from the Nara and Heian period; chipped Edo lacquer, a collection of dusty cigarette packets, a paper lantern and a few dark wooden plates. One *obaachan* shows us an agreement which she says is 150 years old, between the local landowner and the village elders on the amount of rice to be collected each year. It is hand written: the calligraphy is hard and clean and disciplined.

The old women are happy to talk and I ask when electricity first came to the village. I expect them to say some time after the last war. Thinking of the past, the old woman has an innocent smile. "A long time ago," she says. "Before I was born, in 1910 at the end of the Taisho era." We thank the old *obaachans* and go outside and the sun is shining.

The hills are blue as wood smoke and around a corner in the road a man is burning some branches in a field. He's wearing a T-shirt which reads, "That's much better! Good company with a great vision of the future," and his rubber boots have imitation leopard-skin fur trimmings.

We come to a shrine. There are mosquitoes everywhere. As we clap hands before praying I think there must be a *haiku* about this situation: standing before the shrine, clapping one's hands, in a haze of mosquitoes.

The cloud mists moving over the peaks of the mountains remind me of Wang Wei's poem, the song of the Peach Tree

Spring, about the man who followed a river to its source and found himself in a land between the mountains and the clouds, where people had taken refuge from the world and become immortal. Perhaps, like the man when he returned home, I will only remember having gone deep into the hills.

The dragonfly on the wooden pillar in the sunlight; the caterpillar hanging in the air, climbing an invisible thread into the branches of an ilex tree; the thatched barns with the wooden rakes and baskets neatly ranged along their walls; the doors made of straw woven together with bamboo and the little bundle of leaves, tied together, lying across the path in the forest of the shrine: all these things may one day seem as distant as the light from a star on the other side of the universe.

But the sun is bright and the leaves are green and for no particular reason I feel as if I've somehow just woken out of one life into another.

○

It's a sunny day and Tokyo Bay is pretty as a postcard.

I've just been talking with Maria Santini in Administration. She told me about the mechanical massage chair she uses every day when she gets home from work. She has a bath in the *o-furo* and then sits in the chair for twenty minutes having a mechanical massage. It loosens her shoulders nicely for calligraphy.

I assumed she was talking about Chinese calligraphy, with a brush, but then she described how she cuts the points of her own quills. I asked why she practised italic not *shodo* calligraphy. She looked at me as if the answer to my question was hardly worth saying, it was so obvious.

"It's European," she said. "All day I spend with Japanese people. When I get home at night I need to relax, I need to be European."

She's strange. Very few Japanese seem to like her. Her face has a semi-permanent sneer: the expression of a woman who has managed to convince herself that elegance is beauty. There's something sinister about her—sinister and pathetic, as if the person she seems to be, with her rings and handbags and shoes, is the only person she is, and there's no one inside, only the ghost of someone who came to Japan fifteen or twenty years ago. Perhaps that's why she gets on with Laroche; Japan has affected them in similar ways. On the surface they seem like other people. But inwardly they've changed: the person who was there has gone away or something else has entered them.

They're an odd pair; like a late-millennium Mr and Mrs Kurtz, sitting in their air-conditioned offices in Tokyo, organising things.

She wears gold and he wears platinum, but not too much because after living here they know the way to show how much you have is by not showing it. They were here together from the very beginning, when the only other person in the office was that old dragon, Laroche's personal assistant, Noguchi.

They know who everyone is, where everything is, and how it all works. It's all at their fingertips. But that's their business.

○

It's after midnight but there's still a grasshopper making a noise in the next-door garden.

Joe came over this evening and we went for *sushi* at the place on the other side of the railway line. He's thinking about leaving Japan. He's been working for the company for ten years and he wants a change. He feels he's turning into someone he doesn't want to be. "Maybe it's the company, maybe it's Japan," he said. "All I know is I want to begin another life. Before it's too late." It didn't sound as if his problem had anything to do with the company or Japan. I said why worry about time passing? Everyone gets older. Joe said it wasn't just time passing.

"I've been here almost twenty years," he said, "I want to

know what it's like to be me, in a place where they don't speak Japanese." He hasn't told the company yet, but he's more or less decided. He's not sure where he'll go from here; maybe South America, or Indonesia.

It's difficult to believe but I think he means it. Joe's really going to leave Japan. It's almost as strange as a Japanese deciding to emigrate. But it shows that he was there all the time, even when he got drunk and started rambling in Japanese to the barman, using the language a drunken *salariman* would use, not a foreigner, he was still there inside it all.

Fluent Japanese, bi-cultural, ten years in the semi-conductor industry in Japan. The company will have to look hard to find someone like Joe.

We talked about how some Japanese shape their faces into masks, others wear masks which change their faces, and Joe reminded me of the Zen challenge, "Show me your original face, show me the face you had before you were born."

Joe went into a monologue about the way foreign companies operate in Japan. He thinks no one really knows what's going on here. It's a total failure of intelligence: most foreign news agencies and businesses still have representatives who don't speak Japanese, so any foreigner who knows the language is high-profile, and Joe's had enough of it. He doesn't believe there's any particular mystery about Japan, but to know what's really going on here it's necessary to speak the language. He said if people want to understand Japan, but they can't be bothered to learn Japanese, they should read the Analects of Confucius.

"I'm serious," he said. "People can learn more about the secret mind of the Japanese from the Analects of Confucius than all those books about the way Japan works, written by people with university doctorates and degrees from Harvard Business School." I said I didn't know he was a Confucianist. He smiled and told me his favourite quotation from the Analects. "The virtue of the superior man is like wind: the virtue of the ordinary man is like grass. When the wind blows the grass bends.''

Talking about Japan, he sounds like a man who's lost heart, or his heart's no longer in his work. He's tired of trying to explain the situation on the ground in Japan to people in the company at head office. They want to have their prejudices confirmed, they don't want to learn anything new. Either Japan is a trading partner and a friend of democratic capitalism, or it's a materialistic, possibly totalitarian, state which is taking over the world by abusing the free trade system, engineering global markets to its advantage. Either Japan's an ally, or it's an enemy. There's no middle ground, as far as the company is concerned. If Joe tries to give them the Japanese perspective, they say he's making things more complicated than they really are. What the company wants is clear information which can be used for decision making and policy formation.

Reading between the lines, I'd say the company has taken Joe for granted. They assume he's a lifer, they've forgotten he's not one of them and they treat him as if he's gone native.

Living in another country is a difficult art: too close and one loses perspective, too far away and one misses the significant detail. There are no rules because the situation's always changing. Learning to live in another country is something between an instinct and a skill, like a sense of balance.

I told Joe how I thought of Japan, as a labyrinth which anyone who wants to understand the Japanese has to enter in order to find, somewhere in the middle of it, at the centre, the secret of Japan. But the labyrinth has a curious effect on people who enter it; gradually as one gets towards the middle one forgets where one is coming from, who one is and why one is there, so that by the time one actually reaches the centre of the maze and finds the secret of Japan, it has no meaning.

Joe said perhaps the Japanese language was a labyrinth, but not Japan. As far as he's concerned, there's no secret: Japan is Japan. He's heard it described as lots of things: either it's something strange and slightly sinister like a swamp or a slime mould culture, or a headless monster or an octopus, or else it's a shame culture or a vertical society, a homogeneous nation state or a fragile superpower. He's not impressed by the people who claim to know Japan.

"Look at the people who claim to know Japan," he said. "First they make an intellectual model of Japan. Then they take the model to pieces, label the different parts, and write books explaining how the parts fit together to make something they call Japan.

"You know the sort," he said, "read this book and become an expert on Japan." I asked how he would describe it and he looked round at the man behind the *sushi* counter and the people on either side of us. He reckoned each person in the bar would give a different answer. Perhaps the old man in the corner with the red face would describe Japan as *wagawaga no kuni*, and give a lecture about *yamato-damashi*. The *salarimen* with Mitsubishi company buttons in their lapels would know what the old man was talking about, but they'd probably use the language of technocrats, and explain it as a country with a disciplined and educated work force, with the money and technology to do what it likes. The man behind the counter might agree with them, or he might say Japan had a *shima-guni konjo*, an island country complex, which should be more *intanashionaru*.

"This shop," said Joe. "these people, this is Japan. It's like the slogan of the old co-prosperity sphere: 'The whole world under one roof.' "

It was a strange evening.

Joe wasn't drunk, but the way he was talking was different: there was something like a shadow between his sentences which didn't seem to go away, even when he laughed.

We'd finished our *sake* and we were drinking cups of hot green tea. I asked what the matter was. There was a flicker in his eyes and for a moment I thought he was going to cry.

"I don't want to die here," he said. "Living in Japan's killing me. I can't breathe. I want to get out of it." I asked why and he said it was like the fire sermon of the Buddha; a man in a burning house has a different perspective. He'd woken up and he knew what he had to do. I asked what decided him.

"Corporatist Confucianism, post-Buddhist materialism, bureaucratic totalitarianism," he said, "racism, nationalism, every goddamn Japan-ism."

He nodded in the direction of a tiny glass tank full of grey water. There was a big fish with black and white markings, longer than the length of the tank, mouthing at us blindly with its gills over a silver thread of air bubbling through the water. I knew what Joe was going to say before he said it.

◯

Next door the men have finished demolishing the old wooden house. They've cut down all the trees: the ancient pine, the cherry trees, the willow and the maples, they've removed the stone lantern and the stepping stones and cleared away the ornamental pool. Everything's gone and where the garden was there's a large rectangle of bare earth, criss-crossed with bulldozer tracks.

I never spoke to old man Uehara, and in the last few months before he died I hardly saw him. But he was a link with a Japan which has almost ceased to exist. Knowing he was there, somewhere, telling the beads of his rosary in front of the tablets of his ancestors, I felt closer to the past. Like incense in sunlight, his presence was an invisible reminder of another world.

Sometimes, in the evenings, I imagined the old man's spirit walking once again in the garden in the cool of the day: a shadowless memory under the willow tree, listening to the last of the cicadas.

Now it's a building site with half a dozen men in white helmets and pale khaki uniforms sitting on some plywood having their lunch break. James Kirkup said the Japanese look at life through prose-coloured spectacles. It's true. I feel angry with them. The destruction of the garden is like a betrayal because here, in Japan where the past is revered, the destruction of something ancient seems almost like a breaking of the unwritten law that the past is holy.

What was old and beautiful has been lost. But perhaps I'm unfair to the men sitting there cross-legged, smoking cigarettes. They're no more traitors to their tradition than any other Japanese. I remember the same sense of betrayal when I went to Matsushima, and looked at the landscape which Basho looked at, a place known as one of the three most beautiful places in Japan, and there, breaking the line of the horizon, was a row of factory chimneys blowing a cloud of yellow smoke.

The Japanese respect the past but they also respect profits.

Perhaps it's better to think of the disappearance of the garden as another example of *mono-no-aware*, a sign of time passing, like the wind blowing through the cherry flowers, and the falling of the maple leaves.

It's difficult with the sound of a generator turning over and the juddering of a road drill. Even Mozart at full volume can't beat the noise of the past disintegrating.

○

The sun is shining and the market is rising like a thermometer in a heat wave.

This morning Saito told me he's almost certain to buy some stock in the German insurance sector. He also asked me to prepare another model portfolio for the French market. Now that everyone else is buying he feels more confident about entering the market. I couldn't help saying he'd have made more money if he entered the market when I advised, six weeks ago. Last month the market increased by ten per cent. Saito laughed. Then, only a few people were buying and he would have felt nervous. Now more people are buying he wants to buy.

"*Anshin desu,*" he said. "I feel safe. *Shingo akakeba, mina wa-*

*tatte mo kamawanai.* Even when the traffic lights are red, if everyone crosses together, it doesn't matter."

I wanted to ask what he thought of lemmings, but I didn't know how to say "lemming" in Japanese. Now I've looked it up in the dictionary: *ikko-nezumi*.

This morning Yamaguchi told me that the Canadian we interviewed last month is coming to join us in a few weeks' time. "Laroche met him," Yamaguchi smirked, "he liked him." Yamaguchi knows the situation: saying Laroche likes the Canadian, Yamaguchi was reminding me that Laroche doesn't like me and as far as he's concerned, I'm here without his approval.

Talking with someone in accounts about the way the office finances are organised can be an eye-opener. Some branch offices of foreign companies in Tokyo are run like independent companies. Extra costs and expenses are easily explained by the peculiar nature of the Japanese market or the unusual way people do business here. Back in Europe or America or wherever the company has its headquarters no one has enough experience of Japan to ask questions.

Running an office in Tokyo can be a licence to print money. When the markets were expanding, the regulations were changing, there was no law against insider trading and ramping shares was taken for granted. Everyone was making money and no one had the time or the inclination to find out what was happening. In the confusion people made mistakes and errors of judgement which were often to their advantage. Someone sitting on a gold mine either keeps it secret or registers their claim and puts a fence around it. The money kept everyone sweet, and the sweetness was called the harmony of *wa*.

A lot of foreigners convinced themselves they were learning some special Japanese way of doing things, when in fact they were just being corrupted.

Some became members of the *karaoke* club of foreigners who sing the Japanese song. As if by magic, the more malleable they became, the less resistance they met, until eventually they were like glove puppets. They believed they were getting to understand Japan and really they were being manipulated. They behaved like spokesmen for people who were supposed to be their competitors, explaining the success of rival companies and their own failures in terms of Japanese culture, which it was in their interest to make as inscrutable as possible. Although they claimed a special expertise in Japanese matters, few spoke more than half a dozen phrases of Japanese— enough to order a coffee, or direct a taxi home in the evening, but not enough to run an office. They were vulnerable, they needed help and the price was co-operation. It was easy to play on their weaknesses: the Japanese complimented them on their sensitivity to Japanese culture and the speed at which they understood the Japanese way of doing things. There were hints that after a while the understanding might become a profitable friendship. Once there was a profitable friendship, there was always the risk it might for some reason come to an end, and money and goodwill would stop. Pride, greed and fear hollowed them out and they became *karaoke* people, singing other people's songs.

Strange things happen in the no-man's-land between cultures: people change. They lose something of themselves and gain something else. They forget the customs and behaviour of their own country, they ignore the difficult things like religion, conscience and morality, and they pick up the habits of where they are, and they use the one-word language everyone understands: money.

○

It's Saturday afternoon and the sun is shining.

The windows are open and there's the sound of an aeroplane disappearing into the distance and now and again a bang or a crash from the building site next door. The heat haze, the sound of the aeroplane disappearing into the vastness of the sky and the brilliant white of the concrete buildings opposite: the heat, the sound and the light make a pattern of energy with a meaning, like brush strokes form a character.

The garden has ceased to exist.

The pool where the dragonfly flickered in the sunlight has disappeared, the trees are gone and the stone lantern has been sold. This morning I talked with one of the men from the site who told me there's going to be a four-storey residential apartment block. He said he hoped the noise wouldn't disturb me. I said it was sad to see the old place go, but I was looking forward to the new building.

○

It's Sunday evening and Fujiko's just gone back home. There's a Mozart quintet still playing; KV581, composed in the year of the French Revolution. We were listening to it and I was wondering what the music meant to her. Could she hear through the pomp and the pathos, the spirit of the age? She said Mozart is universal. But if Mozart belongs to everyone how can Japan be different from anywhere else? I suppose we were talking about the distances between us. We'd been discussing it, off and on, all day.

It began when I got up this morning. I went to have a shower and there was a hair, a single black hair on the white ceramic surface of the bath. It was like a sign: but its meaning was deeper than language, like the sight of blood or the smell of sex. It was the answer to a question I'd been avoiding for a long time. Looking at it, I knew more clearly than a year of weekends with Fujiko could have taught me, how I felt about her and how I felt about Japan.

The solitary hair was intimate and alien at the same time. It wasn't mine and it wasn't Tanya's. I couldn't hide the difference from myself because I'd just woken up. As it says in the *Tao Te Ching*: "A hair's breadth, and Heaven and Earth are set apart." I turned the shower on and washed it away.

But I kept thinking about it. Later, while we were having

coffee in a *kissaten* near the station, Fujiko asked me what the matter was. She said I was frowning. I was still thinking about the hair and trying to make sense of the feeling I had when I saw it. I didn't mention it. Some Japanese women are sensitive about their hair, they say it's thicker and coarser than foreigners' hair. I didn't want her to feel uncomfortable. I just said something about the differences between people. She said she understood and we had a couple of minutes of silent communication, Japanese style, contemplating the suchness of things.

"*Muzukashi desu ne,*" she said. "It's difficult, isn't it?" and I said yes and she looked relieved because I'd agreed with her, like a Japanese, to make things easier, to reassure her we had something together, even if it was only the same problem. But really I was thinking about something else and the pretence made me feel even farther away from her.

My face could have been a mask belonging to a stranger. The man sitting with Fujiko, drinking coffee, listening to her description of the street bands in Harajuku, was someone else, like a character in a book or a film, and I was sitting there, thinking how she had no idea who I was and I had no way of telling her. I wanted to speak through the mask to her, to apologise for what I could not say; to tell her who I was, how different and how far away I was from her. But it would have been betraying myself or her belief in me and I didn't want her to be unhappy, so I said I would go with her to Harajuku.

I told myself it was just *gaijin* paranoia and it would be over in a few minutes. But the feeling didn't go away. I was thinking of Johnny Tallis. She was close to him. But apart from the evening at Forbes' she never talked about him. I could understand why Johnny's death was something she wouldn't want to talk about: talking about death across culture, in different languages, it's easy to say the wrong thing and perhaps she was embarrassed. But it seemed odd. At least it seemed odd to me. Perhaps I was angry. Perhaps she loved him. I don't know. There are any number of explanations.

She asked me again if there was something the matter and I
said no and her face opened into a smile which reminded me
of why I liked being with her. But the strange feeling didn't go
away. What she didn't say revealed more than what she said.

Under the surface of her new internationalism, the old nationalism of her parents' and grandparents' generation is there,
inside her, but so well hidden and disguised she probably isn't
aware of it. She likes to think of herself as a global citizen and
says the planet is more important than any country, but behind
all the *tatemae* appearances and the way things are supposed
to be, *honne*—the deep-down feeling—who she is and how she
thinks is Japanese. I am a foreigner and she is Japanese.

With Sachiko it was different: we were two people, a man
and a woman together, but Sachiko had grown up abroad.
Fujiko had grown up here. Perhaps the difference is Japan.

I asked Fujiko if she could imagine what it's like being a
foreigner and she said yes, she thought she understood a little.
How about a foreigner knowing what it's like to be Japanese?
That was something else. I asked her why. I knew what she
was going to say.

"The Japanese are unique," she said, "only the Japanese can
understand the Japanese."

I said we were talking in circles and she said Westerners
think in straight lines. It sounded like the start of a typical
Japanese conversation about the cold, inhuman rationalism of
Western logic, as opposed to the warm, human feeling of Eastern intuition. I didn't want any more *nihonjin-ron* so I just
grunted Japanese style. There were a lot of things I might have
said, but I didn't want to lose face by getting angry.

Sometimes silence is the best way to harmony. Even if it's
only *wa*.

We finished our coffee and Fujiko picked up the bill. It was
a relief to get outside again.

A crowd was watching some black men dancing to music
coming from speakers on either side of a temporary stage.

A big silver truck behind the stage was covered in posters advertising a new kind of music system by Mitsubishi. Some Japanese men in Hawaiian shirts and Afro hairstyles were standing at the back of the stage with their arms folded. They looked sullen and aggressive. Maybe they were imitating black "cool." Maybe they were bored and irritable. The presenter was a Middle Eastern man in his mid-twenties in a pink baggy suit with his hair tied back in a pony tail. Now and again he interrupted the music to tell everyone they were having a good time, reminding them that Mitsubishi was the sponsor of the event. His Japanese was fluent.

The dancers were grinning like they'd been told there might be a bonus for the one who smiled the longest. They danced well. They understood their bodies and their bodies were alive to the music, but their smiles reminded me of the expressions of dancers in an early silent film: white flashes in the flickering images of sidewalk musicians cake-walking for the camera somewhere in America in the 1900s, smiling the smiles of people whose fathers and grandfathers wore the grinning masks of slavery: the please-don't-hit-me smile of people living in fear, the cheerfulness of slaves.

I looked at the smiles of the men dancing and the smiles of the Japanese women going among the crowds giving out leaflets: different races, different faces, but the same smile.

We watched the dancing for a while then Fujiko turned to me.

"Black men are *ninki-mono*," she said, "very popular. Many Japanese girls want black boyfriends." Ever since a well-known writer wrote a book describing her experiences with her black lover, young Japanese women have been wanting black boyfriends.

"Black or white," I said, "what's the difference?"

"Black people are natural," said Fujiko. "We Japanese like nature. We like people who are natural. Also maybe, black men are good lovers and it's fun to annoy parents and people who are not international and think all foreigners have AIDS. Walking along the street with a black man is a very big sign of independence, much more than a white man."

"What about brown people?" I asked. Fujiko wasn't sure.

"Maybe between black and white people," she said, "maybe closer to black people. It depends on the colour. The darker the better. A black boyfriend shows a girl is very independent." I wondered what Japanese men thought. She laughed.

"*Tsumuranai desu*. It doesn't matter," she smiled, "it's just fashion. Everything's fashion." She said the word "fashion" with an intonation which seemed to give it another meaning; fa-shion. Something definite and all inclusive, the way things are meant to be. Everything's fashion.

Fujiko wasn't wearing any lipstick, but as she said the word "fashion" her lips seemed very red and her skin seemed very white and her hair was black and shining in the sunlight.

○

I like this.

A piece of music can become part of one's life, like an image. About the time when Mozart was composing this music, here, on the other side of the world, Utamaro was making a wood-block print of a kiss: a man and a woman in a red and black *kimono*. I can see it in my mind's eye.

Her face is hidden, with only the nape of her neck visible. Long before I came to Japan I had a copy of the print in my bedroom. It was like a riddle. I wanted to know who the woman was. In my imagination she was beautiful but the only clue to her character was the way she held the man's face as they kissed, suggesting a certain tenderness, and the finely combed strands of hair drawn up into an elegant arrangement of combs and pins at the top of her head. The lower half of her *kimono* was in disarray revealing the whiteness of a thigh. The self-control required to keep the pins and combs in place was intriguing. Perhaps the man was about to draw the pins, one by one, from her hair, letting it tumble over her shoulders or perhaps everything remained miraculously in place, as she adjusted her *kimono* and cooled herself with a fan inscribed with poetry.

The picture was one of the signs on my way here.

It had a particular fascination: looking at it I felt the attraction bordering on the erotic, of the unknown, the mystery of the unknowable—made in Japan. It was one of the first things from this country to become part of my life and probably it was one of the reasons I came to Japan: to know, and if possible, to uncover any mystery there might be here.

Maybe some art is universal, but Mozart wasn't Japanese. Fujiko and I listen to his music, but it has a different meaning for her and for me. Perhaps. Probably. I don't know. Maybe it's like making love: how was it for you? Almost as close as blood, close enough to make blood, but we don't know, we don't really know, we can only imagine how it is for another person.

Same bed, different dreams.

When I saw the hair this morning I was already some distance away. Seeing it reminded me how far apart we are, not because she has one kind of hair and I have another, but because the world inside her and the world inside me are different places. I like the shape of her eyes, she likes the shape of my lips, our skin is more or less the same colour.

Race has nothing to do with it, the problem is culture.

Perhaps she's too Japanese and if she spent more time outside Japan, she'd see things differently. Perhaps I'm too attached to where I was born and if I lived in Japan longer I'd understand her better.

○

The sky is grey.

The market's up and I'm down.

Saito-san says the German market is too expensive and he's going to wait until it's cheaper before buying any stock. I suggested he go into the French market but he thinks the franc is getting weaker. He's afraid any gains in the market will be lost in the currency. I suggested options or hedging but he didn't want to know. He's a cautious investor who prefers to wait and see.

"I am like your prime minister," he said, "I am very conservative." I wanted to tell him I didn't vote but I'd forgotten the Japanese for "vote." It shows how often I need the word in this country. I didn't want to talk politics in Japanese with Saito-san. It's one of his favourite topics. He knows it's his weak point and he wants to learn. He says foreign politics are difficult: the names of political parties confuse him. He thinks the Japanese Liberal Democratic Party is the best of the old English Liberal Party and the new American Democrat Party, Japanese style. When he wants to understand a foreign political party, he takes his dictionary and looks up the translation of the party's name in Japanese. Sometimes I think Saito-san only takes calls from me for conversation practice. I suggested he buy British.

"*Dai-jishin, dai-rieki,*" I said. Great courage—great advantage, the nearest I could get to "who dares wins" in Japanese.

Saito-san giggled again and asked if he had to be brave to buy British.

Saito-san holds stock in the fifty biggest companies in the five richest countries in Europe. He puts the money in the market and he watches it to see what happens. He once told me he could put in more; "Much more, ten, twenty, maybe even a hundred times more." For the moment he's passive. With the money under his control he could move the prices of several major companies, even influence company decisions. There are a lot of people like Saito-san in Japan, looking after money in pension funds, trust banks, and life-insurance companies. When people ask who is behind Japan's economic domination of the world the answer is Saito-san or someone like him, a person who can't tell the difference between democratic socialism and social democracy, who respects peace, capitalism and democracy, who wants a clean world because he loves nature and believes the individual is important because the individual is creative, and Japan needs creative individuals for its economic growth.

As far as Saito-san is concerned, human rights and civil liberties are things that happen on television. If people live in harmony, it isn't necessary to worry about such things. He wants everyone to live in harmony and peace and become rich and happy. It's a Japanese version of the American dream: a Coca-Cola philosophy with a Disneyland morality.

Saito-san's OK really: he says what he thinks I want to hear, I tell him what he wants to know and one of these days we will do business together. Meanwhile the planet's poisoned, forests burn, animals are slaughtered and war, disease and hunger flatten the human population curve.

Yamaguchi lights another cigarette and the smoke drifts towards the window and unravels against the luminous grey of the sky.

He knows and I know.

We're both hiding behind our screens, pretending everything's normal but it isn't. I know and he knows. It's now only a matter of time, a waiting game.

I could say what I think and what I know, here and now, in the middle of the dealing room, and it wouldn't change a thing. It's deniable: there's almost no evidence, and the evidence there is can be ignored as a series of coincidences.

Whoever reads this probably knows.

It's a waiting game and like the clock in Shinjuku, showing the number of days till the end of the millennium, there's a bit to go.

○

It's four-thirty in the afternoon and our flight leaves in half an hour.

I'm in the duty-free hall at Narita Airport and I've just called Caro to tell her when the plane arrives in Hong Kong. The others are waiting by the flight information screen. There are a dozen or so people in the group.

The senior members of the group are Laroche and Yamaguchi.

It's easy to see how they work together, here in the no-man's-land of an airport departure lounge, away from the closed doors and telephones at the office: Laroche asks Yamaguchi what's happening and what needs to be done, Yamaguchi tells him. Then Laroche tells people what's happening and what they have to do, and Yamaguchi arranges everything. It's a perfect double act: smooth and simple. It takes time for two people to work so well together.

Laroche was looking in my direction. He saw me using the tape-recorder but he was too far away to hear what I was saying. I nodded to him and he looked away. Yamamoto was beside him and noticed what happened. I nodded to her but she dead-faced me and like Laroche she turned away.

○

It's late and I'm sitting by the window, looking at the neon signs on the buildings around Hong Kong harbour.

Caro met me at the airport. I wasn't sure how it was going to be. Last time when I was here in the spring and we went over to the mainland to meet the photographer, we kept getting our signals crossed. But this time we're on the same wavelength.

We had dinner in the hotel and talked about the year we were together in Japan, the old house in Kyoto and the trip to India: remembering past lives by candlelight. She told me about her work with photographers in China and I asked if it was better than working for Warburgs. She had no regrets. The year she spent working in the bank was one of the longest in

her life. Money. It wasn't her style. She said she's forgotten
everything and can't even remember how to calculate earnings
per share or a price-earnings ratio.

She asked how things were in the bank. I told her.

"They make it impossible if they think you're different,"
she said. "But remember they need you more than you need
them."

I looked at her across the candlelight. She was wearing an
Indian cotton shirt. I thought of the ragged blue jumper she
was wearing when we first met and all the places we'd been
together, and how strange it is that we should still be friends.
Suddenly the past was a knife. I heard Caro's voice telling me
not to worry. I didn't have a handkerchief but Caro looked in
her bag and managed to find an old paper tissue so I used that.

I wasn't really unhappy, I suppose I was tired and talking
with Caro, knowing I was with a friend I love and trust, who
understands about screens and masks and *honne* and *tatemae*,
I felt safe. It was OK to take off the armour and be human. I
told her about Laroche and Yamaguchi, the hints and accusation and the things I'd noticed which might or might not have
been part of a pattern, I wasn't sure, and the meaning of the
pattern, if there was one, and she listened frowning or nodding
from time to time, until I'd said everything I had to say.

I asked her what she thought I should do. She didn't answer
for a while and I thought she might not have heard the question. Then she said I already knew. She told me the same thing
last time. Each time we see each other I ask her the same
question and she gives me the same answer. I laughed because
it was true.

We talked about her love affair with the Chinese photographer, what she thought of the foreigners in Hong Kong com-
pared with the foreigners in Japan, and the difference between
being a *guailo* and a *gaijin*. She likes being a *guailo* in Hong
Kong more than being a *gaijin* in Tokyo. I said she'd taken the
easy option and she laughed.

○

I can see why Caro likes it in Hong Kong. Perhaps I could get used to the smell of joss and chicken shit and tiger balm and it would become part of my life.

Disraeli said, "The East is a career." But China's a lifetime, maybe several lifetimes.

In the yoga of the direct path, one life is enough. But it depends on the trajectory.

Something's already passed through nature to eternity. Someone has entered *satori*. I'm here. This is strange. I suppose it's in the nature of things.

Someone should write a *senryu* about this weird existential feeling: looking in the mirror of a hotel bedroom, alone, slightly drunk.

○

It's two-thirty and I've had lunch and I'm taking a walk around the block. It feels good after sitting down all day. The shoe-shine man with no legs is sitting propped up against the wall of the hotel beside his tins of polish and rags. The Englishman has his shoes shined in Hong Kong and the Japanese man visits a brothel in the Philippines. There is a free exchange of goods for services, but there's no equality of bargaining power. Ghosts of Empire walk in the popular imagination. Memories of the past give the actions of the present another meaning. A conversation with the shoe-shine man, a drink with the *mama-san*, keeps things turning over.

It's hot and I'm beginning to sweat.

On the other side of a street there's a group of Japanese tourists outside a shop selling luxury goods. There's another group inside: hundreds of Japanese buying things with French and Italian labels, made in Hong Kong by people from China.

○

The morning meeting was in the hotel. Thirty or forty of us sat around a long table in a conference room decorated in American Louis XVI style. The wallpaper was turquoise with golden birds of paradise trailing their tail feathers in golden trees lit by dazzling chandeliers.

It was good to see Arif again and Sean and Caterina, but Bob couldn't make it. I sat next to a man called Alan who was giving a talk on equity warrants. He was unsure about binomial theory in option pricing models, but he knew the market. He used to work with John Galvanoni at Flemings. I looked round the table at a lot of people in suits, come from all over the world to exchange name cards, put faces to voices and listen to each other talking about money.

Laroche made an appearance in a new, Hong Kong tailored, Prince-of-Wales check suit, four buttons at the cuffs, one button undone to prove it was the real thing. The light-sensitive spectacles gave a Gallic accent to the Hong Kong image of the international gentleman. The light from the chandeliers was so bright it turned the lenses of his spectacles black and it was impossible to see where he was looking. Yamaguchi was sitting next to him. I looked at them and I thought of what Caro said about people who are dead inside, who only know how to live on the outside. I felt I was in a room full of people living on the outside. It wasn't just the night before, although my throat was dry and there was a soft thumping going on somewhere between my eyes and the back of my head.

Laroche got up and made a short speech saying how pleased he was to welcome everyone to this year's international sales conference. He believed it was important for us all to get together.

"This is a people business," he said, "it's made of people." By the angle of his head he could have been looking in my direction. I looked at Yamaguchi, who turned away. Laroche thanked everyone and hoped they would have a pleasant time in Hong Kong. Just as he was sitting down, he stood up again and reminded us about the party on the company junk, tomorrow afternoon. Sean asked if it was compulsory and Laroche said he wanted as many people to be there as possible. I had a curious sensation, like a shadow moving somewhere on the edge of my field of vision; a feeling that something was going on but I wasn't sure what it was. Then the lights were turned down and we watched a couple of films on information technology and data processing, followed by a lecture by someone from London about information and the time-money equation who took an hour to say what he had to say.

There was a break for coffee and everyone stood around in little groups nodding their heads, looking out of the corner of their eyes to see who was talking with who. Most of the people from the Tokyo office kept together while people from the other offices in Asia, Europe and America moved around meeting each other. I talked with Arif. He's fatalistic. He said the United States has borrowed too much money, mostly from Japan, which has more money than any other country in the world. He thinks Japan has the money and the technology to dominate the planet. Even if it doesn't have the resources, it has the technology. Over time, people with more advanced technology dominate those with less advanced technology. In the last couple of years, Japan has overtaken the United States with more world patents for new inventions. By the year 2000 Japan's economy will be bigger than America's.

"The battle's over," he said, "but most people don't even think it's begun." I asked what sort of battle he was talking about and he just laughed and quoted the line in *The Art of War* in which Sun Tzu declares that the best victory is the victory achieved without battle.

After the break we had another couple of lectures: the man called Alan talked about equity warrants and Sean told us about the advantages of synthetic warrants. There was a buffet lunch. Once again the people from Tokyo remained in a group, except for Laroche and Yamaguchi who went out together.

In a Japanese way I could feel the attraction of being with the Tokyo crowd. But I also wanted to be with people from the other offices. In the end I sat next to Yamamoto, but I needn't have bothered because she didn't speak more than a couple of sentences. When I asked what the matter was she said nothing and began talking with Takahashi. I didn't see any point in trying to be part of a group that didn't want me so I joined Sean and Arif and some people from the Hong Kong office. It was good not to be an outsider, although I still felt something like guilt that I wasn't with the people from Tokyo.

○

I'm sitting in a cotton dressing gown, looking at the lights of Hong Kong. I've reached a turning point. I would have liked to talk it through with Bob, but he's not here. It's not something one can do by telephone so I might as well just do it and talk with Bob about it later.

Perhaps this is how actors feel after a performance: something of who one was suddenly vanished into thin air. The charade is over and it's time for everyone to take off their masks. Regret. Relief. Something like dying maybe.

Wearing a mask is like speaking another language. It's possible to become someone else. But wearing a mask for a long time it's easy to forget who one is: one may become someone else, who doesn't really exist.

At first the mask conceals the truth, but gradually it becomes the truth and eventually there is nothing behind the mask. Taking off a mask means losing face. I don't mind. If I look in the mirror I don't want to see a mask.

Talking with Caro, I realised how the situation in Tokyo has affected me when she told me I didn't have to wear a mask with her. I needed someone to say that to me. I asked what she thought of the situation in Tokyo. She could see a pattern but some of it was probably coincidence. I asked if she thought it was my imagination and she said no, she was sure it was real. I hoped she might interpret the pattern but she refused. It was a question that was impossible to answer, she said, it was like asking the meaning of a tree or a picture. She saw it from one angle, I saw it from another and we were both foreigners. There was also a Japanese perspective. Even if there seemed to be a pattern there wasn't necessarily a plan or purpose. It could be a pattern that happened to be there, like the shapes of cliffs and clouds and leaves in computer-generated images of chaos. She wasn't interested in the rights and wrongs of it all anyway. Perhaps there was a conspiracy—perhaps it was my paranoia—it didn't really matter. Why work in a bank in Tokyo? Last time I told her I was writing a book about Japan. Perhaps I should be writing it. Forget about Tokyo. Why worry? Be happy!

Living in Japan I feel different. I've learned to live in a Japanese way. Sometimes I feel Japanese. I look at foreigners, Europeans or Americans, and think how strange they are, and I feel separate from them in the same way as I feel separate when I am with a group of Japanese.

Forget the old lie: "Only connect." It's not enough to connect, one has to belong.

I look like a foreigner but sometimes I think Japanese. Some people have the same problem the other way round; like Koreans who live in Japan, or Japanese who've lived abroad. They look Japanese but they think foreign. It's difficult for people like Yamaguchi, who know life outside Japan. He has a foreign character and he lives in Japan but there's a tension, between what he feels and what he knows. I don't want to be like Yamaguchi when I go back.

Late afternoon.

Part of the tape has been erased. Maybe I did it by mistake or someone did it on purpose. I used the recorder several times during the day. Nothing I said on the junk is on the tape. But I can remember most of it.

We all met down by the quayside and got on to the boat. The paint work was dirty and the varnish was blistered. I had a copy of *Foreign Affairs Quarterly* with an article about Islam which I was looking forward to reading. The sun was shining and everyone was saying what a good idea it was to have a party on a junk and how much they were looking forward to having lunch in Lantau. I remembered the aftermath of my last visit to Lantau, when I had shellfish. It seemed better not to say anything.

It was hot, it was up and down, and it was difficult to concentrate. Laroche appeared in dark blue Hawaiian shorts, decorated with red and yellow flowers. He had a medallion round his neck and a lot of weight round his waist and his shoulders were hairy. He'd pulled his shorts up to his navel to cover the size of his belly.

Most of the party wore swimming costumes. Yamaguchi and Yamamoto, people I saw every day in suits, suddenly walking around with almost nothing on. Some people's characters seemed to change, others were more or less the same. Most of them had no muscles, just fat and bones. Like factory-farm chickens: too much artificial light and not enough exercise. Without their clothes they looked pale and vulnerable.

The man called Alan told me what he was going to do with his money: buy half a dozen terrace-houses in the north of England and put the rest in gold.

"Perfect hedge," he said, "gold goes down, property goes up—property goes down, gold goes up."

We got to Lantau in the early afternoon and went to the restaurant where I ate the shellfish before. The scene had a surreal quality: thirty or forty bankers in shorts and swimming

costumes, sitting at tables on the waterfront in a touristic restaurant against the backdrop of a picturesque slum.

I asked a dealer from New York what he was working for:
how much money did he want and what did he want it for?
He wanted enough to build a big building, which he could look
at and know it was his. I asked why.

"Because it proves you've done something," he said. "The
building's the proof of what you've done." Like a book, I
thought, only different. I wanted to know how much money
he would be happy with. He didn't understand so I rephrased
the question and asked how much money he wanted to have
when he retired. He thought for a couple of seconds and said
one hundred million dollars in today's money. With a bit of
luck he hoped to get it in fifteen years, or at least before he was
fifty. I wished him luck.

A slight breeze was blowing and the rattan awning over the
table was swinging to and fro casting curious shadows over
people's faces and across their bodies. A man in a vest appeared
with the remains of some creature in a bottle of yellow liquid
and Alan said the Chinese will eat anything. Someone else said
it was fascinating how the lessons of famine were preserved in
people's cuisines. I looked at the thing in the bottle again and
thought of someone eating it. I wanted to say something but I
couldn't find the words. I could feel what I wanted to say inside
me as if I'd taken a breath and what I wanted to say was like
a lung full of air imprisoned in my chest. I could feel my heart
beating. This is the moment, I thought, now is the moment to
say what I have to say.

The man next to me asked if I wanted another beer or perhaps
a brandy. A fat, middle-aged man came out of the restaurant
wearing a dirty white vest over cotton shorts and stood looking
at us picking his teeth. His face was unsmiling and the way he
looked at us, his eyes moving from place to place mechanically,
made me feel like I was food, we were all food; sacks of rice
and baskets of vegetables and chickens and pigs and fishes and

shellfish. I got up and went to the lavatory. The smell was sweet and sour. I steadied myself against a wall and thought about the human condition.

I pulled a lever and thought of everything flushing away into the harbour. The soap was covered in a grey scum and the water came out of the tap in a tepid trickle. On the way back to the table the man in the dirty vest and shorts asked if everything was all right. I said it was very good.

I stood where the man had been standing a few minutes before and looked at the party, like shadows silhouetted against the diamond lights of the sun on the water. It was impossible to see the details of their faces: they were just shadows against the light. It was very hot. The scene was oddly artificial, like a set specially constructed to illustrate a metaphysical reality. For a second or two the shadows at the tables and the light on the water seemed like some innocent and terrible truth revealed in a moment of vision, something made of light and darkness that was for a moment timeless and eternal. A waiter in a white jacket carrying a tray passed between me and the rest of the party.

I walked towards the table. I felt I'd been away for a long time. A man in a T-shirt was saying there were two kinds of people—"fuck you" people and "fuck me" people and he preferred to be a "fuck you" person than a "fuck me" person. My glass was half full of brandy. Laroche was sitting back in his chair at the end of the table. His shirt was open and his chest and stomach were bare. There was no hair on his belly. He was wearing his light-sensitive spectacles and smoking a cigar. I was almost sure he knew I was looking at him but he made no reaction. I think we both realised then that something was going to happen between us, because it had to happen.

It was chemical. I could feel it happening inside me. Laroche was watching me. His face was different. I noticed a slow-motion smile spreading across his face. I tried to smile back at him but it was difficult. I didn't feel like smiling. I was wondering how I was going to get through the rest of the afternoon.

Dinner with Caro was a long way away. So was Tokyo and everything to do with Japan.

Laroche's smile didn't seem to belong to his face. It was more like a grin than a smile. Perhaps for a moment he thought there was something funny about the situation. He knew what was going on. Laroche kept the grin in place but the longer it stayed on his face, the harder it was, until it was more like a grimace which could've been mistaken for the bared teeth of a snarl. Then the realisation hit me, like a surge of adrenaline. The expression on his face had nothing to do with goodwill, amusement or aggression. It was fear. He knew that I knew, and he was grinning because he was afraid.

I was on my own, the first time for a long time, and it was a good feeling, like freedom: a lightness, a brightness, a certainty, and the tightness in my chest had gone away. I could feel my heart beating. Thank God, I thought, I'm alive again, like a *kamikaze* pilot before taking off.

The bill was paid and we made our way back in twos and threes through the tables and chairs, along the jetty to the gang plank and onto the junk. The ropes were cast off and the boat moved towards a bay twenty minutes further around the island. It was supposed to be a good place for wind-surfing and water-skiing.

Someone's hand moved slowly down a woman's back. She was wearing red high-heeled shoes and a red bikini. There was a slight swell on the sea. The fingers of the man's hand moved under the top of the woman's bikini bottom. One of the crew came out and emptied a box of cans and bottles and rubbish over the side. It was like a pantomime: a crowd of people drinking and getting drunk on a junk in the afternoon sun, going up and down with the wind in their hair on their way to nowhere in particular. I imagined what the man who threw the rubbish into the sea might think of it all: a ship of fools wanting to stand on water with wind surfers. There was only one pair of water skis and Laroche announced that, as the most senior member of the party, he would use them first.

The place we were aiming for was in sight, but still some way in the distance. I guessed it wouldn't take more than half an hour to get there. I was standing on the roof of the junk. The sun was sparkling on the waves. I just remembered to take a breath before I hit the water.

I surfaced to see the stern of the junk disappearing over the other side of a slow, grey-green wave. I kept my mouth shut. I'd seen what went into the sea around Hong Kong and I didn't want to swallow any of it. The boat reappeared further away. There were a few figures looking in my direction waving. I waved back at them.

Each time I caught sight of the boat it was further away: I could just see the figures at the stern of the boat. One of them was Laroche. I was interested to see his reaction: I wondered if the boat would turn round. I waved. It continued into the distance. After the thudding of the ship's engine and the people in designer swimsuits talking about money and hotels and the latest titles in shopping-and-fucking literature, it was good to be in the sea.

The boat was almost out of sight and the waves seemed bigger than when I was on the boat. I had a moment of doubt. Don't swim after a heavy meal. Of course not. I thought of the beef and oyster sauce, the rice and prawns and beer and beansprouts. And the brandy. I could hardly see the shore over the tops of the waves. I didn't think about tides. I started swimming after the boat. The current was against me. It was more difficult than swimming kilometres in the pool near the office. But the sessions in the pool made a difference.

It seemed a long time before I reached the protection of the headland where the current was gentler and it was easier to think. It made things a lot clearer. Laroche could have told the skipper to turn round but he didn't. He didn't do anything. The people from Tokyo could explain it as someone playing the fool on a company outing.

A motor dinghy was lowered from the boat and some figures

climbed down into it. For a moment I thought the dinghy was coming in my direction but it moved round the other side of the junk.

I swam to the side of the boat, found the rope ladder hanging over the side and climbed aboard. I was tired and I almost fell over as I stepped on to the deck. Arif welcomed me. He'd been worried. He wasn't sure whether I'd dived in or fallen in. I thanked him and said I was fine.

Laroche was water-skiing. He didn't make any mistakes and kept going without a break until people watching him drifted away from the side of the boat and returned to their cushions and international relationships. I had a tepid reception from my Japanese colleagues. I'd broken the taboo against leaving the group, in public, in front of people from other places.

When Yamaguchi saw me his face twisted into an expression which might have been his best imitation of a smile. He asked if I enjoyed my swim. I thanked him. Laroche stopped water-skiing and came back to the boat. He wasn't wearing his spectacles and until he dried his face, the water round his eyes made him look like a small boy who'd been crying. He had to put on his smoky lenses before he caught sight of me. He already had a speech prepared. He was annoyed. Perhaps I'd taken some of the edge off his water-skiing display. He said I did it on purpose. He wanted to take it further. Why couldn't I behave like a normal human being and be like everyone else? It was selfish behaviour.

He knew what he was doing, shouting at me in front of the others. It was a sign to the Japanese: I had threatened the integrity of the group and he was calling on the sacred traditions of the group to defend itself. By the way he was talking to me he was isolating me from the group, trying to pretend his anger was the righteous indignation of the group. I mentioned the line from Confucius that says: "A gentle person should not be an implement: the superior man is not a tool." After that I didn't say much for a while. He was losing face by losing control. But my silence only annoyed him further. I mentioned another line of Confucius, about the man who keeps his virtue in the face of material advantage. He asked what I was getting at.

I said I'd seen behind his mask and there wasn't any purpose keeping up the pretence any longer. I told him about the reports and the information and the analysis and the language and the telephones and the rest of it, the delays and the excuses, the meetings which didn't happen, the messages which weren't received and the letters which weren't delivered and the money, and as I said it I felt better, as if a weight strapped to my body was removed. I could breathe again.

He said I could quote Confucius and the rest of it as much as I liked: he didn't give a damn. In the end it was all very simple. He was the boss and I wasn't. It was his job to tell me what to do and if I didn't like it I could go somewhere else.

The mask slipped a couple of times but he managed to keep it more or less in place. He was really attached to it. He didn't want to lose the smile. Somehow he kept grinning almost the whole time, as if the words coming out of his face belonged to someone else who just happened to be where he was. He didn't know where I got my ideas from. I told him. He said I was making it up and he even managed to laugh; it was all a lot of nonsense, I'd been in the sun too long. I mentioned why it wasn't a lot of nonsense and the person who told me. The smile went then and it didn't come back. He said it was all imagination. I asked him, if it was all imagination, why spend so long discussing it? He said he didn't give a shit.

There wasn't much point continuing the conversation: I'd said what I had to say, people had heard, they'd seen our faces, and they could come to their own conclusions.

I'd had enough of the double game: the double thinking and the double standards.

Time for another game, different players and a new set of rules.

○

I'm lying on a bed in the hotel.

While I was having coffee with Caro I told her I was free and I could see my life like a river moving forward but now I feel strange and playing back the tape my voice sounds different.

I'm lying on the bed looking up at the ceiling with a recorder in my hands talking about the situation. I've lost part of my life. It was real for a while. Thinking of all the people outside turns me over inside but I'm not afraid.

I am the lifeline between who I was and who I will be.

Once I step out of this room I'll be someone in a suit, carrying a case full of papers about money, and brochures for information systems. At the moment I'm between identities, there's still some time before I have to catch the plane and I feel OK.

○

It's Monday afternoon and I'm in the study at Nakameguro. This morning I made my formal resignation from the Tokyo office. I telephoned Laroche's office. It took a long time before the red light on Noguchi's desk went off. I knocked and opened the door. Laroche was sitting at his desk: he was wearing a pink shirt, holding a plastic cup of coffee. He'd taken off his glasses and he looked tired. He was writing something. I closed the door behind me and waited. He didn't look up for a while, for five, maybe ten seconds. Then he glanced at me.

"Hello, Perry," he said. "I'll be with you in a minute."

It was just what I expected him to do.

"Take your time," I said. "I'm not in a hurry." I waited another minute or so and then asked if he minded if I sat down.

"Help yourself." He gestured to the chair on the other side of the desk. I watched him writing. It was the first time I'd seen him do anything other than talking in the office. I suppose he was doing it to keep me waiting, but I didn't mind. There he was, writing something, to prove his time was important, and I was watching him, thinking he was wasting his time. It reminded me of school, watching people writing lines as a punishment. The memory made me smile. Laroche asked if there was anything the matter. I said everything was fine.

"So would you like to share the joke?" he said.

I knew it would annoy him if I said what I was thinking.

"Not particularly," I said. He stopped writing and looked at me.

"You're crazy," he said. I told him what I was thinking. He gave me another look which was probably meant to make me feel uncomfortable and carried on writing. Through the windows behind him, Tokyo lay spread out in a smoky blue haze towards the horizon. Laroche clipped the top of his pen into place and looked at me as if there were a bright light shining over my shoulders.

"What's the matter with you?" he said. "What do you want?"

"Nothing," I said. "I just wanted to talk about things."

"I've nothing to say," he said and his eyes narrowed. "You're not recording this, are you?"

It was almost too good to be true: Laroche asking me if I was wearing a recorder.

"What do you think?" I said.

He ignored the question and asked again if I was using a recorder.

"What difference does it make?" I said. He shrugged. I opened my jacket on both sides and showed him my inside pockets.

"Look, no wires." I said. It wasn't enough. He wanted me to stand up and take off my jacket. I refused. I asked him what he was worried about. He just shrugged and smiled. I stood up and said he could search me. I didn't see why I should tell him if I was using a recorder or not. Maybe he had one. I didn't care. I had nothing to hide. He patted at my pockets and lifted the flap of my jacket. It seemed to satisfy him.

"OK," he said. "What do you want?" I tried to imagine the sort of things Laroche might think I wanted. I looked at him sitting there, on the other side of the desk, framed by the black verticals of the window like something by Francis Bacon.

"What do you think I want?" I said. For a second he lost control.

"Stop . . ." he said and then he checked himself. "Stop wasting my time, Perry. Tell me what you want or get out of here." I didn't say anything. He leaned forward to press the button through to Noguchi.

"What I said on the boat," I began. But I didn't say any more. I wanted to see what he would say. Laroche opened his mouth a little, with a slight sucking noise, almost like a Japanese and showed me his teeth.

"It's a small world, Perry," he said. "I can make it hard for you to get another job in the business." I asked if he was threatening me and he said no, he wasn't threatening me, it was just a statement of fact.

"I'm the boss, you see, Perry," he said. "Who are people going to believe, you or me?"

"I'll tell you what I want," I said. He sat back again, with his head slightly on one side, and a weak smile on his face as if he was trying to convince himself that he didn't really care what I was going to say, but he was listening just in case I said something that might amuse him. I looked at him. Everything I wanted to tell him was there in his face for all the world to see: greed and fear. I told him to have a look in a mirror.

Laroche smiled—it could have been relief or maybe the idea amused him. He said it was all very well but he didn't have time to play games and did I have anything else to say. I told him I didn't want to work with him any more and he said that was fine, he felt the same way.

"I'm sure you've made the right decision, Perry," he said.

"I don't see you in this business. That's what I thought the first time we met. 'This guy's not meant to be here,' I thought. Go and write a book or something—you'll be much happier."

"Maybe I'll write about you," I said.

"Man, I don't give a shit what you do. I just don't want to see you."

It was one of those moments which are made for a smart one-liner, but I couldn't think of anything except goodbye, so that's what I said.

"Goodbye," I said.

"Close the door," he said, and that's what I did. I got up and went over to the door with its plastic imitation wood veneer and put my hand round the aluminium handle and I turned it and stepped into the grey-carpeted reception area where Noguchi was sitting beside the castor oil plant and I closed the door.

○

Last night I went round to see Robin. His face was redder than I remembered and his stomach was bigger. He was wearing athletic shorts and a T-shirt which had written on it "Question: what's the worst blow job you ever had? Answer: Fantastic!"

He got some beers from the kitchen and we sat cross-legged on the floor with the sliding doors open on to the garden and the sound of the cicadas hissing in the darkness and I told him what had happened. When I finished he said, "They got you good and proper, didn't they?" I said I supposed they had.

"It puts a hole in the thing with David," he said and went to get another beer from the kitchen. I looked out of the window at the silhouette of the trees against the evening sky and the white edge of a crescent moon. I wanted to talk about things I hadn't talked about for a long time. I'd just taken the recorder out of my pocket when Robin came back from the kitchen with the beers. He asked if the recorder was turned on. I said it wasn't, but would he mind if I recorded the conversation. He said it was fine, as long as I didn't quote him by name, because there might be problems with the company.

We opened the beers and talked about Japan. With people in the group it's simpler. Things don't need to be explained: we've been through the same experiences and we trust each other. I asked how he saw Japan over the next ten or twenty years. He took a pack of cigarettes off a bookshelf. He doesn't usually smoke. He lit a cigarette before answering.

"The old man was in the army during the Second World War. He was one of the first into Belsen after it was liberated. He operated one of the bulldozers shovelling the bodies into the graves. They had towels soaked in Lysol wrapped round their faces but the smell got to them. He emptied his guts several times a day. He told me because he believed it was his duty to tell me. When I went to Japan he didn't try to stop me. All he said was that the Japanese were allies with the Germans and I shouldn't forget it. And I haven't.

"I've worked here for the last fifteen years. I speak Japanese. I read and write Japanese. I do business in Japanese. Some of my best friends are Japanese. My lady who comes to see me in Kamakura, for instance. But when it comes down to it, you can forget the stuff about economic co-dependency, and mutual interests: when it really comes down to it, it's them or us."

"What do you mean?" I said.

"The Japanese want to be in charge. The way they see it, Europe told the world what to do for a couple of hundred years, then America. Now it's their turn. We've had the age of the white man. Now it's the age of the yellow man. The ones in their seventies and eighties who grew up under the ideology of state Shinto believe it's the sacred duty of the Japanese to bring light to the rest of the world. This country is still half Confucian, it's a gerontocracy—the seventy- and eighty-year-olds rule, although they use front men in their fifties. The war knocked the shit out of a lot of them, but the old guard are still around, behind the scenes, at the top of companies. It goes back to the Occupation. The Americans didn't have enough

Japanese specialists: they had to make do with what they found. Like the Ministry of International Trade and Industry. During the war it was the Ministry of Munitions. They changed the name, but they couldn't change the people in the ministry or the way they were trained to think: strategic planning, mobilising the country, organising industries to build the Great Co-Prosperity Sphere. Bureaucratic traditions survive wars and revolutions."

"But why's it them or us?" I said. Robin looked at me as if he thought I was pretending to be stupid.

"You've done the martial-art bit," he said. "You know how it is. You get the other guy before he gets you. You go for the kill. They learn it at school, practising *kendo*. Maybe it's genetic: all those rice merchants in the eighteenth century, marrying into the *samurai* families—what do you get? Warrior merchants. That's what we're up against. It's them or us."

I looked at him sitting there on the floor, cross-legged in his T-shirt, pulling at his cigarette. His eyes weren't smiling and his mouth was set in a line like someone faced with a difficult decision.

"If it's them or us," I said, "what's the answer?"

"Finish the job. Tell 'em to start behaving or we'll turn the whole lot into a sea of radioactive glass."

I laughed nervously. I knew he was joking but it was too close to what I'd heard a lot of other people say.

"Robin . . ." I said.

"OK," he said. "That's extreme. But someone's got to tell this lot where to get off. They don't know where to stop. That's the problem. Someone has to say 'No.' It's no good thinking market forces will produce some magic solution. In an ideal world, maybe. But this is the real world. Look what happened to the American consumer electronics industry. Or the British car industry. It's OK for people with economics degrees from the right universities to write articles about the discipline of the market. They're safe. It's different for the people in the steel

industry or semi-conductor manufacturing." He lit another cigarette and coughed.

"The discipline of the market is OK as long as there's a
surplus. Otherwise it's the law of the jungle."

Robin got up and went into the kitchen and I switched off
the recorder. The moon had disappeared behind a cloud but
the darkness of the garden was alive with the sound of cicadas.
I thought of Issa, the Japanese poet who loved insects, hearing
the same sound hundreds of years ago and remembered the
conversation with the taxi driver on the way to Robin's, about
*kokoro*, the heart of Japan. *"Nihon no kokoro,"* he said. *"Naku
narimashita,"* he said. "The heart of Japan has gone."

Robin came back with a couple more beers and a mosquito
coil and we sat in silence for a while, with the smoke from the
coil drifting into the room. I think we both knew it might be
the last time we'd be seeing each other for a while.

I stood up and moved over to the open window and looked
at the shadows of the trees and bushes and the strange artificial
glow in the sky. Through the noise of the cicadas I could hear
the sound of a generator and the hum of an air conditioner.

I felt a light touch on my shoulder. I turned round and a fist
shot towards my face and stopped an inch from my nose, so
close I could smell the soap on Robin's fingers. I knocked his
fist away with my left forearm. I stopped a kick and got a punch
through his guard to his neck and he came back with a face
punch which grazed my eye. It lasted less than thirty seconds
but the adrenaline was pumping blood round my body and my
hands were shaking. Robin grinned and said he was glad I still
remembered something.

I was surprised how my body remembered what I'd forgotten. If I'd tried to think of the moves I wouldn't have succeeded
but, somehow, the forms and actions I learned years ago in the
*dojo* came back to me, and the awareness which went with
them. I smiled at Robin and thanked him and bowed and just
as he was bowing in return I put one hand over the back of his

neck and raised my knee within a few inches of his face, so we were quits.

We sat down and finished our beers. It was late, and Robin had a breakfast meeting. He put on a pair of *geta* wooden sandals and went with me to the end of the street, as far as the main road. A taxi arrived almost immediately. We shook hands and said goodbye in the light of a street lamp. I got into the car and as it pulled away I looked back over my shoulder and there was Robin waving, then bowing, and then, just as the taxi turned a corner, I saw him straightening up and once again he was waving.

○

Tony and I had been to Maggie's Revenge. We came out of one of the alleyways by Roppongi crossing and there she was, walking along the street with a girlfriend. I'd been talking about her a couple of minutes before and there she was. It was one of those moments when something happens, like it's supposed to happen—the sort of coincidence that hardly ever happens in real life. I had a strange sensation in my chest as if a bullet had hit me and it was exploding in slow motion but somehow I was still alive and I was saying how good it was to see her and she was looking at me and the way she was smiling I could see she was happy too.

She asked her friend what she wanted to do and I stood there, hoping her friend would say she wanted to go home and worrying in case Tony liked her friend and suggested we all had a drink together. Suddenly her friend wasn't there and Tony said he had to meet someone in a bar, and we were alone together looking at each other and smiling.

We went to a place where a lot of foreigners and Japanese were sitting outside at candlelit tables. Our drinks had just arrived when someone sat down at a neighbouring table, leant over and introduced himself. It was Noubad. He smiled like someone with a secret.

"You're a lucky man to be with such a beautiful woman." I knew the meaning of his smile and it made me smile too, but the cliché annoyed me. I thanked him and said she could probably match him, language for language.

"*Farsi?*" He raised his eyebrows and his eyes looked into mine and for a moment I could see him, like his father and his brothers, in the bazaar in Kabul, pretending indifference, watching me, careful not to miss any detail of my actions which might give a clue to my intentions.

"Not yet," I said. "Perhaps in the future, *Insha' allah.*" He smiled again and I had the same feeling as before, somewhere between amusement and annoyance. It was the first time she and I were alone together and we were spending it with Noubad. I wasn't sure what sort of impression he would make: a Japanese-speaking Afghan, the proprietor of a belly dancing night club in Roppongi, graduate of the American university in Beirut and dealer in sapphires, turquoise, lapis and emeralds.

He was charming, almost too charming. He put her at ease with the humour one might expect from someone who employs young women to perform the Dance of the Seven Veils for *salarimen* in Tokyo. He told her how he liked talking about Persian poetry with me. "I hope you're really happy together," he said and she glanced at me, not nervously, but uncertain whether to smile or keep a straight face.

"We're just getting to know each other," I said. Noubad made a series of flowery apologies. If only he'd known, he wouldn't have disturbed us.

"Listen my friend," he said. I knew he meant it when he said "my friend" but sometimes he speaks like a mobster in a 1930s' film. "Listen my friend," he looked into my eyes so sincerely it seemed like a confession, "you only have to say the word . . ."

It was one of those situations when experience counts and I didn't have enough. I felt angry with myself for not being happy to see an old friend and he spent the next hour with us talking about his adventures in Iran and his life in Japan.

When he first came here twenty-five years ago, there were hardly any foreigners.

"Japanese girls were so curious, you know," he laughed. "They sometimes offered to pay me to go to bed with them." I was intrigued. Did any of them actually pay?

"Sure," he said. "Why not? I was a student from a third-world country, with no money, living in Tokyo. I did what I could. I'm grateful for what I received. *Sobhan' allah.*" He was grinning like the wolf in *Little Red Riding Hood* and I was thinking how the relationship between men changes when there is a woman. He made a few jokes and I smiled, but I wasn't laughing inside. I wanted to laugh but I was tense. I didn't know her well enough to signal how I was feeling with my eyes. Noubad was talking about his experiences with Japanese women.

"They're taught to please," he said. "That's why old guys who've been around Asia all say Japanese wives are the best in the world. If anyone knows, they know." He was like someone playing several games of chess at the same time. The game he was playing with her was a mild-mannered amusement, a soft moving exploration of who she was. His game with me was different and I wasn't sure I liked it.

He was twirling a small, silver object between his fingers, swinging it in tiny glittering circles in the candle-light and talking about the way people really feel, deep down, maybe deeper than their conscious mind. His tone of voice made everything sound sensible and true. It was difficult not to look at the silver thing twirling between his fingers, appearing for a moment as it reached as far as it could spin in one direction, disappearing in a blur of light and rematerialising again the other way, like a pulse between visible and invisible, seemingly in rhythm with the words he was saying. It was fascinating, almost hypnotic. I asked what it was. I had to make a conscious effort. He stopped twirling it and I felt as if a cool hand had been placed on my forehead. He held the object in between his thumb and forefinger. It was an ornate cylinder with one end shaped like an egg. He pressed a trigger and the egg opened, revealing a golden calyx of four shining petals.

"It's nothing," he said. "It's a miniature cocktail shaker—a present from Sapporo." He pulled the trigger and the little flower disappeared into the egg and he began twirling it again, swinging it to and fro in the candle-light, flickering like a luminous moth with golden wings moving between the shadow and the light.

I was trying to hold on to something, like an everyday feeling. I was wondering if he was doing it on purpose, using skills he might have learned in one of the more advanced programmes, or something he picked up in a bazaar from a travelling storyteller. Or maybe it was unintentional. But it was getting to me badly, worse than random interference in a piece of music, because I had the feeling he was doing it on purpose. I just had enough self-control to ask him if he wouldn't mind giving the cocktail shaker a rest.

"What's the matter," he said. "Does it bother you?"

I said it distracted me from what he was saying. He apologised and put it on the table. He did it so quickly I had a moment of doubt, but no regrets. I felt a lot more relaxed. Noubad had lost track of what he was saying. She asked if his wife was Japanese or foreign. He smiled like a schoolboy found cheating at cards.

"Japanese," he said. "*Atarimae*, my wife's Japanese. She used to be a stewardess for Japan Airlines." He loved his wife very much. They wanted children but so far they had none. Fertility rates of Japanese women were falling. All the chemicals and shit poured into the land and rivers getting into the water supply. Heavy metals, chrome, cadmium, mercury, lead.

"The Japanese say they love nature, but they fuck it like a whore." Noubad remembered himself and apologised. I guessed his anger and sadness made him speak like that. I said it was all right. I looked across at her and she looked back at me and I knew what she was thinking. So did Noubad.

He got up from the table and adjusted his cuffs and his suit jacket like a professional gambler repeating a ritual of self-composure. Suddenly I regretted asking him to stop fiddling with the miniature cocktail shaker or whatever it was. I said he needn't go and he hesitated.

"I'd better go," he said. He managed to call up a ghost of the wolfish grin we'd seen earlier. "I'm sure you both have a lot to talk about." He told us to take it easy and with an oddly artificial wave of his hand like an actor in a sixties TV series he disappeared among the passers-by.

I wasn't sure what to say. Noubad had cast a shadow over the brightness of the evening. It wasn't a sinister shadow, but something about the conversation disturbed me.

Perhaps I was imagining it. I sometimes wonder what is real and what is imaginary; old friends, new faces, meetings, the same faces in different places, the memories of journeys. Perhaps it's all imagination, or semi-random patterns of electro-chemical energy in the warm dark of the brain, or the illusion of the Buddha.

We finished our drinks and I asked for the bill. It took a while to get a car at Roppongi crossing. It was late and the drivers were looking for long-distance fares out to Chiba and Narita. When they saw foreigners they stepped on the accelerator. It took so long that finally we stood beside a Japanese couple and when a taxi pulled up and the door opened we pushed past and jumped inside. I knew the Japanese couple would think it was typical late-night behaviour by foreigners. I felt bad about it, but it wasn't the moment to redefine cultural stereotypes.

Her parents were away and she invited me in for coffee. We talked all night till the shape of the trees emerged from the dark and the sky grew pale and there was a pink glow on the white wall opposite the window. It was sunrise and it seemed like a good moment to say goodnight. She said she'd see me to the top of the steps going down to the railway station.

She stood at the top of the steps and I looked at her and thought how it always seems to happen when one least expects it, as if most of the time one is on guard and then, just for a second, one's attention wavers and that's when it happens. I looked at her and wondered if it could last or how long it would take to heal.

The steps were in shadow, but the garden wall beside us was in sunlight. The tops of the trees in the garden were swaying in the morning breeze, and on a branch growing over the wall, there were two wood pigeons in the sunlight.

Sooner or later one of them was going to fly away. I could go before it happened, although we hadn't even begun to say goodbye—or I could wait until one of the birds flew away and like a signal it would be the moment to leave.

I opened my hands as if I was about to clap my hands. She smiled and opened her hands also.

"You," I said.

"No, you," she said.

The birds lifted into the air at almost exactly the same moment. I was on the second flight of steps when I heard her calling to me to wait. I looked back to where she was standing under the branches of the tree silhouetted by the brightness of the sky.

"Wait," she said.

I stood holding on to the white-painted metal handrail, thinking I will remember this for the rest of my life: the coolness of the air, the brightness, the shadows of the trees, the silence and the sight of her standing at the top of the steps, just after calling to me.

As I climbed the steps back to where she was I thought about love and time and I felt sad, even though I was happy.

"You didn't say goodbye," she said as she leaned forward to kiss me.

○

I arranged to meet Sasaki like last time at Shibuya. I was looking forward to our meeting. I regretted not seeing him more often. Perhaps I was too shy, too Japanese with him.

I arrived a few minutes early. There were a lot of foreigners: some tourist types, and men in suits looking at women with shiny shoes and expensive handbags.

Sasaki came towards me smiling and we shook hands. As we went towards the restaurant he patted me gently on my shoulder. I felt even closer to him than the last time. I apologised for not calling him sooner. He told me not to worry about it, over the last few weeks he'd been busy. He'd become a grandfather again, for the third time.

We sat at a table by the window and had a prawn pilaf together. He talked about coming out of prison and meeting his wife; she was ten years younger than he, she'd given him two sons and they'd had a good marriage.

"I'm lucky," he said. "A lot of people of my generation never had the chance."

I asked if he thought he had survived by chance, or did he believe there was a reason why he was alive and so many others died. He nodded and said it's possible to make one's luck, like karma. Perhaps he survived because in a past life he was a good man who helped the poor. Or perhaps he was a monk and by his prayers he accumulated merit, good karma or good luck for future lives.

"We don't know these things," he said. "Nobody knows. All the scriptures, the teachings of the Buddha and the sayings of Jesus tell us: what we sow we harvest. It says in the Bible— we throw our bread on the water and it comes back to us. That's the way it works. It all comes back in the end, it goes round like a circle."

We talked about the books he'd read in prison. He said it was a way for him to be free.

"I used to read this book and experience freedom." He'd forgotten the name of the book. He frowned and tapped his index finger on the table while he tried to remember. "This book, anyway," he went on, "I read the stories in it and I felt I was there. It was so real. That's when I began to explore who I was. Being in prison was like a monastery. It wasn't an ordinary prison. Some people said we were only criminals because we lost the war. Whatever the reason, we were there, it was something we had to endure, *gaman shinakereba*. In such circumstances, a number of us studied books of philosophy and religion. Even now, when I meet people from those days in jail I am surprised how many are religious."

The thought crossed my mind that a lot of people, when they sense their death approaching, take a more lively interest in religion, but I didn't say anything.

He was looking into my eyes to see if I appreciated the meaning of what he was saying. I believed him. I didn't feel like he was putting on a show of religion and I was the audience. He was telling me what he believed, he was showing me who he was, describing his philosophical position and presenting his beliefs. With someone else it could've been embarrassing but there was no false modesty in what he said. From time to time his eyes caught the light.

"This is my body," he said. "This is my country, this is my world, this is my universe." His forehead was smooth and his silver hair was combed back. "This moment belongs to me," he continued, "so does the next moment, and the next, and the next. Knowing this, there is nothing to be afraid of, but the difficult thing is remembering."

"How do you remember?" I said. He frowned.

"What do you call it? I've forgotten how you say it in English. You sit on the floor with your legs crossed and your back straight and you breathe. It's like meditation. You take a breath right down here," he touched somewhere below his navel, just above the belt of his trousers.

"*Hara*," he said. "You breathe towards the centre of your body. You clean your body, then you clean your mind." I couldn't stop a big grin spreading across my face. I was sitting with an ex-war criminal who was telling me how to meditate. I wasn't smiling because of what he was saying. It was more like a smile of recognition.

"You breathe and you think to yourself I am here, I am alive,

I am breathing, like this," he breathed in through his nostrils and out through his mouth. "And you do that for ten, maybe twenty minutes." He laughed "My wife said it keeps me out of mischief, and it's cheaper than golf."

We sat and sipped at our glasses of iced water. Outside the sun was shining and the branches of the willow trees were waving in the wind. I thought of the time he talked about the seasons and described how the passing of the seasons changed people's hearts and their feelings towards each other. I meant to ask him before. When did one season end and another begin?

In the old days it was easy to say. Before there was air conditioning and refrigeration, when people knew the seasons by their bodies, they could feel it with their blood. In the country there were trees and birds and insects and animals, the stars and the weather showing the times of the seasons. In the city there was almost nothing to distinguish one season from another.

"People are living at unnatural speed," he said. "They live by artificial time, they measure everything by money. The seasons are natural."

We talked about the changing weather patterns of the world and he reminded me of the Buddhist doctrine that during the final age in the cycle of the universe, the law of the Buddha will be almost forgotten and the world will become like hell.

"Maybe that's what's happening now," he said. He didn't seem too worried. I asked why.

"I wake up in the morning, I open my eyes and I take one day at a time, I've had a long life. I've seen my grandchildren. Moment by moment. One day at a time. I don't know what's going to happen tomorrow. The best I can do is do my best today. Everything is sacred, so everything one does is an act of reverence. If you believe in God, then God is in everything, and everything you say and do is prayer."

Sometimes he sounded as if he was quoting from the Bible

or a Zen manual of instant enlightenment, like Ron's book: *Handbook to Higher Consciousness*. Other times he was just an old man telling a younger man what he had learned in the course of his life. I looked at his face and thought about his past. Perhaps he was a criminal who had committed atrocities, perhaps he was an innocent man who was convicted and jailed because he was in the wrong place at the wrong time. Guilty or innocent, his life, the journey leading through the bloody coconut grove in the Philippines and the long years in prison changed the meaning of what he said. I had the feeling he was telling me the truth. I suppose we were both aware we might not get another chance to meet and perhaps he was saying things he wouldn't otherwise have said. I didn't want to think about him dying. To my surprise I sensed tears in my eyes.

It was almost four o'clock when we said goodbye at Shibuya station. I bowed like a *deshi* to his *sensei*. Perhaps we should have shaken hands.

○

I've just got back from the cleaners. I told him I would be leaving Tokyo soon. It was strange to hear myself saying so. He said he would miss me. He'd enjoyed our conversations together. I said I had too. He asked what I was going to do and I mentioned an idea I had to go and live in the country and write a book. He was full of polite admiration. He wanted to know what kind of book, a book about Japan? Even if he tried he wouldn't be able to write a book.

"I clean clothes," he said. "I could never write a book about Japan." He was smiling and I was smiling. He's a good man and his smile was genuine but there was also a trace of friendly mockery in the conversation. A foreigner writing about Japan. Perhaps it wasn't so strange after all. He said the only foreign country he'd visited was China, during the war, when he was a soldier in Manchuria. He used to speak some Chinese, but now all he can remember are the numbers one to ten and a few other words. He laughed. He murmured something and looked at me from under his eyebrows to see if I understood. I didn't. He grinned and covered his mouth with his hand, then wrote a character on a piece of paper on the counter.

An electronic bell rang, and an automatic pre-recorded voice greeted another customer coming into the shop. He slipped his hand over the half-finished character on the piece of paper. The customer had a suit to be cleaned but she wanted it done in a special way. Her instructions took a long time. She talked and he nodded and smiled and kept his hand over the scrap of paper.

I looked around the shop at the banks of suits in plastic bags, the single strip of fluorescent lighting over the little white counter with a laundry ticket taped to it, and the sticker sign on the sliding glass door of a big red heart and the words in English "We love leather." It wasn't the first time I'd seen the sign. The old man doesn't look the type who's into black leather. My guess is that he's a *burakumin* and the sign is a gentle symbol of resistance in English, not Japanese. Several times I've been on the point of asking him, but each time something has stopped me.

"Are you a member of the untouchable class?" Whichever way one says it the question sounds bad. Language can dictate a false reality. I've avoided asking the question but I work on the assumption that he's one of the "village people."

Sometimes we talk while the other customers come and go and there's always a warmth to our conversations. It's different from the easy politeness and good humour of a *salariman* who meets foreigners every day, knows which jokes work with Americans but not with Europeans and is fluent in the cocktail-bar chatter of intercontinental hotels.

Propped up against the little white counter surrounded by the suits in plastic bags, he tells me about his problems with the drains and the *sarakin* loan sharks and the cost of land. Sometimes he talks about his time as a soldier; waking up in the morning and tapping his boots to get rid of the scorpions, marching day after day for hundreds of miles and at night going to sleep on the frozen ground, to the sound of artillery fire.

The way he talks reminds me of people in the country. Perhaps there's an understanding between us because we're both outsiders in Japan. Perhaps we knew each other in a past life. We have an understanding anyway.

The woman was still explaining how she wanted him to clean the lining and his hand was still resting over the scrap of paper. I bowed and said I would see him later. On the way back I wondered about the character on the scrap of paper and why he concealed it. He did it so quickly it seemed almost like a reflex action, as if showing me what he had written was something shameful to be hidden from other people. A sign of paranoia, maybe, but it was also a sign of friendship, a secret that we almost shared.

○

I didn't expect to fall in love. Certainly not like this.

I met her in Ebisu at the station exit and we went to a bar nearby where a band was playing reggae music. At first we talked with an African diplomat who was sitting at the table next to us.

"Je suis mal d'amour," he said and leaned towards us like a conspirator. "I am suffering from the sickness of love." His teeth were very white and he laughed a lot as he drank his way through a bottle of brandy, making jokes about the malady of love. After a while we got up to dance and when we returned to our table he was gone. We stayed a couple of hours.

We walked all the way back to Nakameguro and stopped outside her house. I didn't know what to say. I'd fallen in love with her and she was going away, leaving Japan, going to Europe.

I thought of saying I loved her, but the words "I love you"

seemed clumsily big and serious as we stood under the street light. There was a *semi* somewhere in the shadows of the bushes.

I felt Japan closing around me: the darkness of the starless sky and the claustrophobia of the little streets smelling of grilled fish, steamed vegetables and rice, it was all closing around me, preventing me from saying what I would have liked to say. In my imagination it had almost surrounded me and I was disappearing like a ripple in reverse, into Japan.

The scene could have been a panel in a *manga* comic; a man talking with a woman at the end of a street, under a street light. A motorbike screamed along the motorway below followed by the wailing of a police-car siren. I said I hoped we'd meet again, either here or in Europe.

"Wait for me," she said. "Can you wait?"

"Yes," I said. "I think so."

She kissed me and we said goodbye and suddenly she wasn't there and I was standing at the top of the steps where we kissed at sunrise.

○

It's late and I have to get up early tomorrow but I can't sleep. Tomorrow I'm leaving Tokyo for the country. I'm going to write a book. There's a piece of paper in front of me on which I've written some notes: it's autobiographical, and it's written in the first person. It's about going and returning and the brush stroke that comes full circle.

I like the idea of going to the country and writing. It's in the tradition of those Chinese poets a thousand years ago who gave up the quest for power as mandarins and retired to the mountains, where they got drunk on rice wine and wrote tear-stained verses about the beauty of the autumn moon. Not just the Chinese poets. It was about this time of year when Basho wrote his *haiku*: "The first autumn rains, from now on my name shall be 'Traveller,' " and now, three hundred years later, reading the beginning of his book *The Narrow Road to the Deep North* makes my heart beat so that sleep is impossible.

"Days and months are travellers of eternity. So are the years that pass by. Those who steer a boat across the sea, or ride a horse over the earth until they yield to the weight of years, spend every minute of their lives travelling. Many of the men of old died on the road. I have been tempted for a long time by the cloud moving wind, filled with a strong desire to wander."

○

The sky is grey and the leaves are still. The shutters and the sliding paper doors are pushed back and from where I am, sitting cross-legged on the frayed *tatami*, I can just see the river through the trees.

An old *obaachan* is walking along the path. She moves with difficulty—her head is sunk into her shoulders and her back is bent: just looking up from the ground seems an effort. She's stopped for a rest, framed by the branches of a willow tree. She's almost hidden by the tall grass at the bottom of the melon patch, like a ghost resting under the willow. She's looking again in this direction, but there's a willow branch directly in the line of vision between her eyes and my eyes. If I move my head slightly I can see her face. But she's moved her head again so that the willow branch is still between us. I guess she's curious to see who's staying in the old summerhouse.

I bowed to her and she moved her head in a way which could have been a bow or she might have been looking at the path in front of her. I said hello in a voice which was loud enough for her to hear and there was a faint cackle of "*Konni-chiwa.*" Probably she was aware of my presence all the time and the screening of the willow branch was intentional.

Now she's disappeared and I'm listening to the sound of the river wondering what I'm doing here, playing peekaboo with a Japanese grandmother. I've been here a week and I haven't written more than a couple of pages.

I thought it would be the perfect place to write a book about Japan: a dilapidated wooden summerhouse with sun-split walls that let the wind in, but a roof that keeps the rain out, overlooking a melon patch by the side of a river. It's like one of those little huts hidden in the landscape of a scroll painting, only there's a road with lorries going past on the other side of the river and the person sitting in the hut looking at the falling leaves is a foreigner.

This is like the image I had of Japan before I came here: a land of wooded valleys with mountain peaks disappearing in cloud mists and somewhere in the picture a solitary figure gazing at distant hills. And now I've managed to find my way into the scroll painting. There's a red dragonfly on the *tatami*, exactly like a *haiku*. It's as close as I have been to the heart of Japan, to *kokoro*.

Describing what it's like, it becomes something else.

I've found what I was looking for, but it's not what I hoped it would be.

Before I came to Japan it existed in my imagination as an ideal world. My first impressions were disappointing. I gazed through the rain-spattered windows of the airport bus at the rice fields under the pylons and the grey buildings and office blocks of Tokyo and I felt cheated. There wasn't a thatched cottage or a Buddhist monk in sight.

I tried to forget the ideal world I hoped to find. But the memory of it never died away completely. Sometimes, at odd moments, I would see something like a butterfly on a temple bell or a lump of snow falling from the shoulder of a statue of the Buddha and the memory of the world I once imagined came to life again. Those moments helped me to believe in the myth of old Japan.

Some people think the old Japan is the real Japan. I also used to think it was the real Japan and I thought if I was patient, like Daruma, I might one day find enlightenment and understand it all.

Living in the country, in Kashima, the past wasn't far away.

I saw the moon rise over the Kashima shrine like Basho three hundred years before me, and in my mind's eye I hung the moon like a lantern on the branches of a tree, as the old poet once did. At sword practice in the *dojo* I drew my sword in the same shrine as the sword master Sukhara Bokuden, in a pattern of movements he established in the seventeenth century. On New Year's Day I pounded rice cakes and got drunk on *sake* with his several times great grandson.

For a long time I believed the real Japan was anything not disfigured by the present, but gradually I was disillusioned. The Buddha teaches that one must lose illusions to find enlightenment. I learned that disillusionment is not enlightenment.

The colours of the fields and the trees and the sky were the same as they were a thousand years ago but the pylons were there and at night when I went outside to look at the moon, the sky over the Sumitomo steel factory glowed like the background of a painting of hell by Hieronymus Bosch.

Even so, in the country it was possible to pretend the modern world was some kind of aberration, a temporary sickness that had infected the country, a shadow that in time would pass away, and everything would be healed.

In Kyoto something of old Japan survived. There was a McDonald's ten minutes' walk from where we lived in Kittaku, but thirty minutes in the other direction, into the woods at the back of the house, there was a stockade made by the woodcutters to trap the wild boars of the forest. And there were all those temples and monasteries and rock gardens.

Sitting in Ryoanji gazing on waves of raked sand is one way to believe in the myth of Japan. I did a lot of it. Perhaps I needed to believe in the myth to continue living in Japan, because the myth of Japan was Japan. Without the myth, Japan was a wasteland of factories, a vast machine without a purpose, a place without a soul.

The more one believes in a myth, the more powerful it becomes. I believed in the myth of Japan, because almost every Japanese I met believed in it. Now I'm not so sure.

Not long after I arrived in Japan someone told me that to understand Japan it's necessary to understand *kokoro*, so I looked up *kokoro* in the dictionary and found "heart, mind, feeling, thought or mood." The character of *kokoro* is close to the original pictogram. Through half-closed eyes the four curved brush strokes make a stylised picture of a heart. It seemed simple enough: understand the heart, understand the people.

Perhaps at the heart of the myth of Japan is *kokoro*. Perhaps sitting on worn *tatami*, in a one-room shack overlooking a melon patch overgrown with autumn grasses, is close to *kokoro*. In Tokyo it seemed like the perfect place to write a book about Japan but now I'm here I'm thinking about someone on the other side of the world.

I can live where I am, but it's not my home.

Home is where the heart is.

○

I got on the subway train at Roppongi. The carriage was crowded and there weren't any seats so I stood by the door. At Hiro the train stopped, the doors opened and an old man in spectacles stepped into the carriage beside me. I noticed the old man smiling at me and then I recognised him: Sasaki-sensei.

He said he was hoping we would meet another time before I left Japan. He seemed gently amused by our meeting. It took a while to realise he couldn't have known we were going to meet. I kept thinking he must have known it was going to happen. He said how much he enjoyed our last meeting and asked me to give his kind regards to Christina in London. My mind kept swerving away from the coincidence of our meeting. I thought of the Arab saying: A meeting by chance is worth a thousand meetings by appointment. I also thought it might be a sign, his way of saying goodbye, *ichigo-ichie*, and I studied his face in case it was our last meeting.

He didn't say anything particularly memorable, which made

everything seem stranger because it was all so ordinary, as if it was meant to happen and we'd both arranged to meet in the same carriage of a particular subway train, at a certain time: an impossible rendezvous.

He left the train at Ebisu and as the doors closed I heard him say the word "*Sayonara*."

○

This afternoon I went into the office to give the keys of the house back to Maria Santini in Administration. She was sitting with her potted plant and her computer in a glass-walled cubicle in a corner of the room.

"So you've decided to leave us," she said and gave one of her fashion-model smiles. It wasn't a pretty sight, the red lips peeling back to reveal a row of white teeth and the pale blue eyes watching without a change of expression. I wondered if she gave the Japanese people the same feeling she gave me. I said I thought the relief was mutual.

She frowned as if she'd seen something on her screen which shouldn't have been there, but she was still looking at me. She asked if I'd got the keys and I handed them over. She put the keys in an envelope which she sealed and laid on the desk. She took some time. I assumed this was to remind me of my importance relative to the keys in the envelope. Eventually she looked up and asked what happened.

Was there a problem with Takahashi or Yamaguchi? Or was it money? Perhaps there was a headhunter somewhere in the picture? She asked questions in a way which made me think she already knew the answers. But I didn't mind. I said I thought there was a communication problem: not enough information getting through to the people who needed it. With everything on a need-to-know basis, nobody knew what was happening. She took a sip of water from the glass beside her and licked her lips appreciatively. Then she asked where I thought there was a breakdown in communication. I guessed at the ideas going on at the back of her mind. I said something non-committal about the language barrier obstructing the flow of information. She asked me to be more specific. I mentioned Laroche. The head of the office in Tokyo couldn't speak Japanese. How could he know what was going on? She gave another of her smiles and said she was quite sure the head of the Tokyo office had an excellent knowledge of the situation.

"He has his eyes and ears," she said, "like you and me." The smile showed she was pleased with herself. It seemed a good moment to mention Yamaguchi. I said there was also a communication problem between me, Yamaguchi and Laroche. She laughed and told me how Yamaguchi and Laroche have known each other for years. They were friends long before either of them joined the company. They were at the same business school in Switzerland.

I knew Yamaguchi and Laroche had a special relationship, but what she said was like a missing piece, it made sense of other things as well. I thanked her for the information and said it could be useful for the book I was writing. She gave me the sort of look one might expect from one of those creatures pulled out of the sea from several miles down in the Marinas Trench. Then she threw her glass at me.

"Get out!" she screamed. "Get out of here, damn you, get out!"

Some women are supposed to become more beautiful when they're angry, but Maria Santini wasn't one of them. I asked for a cloth to dry my clothes but she didn't seem to hear me. She kept screaming the same words, "Get out of here, get out of here," at the top of her voice. Her reaction took me by surprise; if I had been thinking more clearly I might have asked someone to call a doctor. The noise she was making sounded like she was experiencing an extreme case of sexual harassment. People in the office were looking, their faces were worried. The front of my trousers was soaking wet and she was still screaming, "Get out of here, get out of here." I thought of trying to talk it through but it didn't seem worth it. She was out of control—or else she knew exactly what she was doing. Either way, there was a serious communication problem. I would have liked to know the trigger. It must have been something I said, perhaps it was the word "book."

I got up and went into the main area of the office. As I reached the door I had an idea for an exit line, "Thanks for cleaning my suit, please send me your bill." But she'd gone. I caught the eye of one of the secretaries. She seemed unsure whether to look solemn or laugh. I said something about the weather and closed the door behind me.

I took the lift down to the basement, level three and sat in The Café Human reading the *Japan Times* until my trousers dried. Then I came back here to Joe's and gave the dogs their supper.

○

This afternoon Yoshiko invited me to a tea ceremony at her sister's house in the country. I'd forgotten what time we arranged and I arrived an hour late. While things were being prepared in the tea room I sat near the door watching a quiz game on the television.

Yoshiko appeared in a *kimono* decorated with red and yellow maple leaves, with an orange *obi*. She looked good in a *kimono*, better than in a Western working-woman's suit. She seemed more relaxed and her gestures had a grace which was in harmony with her dress. It was a while since I'd been to a formal tea ceremony and I'd forgotten the correct way to receive a tea bowl, drink tea, and examine the bowl afterwards. I asked her to remind me before we went into the tea room. She told me not to worry. Her sister was used to preparing tea for foreigners; she understood that kneeling on one's heels, *seiza*-style, for hours is difficult for some people.

"Japanese find it painful, too," she said. "But we drink tea for pleasure, not for pain." She said it would be fine if I sat on a cushion.

She drew back a door and we entered the tea room. Her sister was wearing a pale brown *kimono* with a dark red *obi*. Behind her, a paper window was drawn back, through a bamboo lattice I could see the dark green shadows of a bamboo grove.

I knelt and watched her performing the movements of the tea ceremony. I noticed the way she folded the red silk scarf, listened to the sound of the water boiling and watched the threads of steam vanishing. I looked at the scroll picture of three persimmons hanging in the *tokonoma* recess and the *ikebana* flower arrangement of a piece of wood decorated with moss and dried grasses and a single white chrysanthemum.

I made an effort to notice the things I'd been taught to appreciate in the tea ceremony, like the *wabi*, natural simplicity of the wooden utensils, the *sabi*, timeless poetry of autumn, and the *honne*, the true feeling, the spirit of a traditional tea-ceremony ritual, performed by a master of the art of tea. The pain in my knees was excruciating. I tried to concentrate on the stillness of things, the soft turquoise colour of one of the tea bowls, the dark chocolate colour of the other. For a while the pain was almost unbearable. I considered fainting, or pretending to faint, and wondered what the best way would be. Then the pain died away and I lost all sensation in my legs. I remembered something I'd read about the tea ceremony, that it included many elements of Japanese culture and it became like a game trying to identify them: the painting and the poetry of the scroll picture, the pottery ceramics of the tea bowls, the weaving and embroidery of the *kimono*.

I watched Yoshiko's sister scoop the green tea powder into the bowls, pour the steaming water over it and mix the liquid with a bamboo brush. An agonizing cramp gripped my knees. Yoshiko passed me a sweet made of powdery sugar shaped like a crescent moon and then as I leaned forward I managed to ease my legs into a slightly different position. The soles of my feet felt as if they were on fire.

At last it was time to drink the tea. I had the turquoise bowl and the tea inside was a brilliant green, like the surface of a pond, covered in weed, or the Amazon rain forest, seen from the air. I held the bowl in both hands and raised it to my lips. It tasted OK, like a warm, slightly bitter, vichyssoise. I said it was delicious.

Once the bowl was empty it was time to look at it and admire its shape, its glaze and its texture. I liked the colour, but the shape had a commercial line to it which seemed slightly odd for a tea bowl. I complimented Yoshiko's sister on its beautiful and interesting qualities. She said she had chosen it for its colour which she felt had a Persian blue. It was bought in western China, in Xinjiang. The moment she saw it, she knew she would use it as a tea bowl. She chose it for the tea ceremony because she had heard I had been in Afghanistan. She asked if I had noticed the shape of the sweets—crescents like the moon of Islam.

There was a noise outside the bamboo lattice window. Two motor-bikers appeared and halted their machines on the edge of the bamboo grove. They kept their machines running, now and again revving the engines in clouds of blue smoke.

Yoshiko's sister continued speaking but it was difficult to hear what she was saying. We talked about the aesthetics of the tea ceremony and I asked her if, in her teaching, she sometimes came across a pupil who had no talent at all.

Yoshiko's sister smiled. She was reluctant to admit anyone could be without talent, but sometimes, yes, there were people who seemed to have no sense of delicacy, no *yuga*. In such cases, I wondered, what could she do. It wasn't an easy question for her. She didn't want to say that someone was unable to learn. In some cases it took time, two, three or even five years, before there was any noticeable improvement. But in almost every case, even with extremely unpromising pupils, there was always some character development.

The bikers switched off their engines and disappeared into the bamboo grove. Yoshiko's sister's smile suggested a serene approval. I was fascinated; what about the person who had no *yuga,* and after five years had learned nothing at all. Did such people exist? The thought was awesome, like a psychic rhinoceros. Yoshiko's sister gave a nervous titter at the thought of such a grossly insensitive pupil. I persisted. If she had such a pupil what did she do? She smiled again and then her face softened into a look of compassion. "It takes time," she said, "sometimes they just go."

I asked about the modern cult of the tea ceremony and how it sometimes seemed like a social game for one-upping other people. She gave me a blank look. After a couple of attempts to rephrase the question I gave up and Yoshiko asked if the weather in England was similar to the weather here in Japan at this time of year. We all seemed to feel more comfortable talking about the weather and we spent a quarter of an hour or more discussing the colour of the leaves and the wind and rain and then Yoshiko asked if I remembered the *haiku* by Basho: "The first autumn rains, from now on my name shall be 'Traveller.' " I said it was one of my favourite *haiku.* She was pleased. She had asked a friend to carve a *hanko* for me using the characters for journey and man. Tabi and Hito. She hoped that Tabibito was a close enough translation of my name. As I was leaving she presented me with a small square parcel wrapped in silver-blue paper.

I would have liked to open the present, but I did what I thought most Japanese would do; I simply thanked her and put it in my pocket.

Perhaps the Japanese are right to be cautious of opening gifts in front of the giver, in case the present is a disappointment. Perhaps it's a civilised custom. But I would have liked to tell her how much I liked her present.

It's on the table in front of me: a piece of bamboo about the size of my little finger. One end has been trimmed and cut with the characters for Tabibito.

When I pick it up it has another meaning. Close to the base of the *hanko* seal a knot in the bamboo has been trimmed smooth. A natural groove in the bamboo leads to the knot at a point where a stem has been cut away, making a small platform in the wood. Picking up the *hanko* and holding it upright like a *fude* bamboo brush it fits naturally into my hand, in exactly the position it needs to be held to give a good, clear print.

It wasn't possible to appreciate this refinement by looking at it. I only discovered the thoughtfulness of the man who carved the *hanko* when I used it for the first time. Perhaps he thought a foreigner might not know the characters and would use the *hanko* the wrong way round. He chose the wood specially for its shape. The form has a meaning, a silent instruction, how the *hanko* should be used.

As I leave Japan, I receive a Japanese name: Tabibito.

○

The leaves remaining on the trees are like golden faces half hidden in the darkness.

○

I'm at Tony's apartment near Shibuya, and we're watching the enthronement of the Emperor on television. Tony's lying on his *futon* with a fever he picked up in the Philippines. I'm sitting on the floor eating a tangerine. It's possible to hear the sound of the crows near the enthronement ceremony; their cries make it seem as if it's taking place somewhere in the country. It reminds me of watching the previous old Emperor on television, standing in rubber boots in a paddy field, planting the sacred rice.

There's the sound of a siren somewhere in the street.

The slow, measured way the figures on the television are moving has an other-worldly quality, as if they step through the present from another time. I can still hear the crows. It's like a medieval scene, a princess passing, the cawing of crows in the trees. The Emperor of Japan is sitting very still. So is the Empress. Looking at them, motionless in their antique finery, two tiny figures framed by the square of the television screen, it's difficult not to think of the elaborate dolls displayed in Japanese houses during Ningyo Matsuri, the Festival of the Dolls. The sound of a helicopter passes over the house. Tokyo is like a city under martial law. There are police checks everywhere. Last night, on a short walk to the local shrine, I passed four sets of police patrolling the street. People in Tokyo are beginning to complain. A few days ago a policeman was killed by a bomb planted, according to the newspapers, by left-wing extremists. There have been fires at several shrines.

○

With all the heads of state, security has to be tight. An unpleasant incident would be serious loss of face. The Emperor moves. On the television there's a ritual that goes back a thousand years and outside in the street there's another siren, a sound like a wave on a shore, the roar of a crowd watching someone score, and a man's voice shouting through a loudspeaker.

○

It's a demonstration against the Emperor and there are police everywhere, in dark blue uniforms, and riot helmets, carrying shields and staves.

The marchers are wearing blue anoraks and construction helmets. Most of them have covered their faces with scarves and dark glasses. They're marching in rows of four, in groups of a hundred or so, carrying flags and blowing whistles. The group at the head of the march is smaller, maybe twenty or thirty people and at the very front there's a man with his arms held behind him by two people on each side. I guess they're holding him like that so he can't raise a hand to defend himself: a sort of moral battering ram.

The marchers are walking between the lines of police on either side of the road and they're coming to a crossroads.

There are two grey police vans like army patrol vehicles from which police commanders are directing operations. One of the commanders is telling his men to take it easy. The police are closing in on the marchers, they're presenting a wall of shields against them, pushing them against the railing at the side of the road.

It's beginning to get out of control.

The marchers behind are still pushing forward, pressing the people at the front against the police who are holding their ground. A pair of spectacles flies out of the scrum and lands in front of me. The commander is telling his men where to apply pressure. It's getting uglier. A couple of photographers are trying to take pictures over the heads of the marchers and the police. A fist smacks into the face of the man at the front of the demonstration. He's gone down in the crush. I can see his hand. His fingers are moving. The people on either side are holding him up, they've lost their dark glasses and their scarves have been torn from their faces. They're in their early twenties.

The police are telling the journalists and cameramen to get out of the way. The marchers are being squeezed against the railings at the side of the road. A policeman with a video camera is filming the scene. The man at the head of the march has lost his helmet and his face is bloody. It could be fake blood but it looks real. The police chief with his loudspeaker is telling his men to take it easy, and they're backing off slowly, letting the marchers move away from the railings.

It was looking ugly but there don't seem to be any serious injuries. The marchers have got back into rows of four. They're marching again, blowing whistles and moving forward, keeping in rhythm with the chorus of whistles.

The patrol vehicles have pulled away and the police are withdrawing, running ahead of the marchers and taking up new positions a couple of hundred metres down the road.

The marchers are keeping a steady pace, and the leaders are raising their hands above their heads. They're wearing white industrial gloves, the sort carpenters and builders wear, and they're making hand signals to the marchers following them, holding up a fist or pointing to the left or the right.

A man next to me in a baseball hat has a video camera on his shoulder and he's zooming in on one of the marchers whose scarf has been torn aside in the struggle. There are a lot of people with cameras and I can't believe they're all tourists, like the men in casual wear on the edge of things, whose clothes and shoes are too clean and new-looking. After today I guess the people whose scarves have been torn aside will be on police file.

The demonstrators keep marching and the police direct the way they have to go, making a wall of shields diagonally across the road at the next crossroads. The police chief is speaking into a microphone attached to his helmet. It looks like there are receivers in the helmets of his men. They run in groups, often ten or so at a time, and take up position as if they've practised it all lots of times before. It's like one of those shows by people in uniform; a display of discipline, timing and organisation.

There's some kind of thrill seeing a lot of people behaving like machines, even if it's only horror.

The police are wearing boots made of black leather. The marchers are wearing scuffed trainers. The police are standing still, waiting for the demonstrators who are coming towards them. One or two individuals among the passers-by watching the marchers applaud the ranks of people in blue plastic anoraks as they go past. A chorus of whistles. The flag carriers are walking towards the police.

It's a strange feeling; seeing people in conflict, here in Japan, in the land of *wa*, the country of harmony. It's almost like an *omatsuri* festival, only different. The man beside me is clapping applause. The marchers at the front are weaving to the left and the right and the people behind are following. They're moving together, in a serpentine formation, like a Chinese dragon, a couple of hundred people in rows of four, holding on to each other, moving in a single body, like a dragon at a Chinese New Year celebration. The dragon flows towards the wall of shields and at the last moment it swerves away without breaking it and it's turning to the right, up a lane towards a small park where it swerves through the trees and comes to rest in a children's playground.

I ask an *obaachan* next to me what she thinks of it all.

"*Baka desu*," she says, "It's silly." It reminds me of the Zen monk who said: "In the end, truth is nothing but the wisdom of old women."

The marchers going past now are different from the ones at the front. They're not wearing helmets or scarves over their faces. They're middle-aged or older, they look like labourers and school teachers from the country: farmers from Narita; Christians demonstrating against the idea that a man should be worshipped as a God, in the person of the Emperor; even a few old-style communists.

There's a line of people in wheelchairs and then a lot of families with children. They're almost all wearing trainers and their clothes have a sameness as if everything was bought from the same store: the uniform of the poor.

The police lining the road are standing still and the demonstrators are moving past them, towards the little park and children's playground where the leaders of the march are already making speeches from the top of a climbing frame.

Walking among the marchers, listening to the speeches, asking people why they've come, I keep hearing the same reasons: the Emperor system was used by the military before the Second World War; without the Emperor the war might not have happened. They say he is a man like anyone else and it's only the politicians who want to have the enthronement ceremony. Some see it as evidence of a capitalist conspiracy by the ancient power brokers of Japan. They criticise it for being a waste of money and they complain that they, the people, were not consulted. They mention constitutional problems. How is it possible in a democracy to recognise the legitimacy of inherited authority? Why is the state paying for a ceremony which is supposed to be religious, unless it's really a celebration of the state religion? One or two quoted the Japanese constitution forbidding religious organisations to receive any privilege from the state. And who is paying?

Some refuse to answer. Either they suspect, even though I am a foreigner, that I may be some kind of agent working for the police or else, like the ones with brand-new trainers and white golfing hats, they themselves are undercover agents. When I put questions to them or the plain-clothes policemen standing around the edge of the park with their earphones in their ears like old-fashioned hearing aids, I know I'm doing something I'm not supposed to do. It's not wrong, or against the law. I suppose it's like putting a chameleon on a tartan rug, to see what happens. *Reigi tadashii nai*—it's not good manners. I asked one man why he was there and he looked at me. "For peace," he said and there was a humorous light in his eye, as if it was all an exercise in public relations, but the two men beside him were not amused.

The lanes leading to the park are guarded by police with helmets and shields and batons. The speeches are coming to an end. They all said more or less the same thing and everyone clapped at predictable words and phrases, like an audience applauding the lines of a famous play.

I was waiting for some kind of dramatic climax but this is Japan and the marchers' organisers are telling people where the nearest underground stations are. They are packing their rucksacks like well-behaved picnickers. There's a matter-of-fact, end-of-the-meeting atmosphere. It's more like a crowd of commuters from out of town than a demonstration against the Emperor—a whole lot of Japanese with trains to catch.

They file past the lines of police to the entrance of the underground. People are watching from the windows and balconies. I wonder if it's the same for them as it is for me, watching the marchers from the demonstration going into the underground like names vanishing at the end of a film.

The sky through the trees in the park is a luminous Chinese

pink shading to lilac overhead. The neon signs of the shops have been switched on and there's a darkness on the other side of the light.

The marchers have all gone. The police are blowing their whistles and moving in groups, towards a line of grey buses.

Walking back to Tony's flat I passed a row of televisions in a shop window and on the screens was the image of the man who was at the front of the march, with the bloody face. There was one big-size high definition television screen image and ten or twelve smaller ordinary images of the man moving around in synch with each other and then the picture switched to a man in a suit at a desk reading the news.

○

I suppose I feel nervous about leaving. I don't know when I'll be here again. If I'm here again, it'll be different. It always is. Endings in life are never like stories and fables, where the meaning or the moral comes at the end of the tale, like a journey makes sense when one arrives at the end of it.

Living here for a while and then leaving is more like a beginning: coming from somewhere in the future and somewhere in the past at the same time, arriving at the present, in a place that isn't Japan.

○

I'm on the bus to the airport and I hope I've got everything. I called Larry to tell him I was leaving and we arranged to meet at Shibuya. He helped me with my cases and the *pachinko* machine. We went for a quick meal at a noodle bar. It was difficult to believe it was happening; slurping noodles with Larry, thinking of being in another country, knowing some things only happen in Japan, and remembering how easy it is to forget them; like eating noodles with a friend.

We talked about Japan and the way foreigners see it. Larry said whichever way one looks at Japan, it's really a poor country and we had a good time arguing over the wealth of nations. Then we caught a taxi, collected the cases and the *pachinko* machine and headed towards the bus terminal.

The traffic was bad. There was a demonstration by rice farmers against the opening of the market to foreign imports. I began to worry about missing the plane. Larry was running late for another appointment and got out at some traffic lights.

"Read Adam Smith. Ask yourself if the invisible hand knows its left from its right." He waved as the taxi pulled away.

It could have been the answer to a *koan* or a *mondai*.

I waved back as a white Mitsubishi truck carrying a single, red-leafed maple tree came between us.

○

I didn't see any point in telling the baggage handlers about the package containing the *pachinko* machine. It was wrapped in cardboard. I watched the face of the man operating the baggage scanner. He frowned and then smiled and asked me what was in the package. I said it was a souvenir of my time in Japan.

The plastic colours and the flashing lights and the noises and the wheels spinning and the bells ringing and all the identical silver balls rolling around, the patience, the skill, the luck, the money, a way of passing the time; Japan is *pachinko*. *Pachinko* is Japan.

"It's *nihon-teki*," I said. "Very Japanese.

The man grinned and nodded and told me how much it would cost by air cargo.

I showed him the money I had. He sucked the air in through his teeth and asked if I had a credit card. I said I was hoping to take a bit of Japan home with me—something of the real Japan. I didn't think it was going to be so expensive. He sucked some more air in through his teeth and put his head on one side. How much did I want to pay? I wasn't sure what to say.

I didn't say anything. It was one of those occasions which sometimes happen in Japan when one has to behave like a dumb foreigner; the less said the better. Saying anything only complicates the situation.

He wanted to help me, but there were rules and regulations. He liked *pachinko*, but he had a duty to his company. He apologised for keeping me waiting, he had to consult someone. When he came back he was smiling. The money I had was enough. He wished me a safe journey and hoped I would have fun at home playing *pachinko*.

○

Things aren't so different here.

The sky is grey. The trees are bare.

Japanese people seem to like this part of town. I see them in smart clothes in little groups and I hear fragments of their conversation. They think we're stupid and dirty and we smell bad, but they like all the old buildings; it's like a big museum, a historical Disneyland, where they can buy things and take pictures of each other.

The other day I was walking up the hill. There was a small crowd of people by the war memorial. Three Japanese-looking men with a camera and sound unit were filming another young man dancing on the war memorial, between a pile of red poppies and a sound system playing a song with a synthetic beat. The dancer was moving like a robot, a man-made machine programmed to move in synch with the beat of the music. It was a slick act. He must have practised a lot. The passers-by who stopped to watch were fascinated: a Japanese man dancing like a robot on a war memorial.

I watched for a while and then I went up to him and said hello in Japanese.

"*Konnichiwa*," I said. He made no reaction.

I was curious. I wanted to know where he came from and what he was doing. He ignored my questions. He was in the middle of his act, pretending to be a robot, and I was asking him questions in Japanese. There was no reason why he should reply. For a moment I thought he might be Chinese, but then I noticed the guidebook beside him and saw its title was in Japanese. I asked him again what he was doing, but still he made no reaction. Finally I said that he didn't have to answer but I wanted to tell him that I really liked his act but perhaps he didn't realise, he was dancing on a war memorial and there were some people, maybe of an older generation, who might prefer him to dance somewhere else. He must have heard what I said. It was simple to understand. But he gave no sign of hearing or understanding. It was a typically Japanese reaction: no reaction.

Ignore a problem until it goes away. Deny something and there's nothing—nothing to disturb the harmony, nothing to worry about.

I thought about it.

Perhaps the dead, some of the dead, might be amused. Perhaps their death was not in vain if a young man could dance on their memorial in the autumn sunlight and perhaps it was really some kind of exorcism, a dance of peace and a celebration of life.

I said he could ignore me but I knew he could understand me and I told him about going to the Yasakuni shrine in Tokyo which was like the war memorial he was dancing on, dedicated to the spirits of those killed in war. Perhaps my attitude to the dead was a bit Japanese because I was in Japan: when in Rome do as the Romans, and of course it's a free country. But why didn't he respond to what I was saying?

He looked at me out of the corner of his eye and I knew then that he'd understood what I'd said. He didn't stop immediately—he went on until the end of the track and he finished his performance with a funny, disjointed-looking bow, like an electrical toy with the current suddenly switched off.

It was a great act.

o

It's getting darker.

A few minutes ago I was walking in the park looking at the sky which was cold and clear and thinking about putting my notes and recordings in some kind of order. They're like foreign objects. Their meaning is different, almost as if they belong to someone else.

It's difficult to know where to begin.

A figure on roller-skates came towards me, wearing a Tokyo Giants T-shirt. He was in his twenties, maybe a *salariman* working here. I looked at him as he swept past and he was smiling, not a mask smile or a Buddha smile; just a smile, roller-skating in the light of the big red sun in the West.

# GLOSSARY

*Ainu* The original inhabitants of Japan.
*Amae* Indulgence or induced dependence.
*Anshin* Peace of mind.
*Atarimae* Naturally; of course; as one would expect.
*Atsui* Hot.
*Banzai* Cheers; Hurrah (lit. ten thousand years.)
*Basho* Japan's greatest haiku poet (1644–94).
*Bento* A lunch box.
*Besso* Summer residence, cottage in the country.
*Bifubaaga* A beefburger.
*Burakumin* Village people.
*Buriko* Pretending to be a child: false cute.
*Bushi* An armed warrior.
*Bushido* The way of the armed warrior.
*Butsudan* A Buddha shelf; a family altar.
*Buzaki* Blossom.
*Chan* A suffix denoting affection.
*Chanko-nabe* A nourishing stew eaten in vast quantities by sumo wrestlers.
*Chienpira* A punk; a trainee yakuza gangster.
*Chotto* A little.
*Dai-jishin* Great confidence.
*Daikon-ashi* Radish legs.
*Dai-rieki* Great advantage.
*Da-me* No way; no go.
*Desu-ka* Is that so? Really? An interrogative suffix.
*Dojo* An exercise hall; training place (lit. way place).
*Domo* Thanks; sorry; good to meet you.
*Don-buri* A bowl of food.
*Dozo* Please; go ahead; be my guest.
*Erebeta* Elevator.
*Fude* Writing brush.
*Furu-sato* Birth place (lit. old village).
*Gaijin* A foreigner; an alien (lit. outside person).

*Gaijin-kusai* Foreigner-smelling.

*Gaman* Endurance; perseverance.

*Gaman shinakereba* One must endure.

*Gaman-tsuyoi* Good-at-enduring; strong-at-persevering.

*Ganbaru* To do one's best; Ganbarimasu—I shall do my best (often said in reply to "Ganbatte!"—Good luck! or Do your best!)

*Geisha* A person of artistic accomplishments; a multi-talented entertainer.

*Genki* Spirits; courage; energy; healthy (lit. original spirit).

*Geta* Wooden sandals.

*Gimu* Official duty; social obligation.

*Giri* Loyalty.

*Go* The game of go.

*Hadaka* Naked.

*Hai* Yes! Okay! Understood! Right! (Hai is not equivalent to "yes" in the English sense, which can sometimes lead to misunderstandings).

*Haiku* A seventeen-syllable poem containing a kigo or season-word.

*Hakuin* A Zen monk of the seventeenth century, famous for his use of the phrase "the sound of one hand clapping"; one of the principal figures of the Rinzai school of Zen.

*Hanko* A seal; stamp.

*Happi* A light coat of silk or cotton, like a short kimono.

*Hara* Belly; abdomen; heart; a centre of vital energy.

*Hashi* A bridge; also, depending on intonation, chopsticks, or the edge or border of something.

*Henken* Prejudice.

*Hi-no-maru* The Japanese sun flag (lit. hi—sun and maru—circle).

*Hisashiburi* It's been a long time.

*Hitotsu* One.

*Honne* Original feeling; a person's true intentions.

*Honto* True; real; genuine.

*Iada* Nasty!

*Ichiban* Number one; the best.

*Ichi-buzaki* The first stage of blossom that continues through to manbuzaki, full blossom.

*Ichigo-ichie* A once-in-a-lifetime meeting.

*Ii* Good; nice; fine.

*Ika* Dried cuttlefish

*Ikebana* Flower arrangement.

*Ikko-nezumi* Lemming.

*Ingin-burei* False politeness; dumb insolence.

*Intanashionaru* International.

*Irashai* Welcome!

*Iroha* The Japanese alphabet in the form of a poem which can be translated as: "Leaves and blossoms in all their brilliance fall. Who among us will tarry in this world? We shall cross the deepest mountains of this Samsara, the world of illusion, and dream no more shallow dreams, nor yield to drunkenness." This poem used to be learned by every Japanese.

*Ishin-denshin* Telepathy; intuitively shared thoughts or feelings.

*Ishi-no-ue-ni sannen* Ishi-stone. (lit. "On top of a stone—three years" which refers to the meditation by Daruma, who sat on a stone for three years in an attempt to understand the meaning of life. Nowadays the meaning of the saying is something like "Try, try, try again.")

*Jibun-kata* Selfish; thinking of oneself at the expense of others.

*Jinja* Shrine

*Kaibashira* A shellfish.

*Kaisha* A company; corporation; firm.

*Kami-sama* God; deity; divinity.

*Kanji* Chinese characters; ideograms.

*Karaoke* Sing-along soundtrack (lit. empty-voice).

*Katana* Sword; blade.

*Kawaii* Cute; sweet; charming.

*Keigo* Respect language.

*Ki* Spirit.

*Kiipuseiku* Keep-sake.

*Kimochi* Feeling. Kimochi-ga-ii—That feels good!; Kimochi yokatta—That was good—the feeling was good.

*Kimono* Clothing; clothes; kimono.

*Kinben-bitoku* "Work is virtue."

*Kirei* Pretty; beautiful; good-looking.

*Kissaten* Tea room; coffee shop.

*Kitanai-mon* Nasty! Ugh! (lit. dirty thing).

*Koan* An idea; a type of conundrum that defies logical analysis often used in Zen teaching, e.g. "the sound of one hand clapping."

*Kohai* A junior or, in an office, an inferior.

*Kohi* Coffee.

*Kokoro* Heart; mind; feeling.

*Kokuminsei* Nation-spirit; the character of a country's people.

*Konnichiwa* Hallo (lit. this is the day).

*Kotatsu* A foot warmer with a quilt over it.

*Koto* A Japanese harp.

*Kowai* Scary; frightening.

*Kudasai* Please; kudasai is added on to the end of requests (lit. to give).

*Kuni* A country; a land.

*Kusai* Bad-smelling; stinking. *Wah! kusai!* is the Japanese way of saying Pooh! what a smell!

*Kyokai* An association; league; society.

*Mai-peisu* My pace, i.e. in one's own time, at one's own speed.

*Majime* Serious; sober; earnest.

*Makoto* Sinceiity; truth; real; genuine; faithful.

*Makudonarudo* McDonald's, a fast-food eatery which some Japanese believe is a Japanese company; when they go abroad they are shocked to discover McDonald's also has outlets in other countries.

*Mama-san* A mature woman in charge of a bar and the girls who work in it.

*Manga* A cartoon; comic strip.

*Manju* A bean jam dumpling.

*Matte-imasu* I'm waiting.

*Meiji* The throne name of Mitsuhito, Emperor of Japan, 1867–1912 (lit. enlightened government).

*Meishi* A visiting card or calling card.

*Mina-san* Everyone; all together; one and all.

*Mizuwari* A whisky and water.

*Mondai* A question; a problem; a difficulty.

*Mono-no-aware* The passing of things; the ephemeral nature of existence.

*Mushi-atsui* Sultry; close; muggy.

*Muzukashi* Difficult; hard.

*Nai* A negative suffix attached to the end of words.

*Naku narimashita* It's gone; it's disappeared (lit. it has become nothing; sometimes used as a euphemism for dying).

*Nanda* What's that? (colloquial).

*Naruhodo* Really; I see; of course; as one would expect; sure.

*Nihonjin-ron* Conversations about Japan and the Japanese; a fairly popular pastime among foreigners living in Japan, sometimes described as "Japan-bashing" by the Japanese.

*Nihon-sei* Made in Japan.

*Nikkei-Shinbun* Financial Times (lit. the Japanese Economic Newspaper).

*Ningen-kankei* Human relationships.

*Ninjo* Humanity; sympathy; warm-hearted.

*Ninki-mono* Popular; the current thing.

*Nisei* An American-born Japanese.

*Nomiya* A tavern; bar; pub.

*Obaachan* An affectionate name for an old lady; Granma; sometimes used with a hint of condescension.

*Obi* A sash; a wide silk belt.

*O-furo* A bath; bathroom; bath tub.

*Ohaiyo-gozaimasu* Good morning (lit. it's early).

*O-jo-sama* Princess; a nice girl (slang).

*Okaa-san* Mother.

*O-mae* You (impolite).

*On* A kindness; favour; obligation; a debt of gratitude.

*Onsen* A hot-spring; spa; watering place.

*O-yasumi-nasai* Good night (lit. please take a rest).

*Pachinko* Pinball.

*Rāmen* Noodle soup.

*Reigi* Manners; the proper way of doing things.

*Rieki* Advantage; profit; gain.

*Romaji* The Roman letters; the Latin alphabet.

*Rorikon* A Japanese mispronunciation of "Lolita complex."

*Rotenburo* An open air bath.

*Ryokan* An inn; hotel.

*Saah* An exclamation of indecision or consternation at the beginning of a sentence.

*Sabi* Tranquillity; serenity; a pleasurable sense of loneliness.

*Sake* Rice wine.

*Sakura* Cherry blossom.

*Salariman* A man employed by a company.

*Samurai* A warrior.

*Sashimi* Raw fish.

*Sato* A village; the country; home.

*Satori* Awakening; realisation; enlightenment.

*Seiza* Sitting still; sitting quietly (usually in a kneeling position, sitting back on one's feet).

*Semi* A cicada.

*Senbei* A rice cracker.

*Senko* A joss stick; incense.

*Senpai* A senior; superior.

*Sensei* A teacher; master (often added to the end of a person's name as a sign of respect).

*Shibui* Simple; uncomplicated; aesthetic.

*Shima-guni konjo* An island-country complex.

*Shimasho* "Let's do (it)."

*Shingo akakeba, mina wattate mo kamawanai* Even if the traffic lights are red, when everyone crosses over together it doesn't matter, i.e. the majority are stronger than the law.

*Shishi* A lion-dog.

*Shodo* Calligraphy.

*Shogun* A general; commander-in-chief.

*Shoji* A paper sliding door.

*Shunga* An erotic print or drawing.

*So desho* "Oh really" "Is that so?"

*Suki* To like; to be attached to something.

*Sumimasen* "Excuse me" "I'm sorry."

*Sumo* Sumo wrestling.

*Suppai* Sour; acid; bitter.

*Sushi* Sushi; strips of raw fish on handfuls of boiled rice.

*Tadashii* Correct; proper; just.

*Tanuki* An animal like a raccoon dog.

*Tarento* A show business personality (lit. a talent).

*Tatami* Rice straw matting.

*Tatemae* Appearances; the way things seem to other people.

*Tokonoma* An alcove in the living room of a house where scroll paintings are hung and flower arrangements are displayed.

*Tokugawa* The name of the shogunate that lasted from 1603 to 1867.

*Tsumaranai* Pointless; useless; meaningless.

*Tsunami* A tidal wave.

*Tsuyu* The rainy season.

*Uchi* Inside; indoors; home; one's own people.

*Wa* Peace, harmony.

*Wabi* A pleasant feeling of simplicity.

*Waga kuni* Our country (the way some of the more nationalistic Japanese refer to Japan).

*Wagamama* Selfishness; egoism.

*Wah!* An exclamation of surprise or disgust.

*Wakatta* Understood.

*Washi* Japanese paper.

*Yakitori* A chicken grill.

*Yakuza* A gangster; the Japanese equivalent of the Mafia.

*Yama-bushi* A travelling monk; an ascetic in the mountains.

*Yamato-damashi* The pure (Japanese) spirit; the soul of Japan.

*Yamete* Stop!

*Yappari* "Of course" "as I thought" "as one might have expected."

*Yo* Suffix added to words to give extra emphasis.

*Yuga* Elegance; grace; refinement.

*Zen* A form of Buddhism, from the Indian dhyana meditation, and the Chinese chan doctrine of enlightenment.

*Zenrin* Neighbourly friendship.

A NOTE ON THE TYPE

The text of this book was composed in a digitized version of Palatino, a typeface designed by the noted German typographer Hermann Zapf. Named after Giovanbattista Palatino, a writing master of Renaissance Italy, Palatino was the first of Zapf's typefaces to be introduced in America. The first designs for the face were made in 1948, and the fonts for the complete face were issued between 1950 and 1952. Like all Zapf-designed typefaces, Palatino is beautifully balanced and exceedingly readable.

Composed by Crane Typesetting Service,
West Barnstable, Massachusetts

Printed and bound by R. R. Donnelley &
Sons, Harrisonburg, Virginia

Designed by Brooke Zimmer